Lecture Notes in Computer Science 8459

Commenced Publication in 1973
Founding and Former Series Editors:
Gerhard Goos, Juris Hartmanis, and Jan van Leeuwen

Eva Kühn   Rosario Pugliese (Eds.)

Coordination Models and Languages

16th IFIP WG 6.1 International Conference,
COORDINATION 2014
Held as Part of the 9th International Federated Conference
on Distributed Computing Techniques, DisCoTec 2014
Berlin, Germany, June 3-5, 2014
Proceedings

 Springer

Volume Editors

Eva Kühn
Vienna University of Technology
Institute of Computer Languages
Argentinierstr. 8, 1040 Vienna, Austria
E-mail: eva.kuehn@tuwien.ac.at

Rosario Pugliese
University of Florence
Dept. of Statistics, Informatics, Applications
Viale G.B. Morgagni, 65, 50134 Florence, Italy
E-mail: rosario.pugliese@unifi.it

ISSN 0302-9743   e-ISSN 1611-3349
ISBN 978-3-662-43375-1   e-ISBN 978-3-662-43376-8
DOI 10.1007/978-3-662-43376-8
Springer Heidelberg New York Dordrecht London

Library of Congress Control Number: 2014938482

LNCS Sublibrary: SL 2 – Programming and Software Engineering

Typesetting: Camera-ready by author, data conversion by Scientific Publishing Services, Chennai, India

Printed on acid-free paper

Springer is part of Springer Science+Business Media (www.springer.com)

Foreword

In 2014, the 9th International Federated Conference on Distributed Computing Techniques (DisCoTec) took place in Berlin, Germany, during June 3–5. It was hosted and organized by the Technische Universität Berlin. The DisCoTec series, one of the major events sponsored by the International Federation for Information Processing (IFIP), included three conferences:

- COORDINATION 2014, the 16th IFIP WG 6.1 International Conference on Coordination Models and Languages
- DAIS 2014, the 14th IFIP WG 6.1 International Conference on Distributed Applications and Interoperable Systems
- FORTE 2014, the 34th IFIP WG 6.1 International Conference on Formal Techniques for Distributed Objects, Components and Systems

Together, these conferences cover the complete spectrum of distributed computing subjects ranging from theoretical foundations over formal specification techniques to systems research issues.

Each day of the federated event began with a plenary speaker nominated by one of the conferences. The three invited speakers were:

- Frank Leymann (University of Stuttgart, Germany)
- Maarten van Steen (VU University Amsterdam, The Netherlands)
- Joachim Parrow (Uppsala University, Sweden)

There were also three satellite events, taking place during June 6–7:

1. The 5th International Workshop on *Interactions Between Computer Science and Biology* (CS2BIO) with keynote lectures by Marco Pettini (Université de la Mediterranée, France) and Vincent Danos (University of Edinburgh, UK) and a tutorial by Jeffrey Johnson (Open University, UK)
2. The 7th Workshop on *Interaction and Concurrency Experience* (ICE) with keynote lectures by Kim Larsen (Aalborg University, Denmark) and Pavol Cerny (University of Colorado at Boulder, USA)
3. The First International Workshop on *Meta Models for Process Languages* (MeMo) with keynote lectures by Joachim Parrow (Uppsala University, Sweden) and Marino Miculan (Università degli Studi di Udine, Italy)

This program was an interesting and stimulating event for the participants. Sincere thanks go the chairs and members of the Program Committees of the involved conferences and workshops for their highly appreciated effort. Moreover, organizing DisCoTec 2014 was only possible thanks to the dedicated work of the Organizing Committee from TU Berlin, including Margit Russ, Kirstin Peters (also publicity and workshop chair), and Christoph Wagner. Finally, many thanks go to IFIP WG 6.1 for providing the umbrella for this event, to EATCS and TU Berlin for their support and sponsorship, and to EasyChair for providing the refereeing infrastructure.

June 2014   Uwe Nestmann

Preface

This volume contains the papers presented at COORDINATION 2014: the 16th IFIP WG 6.1 International Conference on Coordination Models and Languages held during June 3–4, 2014, in Berlin. The conference is the premier forum for publishing research results and experience reports on software technologies for collaboration and coordination in concurrent, distributed, and complex systems. Its distinctive feature is the emphasis on high-level abstractions that capture interaction patterns manifest at all levels of the software architecture and extending into the realm of the end-user domain. COORDINATION 2014 called for high-quality contributions on the usage, study, design, and implementation of languages, models, and techniques for coordination in distributed, concurrent, pervasive, and multicore software systems.

The Program Committee (PC) of COORDINATION 2014 consisted of 26 top researchers from 12 different countries. We received 37 abstracts that materialized in a total of 31 submissions out of which the PC selected 12 papers for inclusion in the program. All submissions were reviewed by three to four independent referees; papers were selected based on their quality, originality, contribution, clarity of presentation, and relevance to the conference topics. The review process included an in-depth discussion phase, during which the merits of all papers were discussed by the PC. The process culminated in a shepherding phase whereby some of the authors received active guidance by one member of the PC in order to produce a high-quality final version. The selected papers constituted a program covering a varied range of the conference topics: programming abstractions and languages, coordination models and paradigms, applied software engineering principles, specification and verification, foundations and types, distributed middleware architectures, multicore programming, collaborative adaptive systems, and coordination related use cases. The program was further enhanced by an invited talk by Frank Leymann from the University of Stuttgart (Germany) entitled "Orchestrating Management Behavior of Cloud Applications."

The success of COORDINATION 2014 was due to the dedication of many people. We thank the authors for submitting high-quality papers and the PC and their sub-reviewers for their careful reviews and lively discussions during the final selection process. We thank the providers of the EasyChair conference management system, which was used to run the review process and to facilitate the preparation of the proceedings. Finally, we thank the Distributed Computing Techniques Organizing Committee from TU Berlin, led by Uwe Nestmann, for its contribution in making the logistical aspects of COORDINATION 2014 a success.

June 2014

Eva Kühn
Rosario Pugliese

Organization

Steering Committee

Farhad Arbab (Chair)	CWI and Leiden University, The Netherlands
Gul Agha	University of Illinois at Urbana Champaign, USA
Dave Clarke	Uppsala University, Sweden
Wolfgang De Meuter	Vrije Universiteit Brussel, Belgium
Rocco De Nicola	IMT - Institute for Advanced Studies Lucca, Italy
Jean-Marie Jacquet	University of Namur, Belgium
Christine Julien	University of Texas at Austin, USA
Marjan Sirjani	Reykjavik University, Iceland
Carolyn Talcott	SRI International, USA
Vasco T. Vasconcelos	University of Lisbon, Portugal
Gianluigi Zavattaro	University of Bologna, Italy

Program Committee

Marco Aldinucci	University of Turin, Italy
Farhad Arbab	CWI and Leiden University, The Netherlands
Luis Caires	Universidade Nova de Lisboa, Portugal
Wolfgang De Meuter	Vrije Universiteit Brussel, Belgium
Rocco De Nicola	IMT - Institute for Advanced Studies, Italy
Schahram Dustdar	Vienna University of Technology, Austria
Gianluigi Ferrari	University of Pisa, Italy
José Luiz Fiadeiro	Royal Holloway, University of London, UK
Valérie Issarny	Inria, France
Jean-Marie Jacquet	University of Namur, Belgium
Christine Julien	University of Texas at Austin, USA
Rania Khalaf	IBM T.J. Watson Research Center, USA
Eva Kühn (Chair)	Vienna University of Technology, Austria
Michele Loreti	University of Florence, Italy
Hanne Riis Nielson	Technical University of Denmark, Denmark
Andrea Omicini	University of Bologna, Italy
Kirstin Peters	Technische Universität Berlin, Germany
Paolo Petta	Austrian Research Institute for Artificial Intelligence, Austria
Anna Philippou	University of Cyprus, Cyprus
Rosario Pugliese (Chair)	University of Florence, Italy

Marjan Sirjani	Reykjavik University, Iceland
Carolyn Talcott	SRI International, USA
Emilio Tuosto	University of Leicester, UK
Herbert Wiklicky	Imperial College London, UK
Martin Wirsing	Ludwig-Maximilians-Universität München, Germany
Gianluigi Zavattaro	University of Bologna, Italy

Additional Reviewers

Basile, Davide
Bernardo, Marco
Bettini, Lorenzo
Boix, Elisa Gonzalez
Bono, Viviana
Canciani, Andrea
Cardozo, Nicolas
Cejka, Stephan
Ciancia, Vincenzo
Craß, Stefan
Dalla Preda, Mila
Damiani, Ferruccio
Dardha, Ornela
Dinges, Peter
Ferreira, Carla
Galletta, Letterio
Garrett, Deon
Giallorenzo, Saverio
Jafari, Ali
Jaghoori, Mohammad Mahdi
Kilpatrick, Peter

Kouzapas, Dimitrios
Lange, Julien
Lienhardt, Michael
Marek, Alexander
Mariani, Stefano
Melgratti, Hernan
Mezzetti, Gianluca
Nigam, Vivek
Oostvogels, Nathalie
Peretti Pezzi, Guilherme
Petrocchi, Marinella
Philips, Eline
Ravara, Antonio
Sabouri, Hamideh
Sammartino, Matteo
Scholliers, Christophe
Schwayer, Matthias
Seco, João Costa
Tiezzi, Francesco
Tinacci, Marco
Vandin, Andrea

Invited Talk

Orchestrating Management Behavior of Cloud Applications

Frank Leymann

Institute of Architecture of Application Systems (IAAS)
University of Stuttgart, Germany
Leymann@iaas.uni-stuttgart.de

Ensuring quality of services of applications in the cloud is a major concern. Applications that should benefit from the desirable properties of the cloud must follow certain architectural principles. The most fundamental of such principles have been described as patterns that we will motivate. In particular, the IDEAL principle recommending Isolated state, Distribution, Elasticity, Automated management, and Loose coupling for a cloud application is described.

Just turning an application into a virtual image and running it in the cloud does not make appropriate use of cloud properties. For example, scalability cannot be ensured without introducing redundant componentry that often comes with unexpected high cost and consistency problems. Thus, an application that should adequately run in the cloud must consist of a collection of more fine-grained components. To allow the cloud environment to perform management actions on it, specific relations between the former components must be defined. Together, the topology of the application must be specified.

The topology of a (not too complex) application allows for automatically deriving the basic management behavior of the application, e.g., how it is provisioned and decommissioned. More complex management behavior requires the specification of plans, i.e., workflows that define how to perform management actions in terms of the topology of the to-be-managed application. Pros and cons of the former (declarative) approach and the latter (imperative) approach are discussed.

A language (called TOSCA - Topology and Orchestration Specification for Cloud Applications) to define the topology and associated plans of an application has been standardized. This language is sketched. An architecture of an environment supporting this language is outlined and an open source implementation of a such an environment (called OpenTOSCA) is briefly introduced.

Table of Contents

Encoding Synchronous Interactions
Using Labelled Petri Nets*

Paolo Baldan[1], Filippo Bonchi[2], Fabio Gadducci[3], and Giacoma V. Monreale[3]

[1] Dipartimento di Matematica, Università di Padova, Padova, Italy
[2] LIP, ENS Lyon, Université de Lyon (UMR CNRS - INRIA 5668), Lyon, France
[3] Dipartimento di Informatica, Università di Pisa, Pisa, Italy

Abstract. We present an encoding of (bound) CSP processes with replication into Petri nets with labelled transitions. Through the encoding, the firing semantics of Petri nets models the standard operational semantics of CSP processes, which is both preserved and reflected. This correspondence allows for describing by net semantics the standard CSP observational equivalences. Since the encoding is modular with respect to process syntax, the paper puts on a firm ground the technology transfer between the two formalisms, e.g. recasting into the CSP framework well-established results like decidability of coverability for nets. This work complements previous results concerning the encoding of asynchronous interactions, thus witnessing the expressiveness of (open) labelled nets in modelling process calculi with alternative communication patterns.

Keywords: Communicating sequential processes (CSP), labelled Petri nets, net encoding of processes, synchronous interaction.

1 Introduction

Petri nets [17] are among the most widely used formalisms for the visual specification of concurrent and distributed systems. Their appeal lies in the ease of use as well as in the expressiveness. Indeed, their graphical presentation allows for a simple description of possibly complex interaction patterns, in such a way that both synchronous and asynchronous features are plainly represented. Also, in a Petri net the behavioural relations between computational steps, such as causal dependencies and nondeterministic choices, are explicit and easier to analyse.

These characteristics also favoured Petri nets as the target for the encoding of many textual formalisms, such as different process calculi. This is partly due to the availability of many tools and techniques for the analysis of net behavioural properties, like coverability, boundedness, and deadlock-freedom, so that any suitable encoding might offer the possibility of a fruitful technology transfer. However, it is the same simple and immediate graphical presentation of nets that attracted the attention of researchers, in the hope of clarifying the nature of concurrency and distributivity in the formalism at hand. Indeed, there has

* Supported by EU FP7-ICT IP ASCENS, MIUR PRIN CINA and ANR PACE.

E. Kühn and R. Pugliese (Eds.): COORDINATION 2014, LNCS 8459, pp. 1–16, 2014.

been since a long time an interest for the encoding of synchronous calculi such as Milner's CCS. Intuitively, the handshaking communication pattern of CCS and π-calculus can be implemented via nets in such a way that the operational behaviour of a process is (at least) preserved by the encoding [10,7].

In a recent work we offered a further witness to the flexibility of nets by providing an encoding for asynchronous CCS [1]. More precisely, our encoding preserves the operational behaviour of processes as well as asynchronous bisimilarity, captured by standard net bisimilarity. In order to model the intrinsic reactivity of CCS processes, the encoding resorted to open Petri nets [2], i.e., nets extended with the possibility of interacting with the environment through an interface. Specifically, the interface consists of a set of places designated as open, where the environment can create and consume tokens. Interfaces were also essential to define composition operations on nets, thus allowing for a modular definition of the encoding. The need of considering reactive extensions of Petri nets in order to have a modular model, with compositional semantics, have been felt by several authors, leading to the Box Calculus [3], the Petri net components [13] and other open net models [15,4], just to mention a few.

This paper aims at further extending our results by moving back to synchronous processes, yet taking into account the broadcast communication pattern, as provided by Hoare's CSP [12]. More precisely, we identify an expressive fragment of CSP which can be mapped modularly into Petri nets via an encoding that is preserving as well as reflecting the operational semantics. Since most of CSP semantics are based on traces, the encoding is guaranteed to preserve and reflect also the common observational equivalences for the calculus. This allows some immediate technology transfer from nets to processes. For instance, coverability, the maximal degree of parallelism of a process (given by the number of its sub-processes occurring in parallel) and convergence (i.e., the possibility of termination) can be proved to be decidable in the CSP setting. Some of these decidability results seem to be the first of their kind for (bound) CSP processes.

The idea of mapping CSP processes into nets arose early on, see among others [9,16,6]. Conceptually, all these encodings are syntax-driven: each process is split into a family of sequential components, which represent the places of a net, and a (possibly concurrent) semantics for the calculus is thus obtained. As of more recent advances, we are aware of [14]. There, an on-the-fly algorithm is devised for building (and optimising) a net from a CSP process by exploiting its transition system. In our encoding we followed the spirit of the former proposals, striving for modularity: the encoding itself has a denotational flavor, mapping each operator of the calculus into an operator on nets, and as a consequence preservation and reflection of CSP standard operational semantics are easily stated and proved. We believe that such clarity is due to the identification of the right CSP fragment. Indeed, it is noteworthy that in all the papers mentioned above the recursion of nested parallel processes is not allowed "because the set of places of the generated Petri net would be infinite" [14, p.111]. Our paper lifts such a constraint: our chosen CSP fragment is not finite state, but rather it bounds the number of parallel processes synchronising on the same channel.

$$P \quad ::= \quad STOP \qquad\qquad\qquad\qquad \text{inactive process}$$

$$\oplus_{i=1}^{n} a_i.P_i \qquad\qquad\qquad \text{guarded alternative}$$

$$P + Q \qquad\qquad\qquad\quad \text{nondeterministic choice}$$

$$P \mid_X Q \qquad\qquad\qquad\quad \text{parallel composition}$$

$$P \backslash X \qquad\qquad\qquad\quad\; \text{hiding}$$

$$!_a.P \qquad\qquad\qquad\quad\; \text{replication}$$

Fig. 1. CSP processes

The paper is structured as follows. Section 2 recalls the syntax and the operational semantics of CSP, while Section 3 introduces labelled nets with interfaces, as well as a suitable algebra for them. The core of the paper is Section 4, which presents the modular encoding from (bound) CSP processes into labelled nets. In Section 5 the encoding is proved to preserve and reflect the operational semantics, and hence the standard observational equivalences of the calculus (such as trace equivalence). The encoding is exploited in Section 6, which provides some examples of its effects on the technology transfer between the two formalisms. Finally, Section 7 discusses some expressiveness issues for the considered models, taking advantage from the encoding, and it draws some conclusions while providing a few pointers to future works.

2   Communicating Sequential Processes

In this section we briefly review the calculus of Communicating Sequential Processes (CSP) [12], presenting its syntax and operational semantics. We actually focus on a fragment of the calculus, which will be used throughout the paper.

Definition 1 (CSP processes). *Let Σ be the alphabet of communication events, ranged over by $a, b, c \ldots$ The set of CSP processes $\mathcal{P}$, ranged over by $P, Q, R, \ldots$, is generated by the grammar in Fig. 1, where $X \subseteq \Sigma$ is a finite set of events.*

The process $STOP$ cannot perform any event, i.e., it is a deadlocked process. The guarded alternative $\oplus_{i=1}^{n} a_i.P_i$ can perform any event a_i, for $i \in \{1, \ldots, n\}$, and then behave as P_i. For the sake of simplicity, we assume that $\forall j, \forall z. a_j \neq a_z$. The nondeterministic choice $P + Q$ can behave as either P or Q. The operators $\oplus$ and $+$ differs for the fact that for $\oplus$ the choice is external, i.e., it is the environment that determines the branch to be chosen, while for $+$ the choice is internal to the process. The process $P \mid_X Q$ is the parallel composition of P and Q, where the events in X are forced to synchronise, while those in $\Sigma \setminus X$ can be performed by P and Q independently. The hiding $P \backslash X$ behaves like P except for the fact that the events in X are hidden to the environment, that is, they become internal to the process. Finally, the replication $!_a.P$ can indefinitely perform an event a and spawn a parallel copy of P.

$$(Alt) \quad \frac{j \in \{1, \ldots, n\}}{\oplus_{i=1}^{n} a_i.P_i \xrightarrow{a_j} P_j}$$

$$(Cho_1) \; \frac{}{P + Q \xrightarrow{\tau} P} \qquad\qquad (Cho_2) \; \frac{}{P + Q \xrightarrow{\tau} Q}$$

$$(Syn_1) \; \frac{P \xrightarrow{\mu} P' \quad \mu \notin X}{P \mid_X Q \xrightarrow{\mu} P' \mid_X Q} \qquad (Syn_2) \; \frac{Q \xrightarrow{\mu} Q' \quad \mu \notin X}{P \mid_X Q \xrightarrow{\mu} P \mid_X Q'}$$

$$(Syn_3) \; \frac{P \xrightarrow{a} P' \quad Q \xrightarrow{a} Q' \quad a \in X}{P \mid_X Q \xrightarrow{a} P' \mid_X Q'}$$

$$(Hid_1) \; \frac{P \xrightarrow{\mu} P' \quad \mu \notin X}{P \backslash X \xrightarrow{\mu} P' \backslash X} \qquad (Hid_2) \; \frac{P \xrightarrow{a} P' \quad a \in X}{P \backslash X \xrightarrow{\tau} P' \backslash X}$$

$$(Repl) \; \frac{}{!_a.P \xrightarrow{a} !_a.P \mid_\varnothing P}$$

Fig. 2. CSP operational semantics

The guarded alternative is a specialisation of the external choice operator. This restriction does not represent a serious limitation since, as explained in [18], it is rare to find a usage of the external choice which cannot be expressed as a guarded alternative. More interestingly, we consider guarded replication in place of recursion. This will be important for ensuring the existence of a finite Petri net encoding for the class of CSP processes considered (see Section 5).

The behaviour of CSP processes, intuitively described above, is formalised in terms of a set of syntax directed rules which axiomatise a transition relation.

Definition 2 (operational semantics of CSP). *The labelled transition system (LTS) for CSP processes is the relation* $\rightarrow \subseteq \mathcal{P} \times (\Sigma \uplus \{\tau\}) \times \mathcal{P}$ *inductively defined by the rules in Fig. 2, where we write* $P \xrightarrow{\mu} P'$ *for* $\langle P, \mu, P' \rangle \in \rightarrow$.

We write $P \xrightarrow{s}{}^* P'$ for a sequence $P = P_1 \xrightarrow{\mu_1} P_2 \xrightarrow{\mu_2} \ldots \xrightarrow{\mu_{n-1}} P'$ with $s = \mu_1\mu_2 \ldots \mu_{n-1}$. Moreover, we write $P \xRightarrow{s} P'$ when $P \xrightarrow{s'}{}^* P'$ for some s' such that s is obtained from s' by removing the τ's. We write simply $P \rightarrow P'$ and $P \rightarrow^* P'$ instead of $P \xrightarrow{\mu} P'$ and $P \xrightarrow{s}{}^* P'$, respectively, whenever we are not interested in identifying the labels.

Definition 3 (bound processes). *A CSP process* $P \in \mathcal{P}$ *is called* bound *if parallel compositions* $\_ \mid_X \_$ *occur under the scope of replications only with* $X = \emptyset$.

In a bound process only pure parallel composition, without synchronisation, is allowed under the scope of replications. This avoids the possibility of having an unbounded number of parallel components synchronising on the same event. Additionally, a synchronisation under a replication would possibly lead to the generation of an unbounded number of conceptually different names as in

$!_a.(b.b.STOP \mid_{\{b\}} b.STOP)$. As discussed in Section 4, this fact will be essential for defining a finite encoding of bound CSP processes into Petri nets.

Relying on the LTS defined above several observational semantics can be defined over CSP processes. In this paper, we will focus on the one based on traces, i.e., sequences of visible transitions.

Definition 4 (traces). *Let* $P \in \mathcal{P}$ *be a CSP process. We define* $traces(P) = \{s \in \Sigma^* : \exists Q. P \stackrel{s}{\Rightarrow} Q\}$.

Traces are exploited to provide a behavioral equivalence for processes.

Definition 5 (trace equivalence). *Let* $P, Q \in \mathcal{P}$ *be two CSP processes. They are called* trace equivalent, *written* $P =_T Q$, *if* $traces(P) = traces(Q)$.

Example 1. Consider the processes $P = a.(d.b.STOP \backslash d) \oplus b.a.STOP$ and $Q = (c.a.STOP \mid_{\{c\}} c.b.STOP)\backslash c$. It is easy to see that $traces(P) = traces(Q) = \{\epsilon, a, ab, b, ba\}$. Hence they are trace equivalent.

3 Labelled Petri Nets with Interfaces

This section reviews *labelled Petri nets*, i.e., ordinary P/T nets with labelled transitions [17]. Nets are also enriched with interfaces and endowed with composition operators in order to allow for an inductive encoding of CSP processes.

3.1 Labelled Petri Nets

Let $X^{\oplus}$ be the free commutative monoid over a set X. An element $m \in X^{\oplus}$, a *multiset* over X, is often viewed as a function $m : X \to \mathbb{N}$ (the set of natural numbers) that associates a multiplicity with every element of X. We write $m_1 \subseteq m_2$ if $\forall x \in X, m_1(x) \leq m_2(x)$. The symbol 0 denotes the empty multiset. Given $f : X \to Y$ we denote its extension to multisets by $f^{\oplus} : X^{\oplus} \to Y^{\oplus}$.

Hereafter Σ denotes a fixed set over which all nets are labelled. In the encoding of processes into nets, Σ is the set of CSP communication events.

Definition 6 (labelled Petri net). *A* labelled Petri net *is a tuple* $N = (S, T, {}^{\bullet}(.), (.)^{\bullet}, \lambda)$ *where* S *is the set of places,* T *is the set of transitions,* ${}^{\bullet}(.), (.)^{\bullet} : T \to S^{\oplus}$ *are functions mapping each transition to its pre- and post-set and* $\lambda : T \to \Sigma$ *is the labelling of transitions.*

The state of a net is given by a *marking*, i.e., a multiset of places $m \in S^{\oplus}$. Hereafter, the components of a net N will be assumed S, T, ${}^{\bullet}(.)$, $(.)^{\bullet}$ and λ, possibly with subscripts. We will often write ${}^{\bullet}t$ and $t^{\bullet}$ instead of ${}^{\bullet}(t)$ and $(t)^{\bullet}$.

Definition 7 (net morphism). *Let* N_1, N_2 *be two labelled nets. A net morphism* $f : N_1 \to N_2$ *is a pair of functions* $f = \langle f_S, f_T \rangle$ *where* $f_S : S_1 \to S_2$, $f_T : T_1 \to T_2$ *satisfy for any* $t \in T_1$:

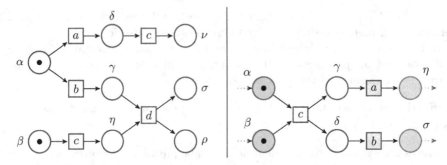

Fig. 3. Graphical representation of labelled nets, the rightmost with interfaces

1. $f_S^{\oplus}({}^{\bullet}t) \subseteq {}^{\bullet}f_T(t)$ *(reflection of pre-set)*
2. $f_S^{\oplus}(t^{\bullet}) \subseteq f_T(t)^{\bullet}$ *(reflection of post-set)*
3. $\lambda_1(t) = \lambda_2(f_T(t))$ *(preservation of labels).*

Net morphisms roughly represent the insertion of a net into a context. As a consequence the pre- and post-set of transitions can be larger in the target net.

Example 2. Fig. 3 (left) shows a labelled net. As usual, circles represent places and rectangles transitions. Arrows represent pre- and post-sets of transitions. Bullets in places, referred to as tokens, represent the current marking m of the net. Transition labels are placed inside the corresponding rectangle. For the sake of readability, also some places are provided with an identifier, yet positioned outside of the corresponding circle.

3.2   Petri Nets with Interfaces

In order to define the encoding of CSP processes into Petri nets inductively, we equip nets with "handles" for interacting with the environment and define operations for composing them.

Definition 8 (Petri net with interfaces). *A Petri net with interfaces is a tuple* $\mathbf{N} = \langle I, O, N, V \rangle$, *where N is a labelled net, I and O are subsets of places, the input and output places, and V is a subset of transitions, the visible transitions.*

Hereafter, the components of a net with interfaces $\mathbf{N}$ will be assumed to be I, N, O, and V, possibly with subscripts.

The standard operational semantics on Petri nets naturally induces a semantics for nets with interfaces, where the firing of a transition that is not visible is turned into a silent action τ. This is expressed by the rules in Fig. 4.

Graphically, a net with interfaces is depicted as a net with input interface on the left and output interface on the right, marked with incoming and outgoing dotted arrows, respectively. Places in the input and output interface are in blue and red, respectively (grey if in b&w), while internal places are white. Moreover, visible transitions are green (grey if in b&w) and hidden ones are white.

$$(\text{VIS}) \ \frac{m = {}^\bullet t \oplus m' \quad t \in V}{m \xrightarrow{\lambda(t)} t^\bullet \oplus m'} \qquad (\text{HID}) \ \frac{m = {}^\bullet t \oplus m' \quad t \in T \setminus V}{m \xrightarrow{\tau} t^\bullet \oplus m'}$$

Fig. 4. Operational semantics of nets with interfaces

Example 3. An example of net with interfaces is shown in Fig. 3 (right). The input interface consists of the places α and β, while the output interface contains the places η and σ. The white places γ and δ are internal, i.e., they do not belong to the interfaces. The white transition labelled c is hidden, while those labelled a and b are visible. Finally, in the current marking m_0 of the net, the places α and β are marked. By applying the (HID) rule in Fig. 4 we obtain the firing $m_0 \xrightarrow{\tau} m_1 = \{\gamma, \delta\}$. By rule (VIS), we get $m_1 \xrightarrow{a} m_2 = \{\eta, \delta\}$ and $m_1 \xrightarrow{b} m_3 = \{\gamma, \sigma\}$. Finally, $m_2 \xrightarrow{b} m_4$ and $m_3 \xrightarrow{a} m_4$, with $m_4 = \{\eta, \sigma\}$.

As in the case of CSP processes, we write $m \xrightarrow{s}{}^* m'$ when there is a sequence $m = m_1 \xrightarrow{\mu_1} m_2 \xrightarrow{\mu_2} \dots \xrightarrow{\mu_{n-1}} m'$ with $s = \mu_1 \mu_2 \dots \mu_{n-1}$. We also write $m \xRightarrow{s} m'$ when $m \xrightarrow{s'}{}^* m'$ for some s' such that s is obtained from s' by removing the τ's.

We next define suitable composition operators on nets with interfaces.

Definition 9 (sequential composition). *Let $\mathbf{N}_1$ and $\mathbf{N}_2$ be nets with interfaces such that $O_1 = I_2 = S_1 \cap S_2$ and $T_1 \cap T_2 = \emptyset$. Their sequential composition is the net with interfaces $\mathbf{N}_1 \circ \mathbf{N}_2 = \langle I_1, O_2, N, V_1 \cup V_2 \rangle$, where N is the pointwise union $N_1 \cup N_2$, with the obvious pre-set, post-set and labelling functions.*

Intuitively, the sequential composition $\mathbf{N}_1 \circ \mathbf{N}_2$ is obtained by taking the disjoint union of the nets underlying $\mathbf{N}_1$ and $\mathbf{N}_2$, and gluing the output places of N_1 with the corresponding input places of N_2. For the sake of presentation, it is convenient to assume that the two nets intersect only on the input/output interfaces and take the plain union. This could require some alpha-renaming.

In the following, given a net with interfaces $\mathbf{N}$ and a set $X \subseteq \Sigma$, we denote by $V^X = \{t \in V : \lambda(t) \in X\}$ the set of transitions labelled with an event in X.

Definition 10 (synchronised parallel composition). *Let $\mathbf{N}_1$ and $\mathbf{N}_2$ be nets with interfaces such that $S_1 \cap S_2 = \emptyset$ and $T_1 \cap T_2 = \emptyset$, and let $X \subseteq \Sigma$. Their synchronised parallel composition on X is the net with interfaces $\mathbf{N}_1 \otimes_X \mathbf{N}_2 = \langle I_1 \cup I_2, O_1 \cup O_2, N, V \rangle$, where the set of visible transitions is*

$$V = V_1 \otimes_X V_2 = \{\langle t_1, t_2 \rangle : t_1 \in V_1^X \wedge t_2 \in V_2^X \wedge \lambda_1(t_1) = \lambda_2(t_2)\}$$
$$\cup \{\langle t_1, * \rangle : t_1 \in V_1^X \wedge V_2^{\lambda_1(t_1)} = \emptyset\}$$
$$\cup \{\langle *, t_2 \rangle : t_2 \in V_2^X \wedge V_1^{\lambda_2(t_2)} = \emptyset\}$$
$$\cup \{t : t \in V_i \setminus V_i^X\}$$

and $N = (S, T, {}^\bullet(.), (.)^\bullet, \lambda)$ defined as follows

- $S = S_1 \cup S_2 \uplus \{p\}$
- $T = (T_1 \setminus V_1) \cup (T_2 \setminus V_2) \cup V$

$$- {}^\bullet t = \begin{cases} {}^\bullet t & \text{if } t \in T_i \setminus V_i^X \\ {}^\bullet t_1 \oplus {}^\bullet t_2 & \text{if } t = \langle t_1, t_2 \rangle \text{ with the convention } {}^\bullet * = p \end{cases}$$

$$- t^\bullet = \begin{cases} t^\bullet & \text{if } t \in T_i \setminus V_i^X \\ t_1{}^\bullet \oplus t_2{}^\bullet & \text{if } t = \langle t_1, t_2 \rangle, \text{ with the convention } *^\bullet = 0 \end{cases}$$

$$- \lambda(t) = \begin{cases} \lambda_i(t_i) & \text{if } t \in T_i \setminus V_i^X \\ \lambda_1(t_1) & \text{if } t = \langle t_1, t_2 \rangle \wedge t_1 \neq * \\ \lambda_2(t_2) & \text{if } t = \langle t_1, t_2 \rangle \wedge t_2 \neq *. \end{cases}$$

We write $\mathbf{N}_1 \otimes \mathbf{N}_2$ for $\mathbf{N}_1 \otimes_\emptyset \mathbf{N}_2$. Intuitively, the synchronised parallel composition $\mathbf{N}_1 \otimes_X \mathbf{N}_2$ is obtained by taking the disjoint union of the nets N_1 and N_2, except for those visible transitions labelled with a symbol $x \in X$, which are forced to fire synchronously. Concretely, for each pair of transitions $t_1 \in V_1$ and $t_2 \in V_2$, with identical label in X, a new transition $\langle t_1, t_2 \rangle$ is inserted whose pre- and post-set is obtained as the union of the pre- and post-set of t_1 and t_2. If a transition t_1 in N_1 has no possibility of synchronising with a transition of N_2 since V_2 does not include transitions with the same label ($V_2^{\lambda_1(t_1)} = \emptyset$), it will not be executable in the synchronised product. This is obtained by turning transition t_1 into $\langle t_1, * \rangle$ and adding to its pre-set a new place p, which will never be marked. The same happens for transitions in N_2 that cannot synchronise with any transition in N_1. An alternative solution, equivalent from the point of view of the behaviour, would be the removal of the dead transitions. We preferred this solution since, when used for the encoding of CSP processes into nets, it will ensure a closer structural correspondence between reducts of a process and the markings of the net encoding. Finally, transitions which are labelled outside X can fire asynchronously and thus are kept unchanged.

Lastly, we introduce an operation for restricting the set of visible transitions of a net. It is called hiding as it has an obvious analogy with the corresponding operation of CSP processes.

Definition 11 (hiding). *Let $\mathbf{N}$ be a net with interfaces and let $X \subseteq \Sigma$. The hiding of $\mathbf{N}$ with respect to X is the net $\mathbf{N} \setminus X = \langle I, O, N, V' \rangle$ where $V' = V \setminus V^X$.*

Given a net $\mathbf{N}$, the restriction $\mathbf{N} \setminus X$ behaves exactly as $\mathbf{N}$, but transitions labelled in X, which were previously visible, are now hidden.

When a starting state is fixed, nets are called marked.

Definition 12 (marked nets). *A marked net with interface $\mathbf{N}$ is a pair $\langle \mathbf{N}, m \rangle$, where $\mathbf{N}$ is a net with interfaces and $m \in S^\oplus$ is the initial marking.*

For marked nets we can consider the language of traces starting from the initial marking and the corresponding equivalence.

Definition 13 (traces). *Let $\mathbb{N}$ be a marked net with interfaces. Its set of traces is $traces(\mathbb{N}) = \{s \in \Sigma^* : \exists n. \, m \overset{s}{\Rightarrow} n\}$. Two marked nets with interfaces $\mathbb{N}_1$ and $\mathbb{N}_2$ are trace equivalent, written $\mathbb{N}_1 =_T \mathbb{N}_2$, if $traces(\mathbb{N}_1) = traces(\mathbb{N}_2)$.*

After building the net encoding of a CSP process, we need to mark its input places in order to fix the initial state. The following operation will then be used.

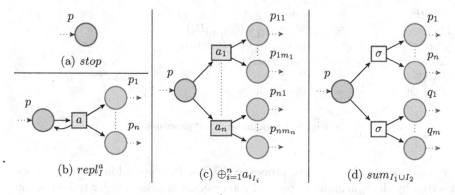

Fig. 5. The constant nets $stop$, $repl_I^a$, $\oplus_{i=1}^n a_{i_{I_i}}$ and $sum_{I_1 \cup I_2}$

Definition 14 (closing). *Let* **N** *be a net with interfaces. We denote by* $Cl(\mathbf{N})$ *the marked net with interfaces* $\langle\langle \emptyset, O, N, V\rangle, I\rangle$.

4   From Processes to Nets

This section introduces an encoding for CSP processes into nets with interfaces. It is defined inductively by exploiting the composition operators for nets introduced in Section 3. As anticipated, the encoding is restricted to bound processes.

The encoding relies on a set of constant nets, depicted in Fig. 5, which are combined using the composition operators on nets. The net $stop$ in Fig. 5(a) consists of a single place. The net $repl_I^a$ in Fig. 5(b), where $a \in \Sigma$ and $I = \{p_1, \ldots, p_n\}$, by repeated firing of transition a allows for an arbitrary number of "parallel activations" of the net which follows. This will be used as a combinator for replication. The set I is the set of input places of the encoding of the process under the replication operator. The net $\oplus_{i=1}^n a_{i_{I_i}}$ in Fig. 5(c), where $a_i \in \Sigma$ and each I_i is a set of places, is intended to provide a combinator for the guarded alternative. It consists of n transitions, labelled $a_1, \ldots, a_n$, all competing for the token in their common pre-set. Each transition a_i has $I_i = \{p_{i1}, \ldots, p_{im_i}\}$ as post-set, corresponding to the input places of the encoding of the continuation of a_i. Finally, the net $sum_{I_1 \cup I_2}$ in Fig. 5(d) is a combinator for nondeterministic (internal) choice. As above, $I_1 = \{p_1, \ldots, p_n\}$ and $I_2 = \{q_1, \ldots, q_n\}$ are sets of places which are the input places of the encodings of the processes involved in the choice. Note that the two transitions are hidden, so by definition of the operational semantics they will be turned into silent actions τ. Hence the label $\sigma \in \Sigma$, fixed for the hidden transitions of the internal choice, is totally irrelevant.

Definition 15 (encoding for processes). *Let* P *be a bound process. The encoding of* P, *denoted by* $[\![P]\!]$, *is defined as* $[\![P]\!] = Cl(|P|)$, *where* $|.|$ *is given inductively according to the rules in Fig. 6.*

The encoding of a process P is obtained by composing the encoding of its subprocesses and finally marking the input places. It therefore contains one place

$$
\begin{aligned}
|STOP| &= stop \\
|\oplus_{i=1}^{n} a_i.P_i| &= \oplus_{i=1}^{n} a_i I_{|P_i|} \circ \left(\bigotimes_{i=1}^{n} |P_i|\right) \\
|P + Q| &= sum_{I_{|P|} \cup I_{|Q|}} \circ (|P| \otimes |Q|) \\
|!_a.P| &= repl^{a}_{I_{|P|}} \circ |P| \\
|P\backslash X| &= |P| \backslash X \\
|P \mid_X Q| &= |P| \otimes_X |Q|
\end{aligned}
$$

Fig. 6. Encoding for CSP processes

for each operator !, +, $\oplus$ and process $STOP$ of P. Some additional places are inserted by the synchronised parallel composition of nets in order to keep some components inactive (see Definition 10). Note that, in the following examples, we avoid to represent such places when they are isolated. Recall that whenever two components are in a synchronised parallel composition a transition is inserted for each possible synchronisation, i.e., for each pair of events with the same name.

Example 4 (prefix and parallel synchronised processes). Consider the process $P = (a.c.STOP \oplus b.d.STOP) \mid_{\{d\}} c.d.STOP$. Its encoding is depicted in Fig. 7 (right), where input and output interfaces are empty and all transitions are visible. It is obtained by closing the net $|P|$, the result of the parallel composition, synchronised on d, of the encodings $|a.c.STOP \oplus b.d.STOP|$ and $|c.d.STOP|$, in turn depicted in the left part of Fig. 7. More precisely, the net on the upper part illustrates $|a.c.STOP \oplus b.d.STOP|$. The places ν and σ represent the subnets encoding the $STOP$ processes (those reached after the events c and d, respectively). The subnet rooted at place δ is the encoding of the subprocess $c.STOP$. Analogously, the subnet rooted γ is the encoding of the subprocess $d.STOP$. The encoding of the subprocess $a.c.STOP \oplus b.d.STOP$ is obtained by sequentially composing the net $a.I_{\{\delta\}} \oplus b.I_{\{\gamma\}}$ with $|c.STOP| \otimes |d.STOP|$. The net in the lower part represents the encoding $|c.d.STOP|$ of $c.d.STOP$.

Example 5 (bound processes). Consider the process $Q = a.a.STOP \mid_{\{a\}} a.STOP$. The encodings $|a.a.STOP|$ and $|a.STOP|$ are depicted in Fig. 8(a) and (b). The encoding $|Q|$ is obtained as their parallel composition, synchronised on a, as shown in Fig. 8(c). Each transition labelled by a of $|a.a.STOP|$ is "combined" with any other transition labelled by a in $|a.STOP|$. Observe that the second a-labelled transition in the encoding of Q cannot fire since after the firing of the first a-labelled transition, place δ is emptied and never filled again. This is consistent with the operational semantics of CSP where $Q \xrightarrow{a} a.STOP \mid_{\{a\}} STOP$, in such a way that the remaining occurrence of a cannot be executed since it has no counterpart in the parallel subprocess.

Now consider the process $R = !_b.Q = !_b.(a.a.STOP \mid_{\{a\}} a.STOP)$, that is the process Q inserted in a replication. Observe that R is not bound as it contains a non-trivial parallel synchronised product (where synchronisation is on a non-empty set of events) under the scope of a replication.

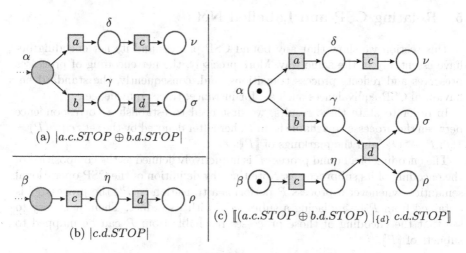

(a) $|a.c.STOP \oplus b.d.STOP|$

(b) $|c.d.STOP|$

(c) $[\![(a.c.STOP \oplus b.d.STOP) \mid_{\{d\}} c.d.STOP]\!]$

Fig. 7. Some process encodings

The net $[\![R]\!]$ in Fig. 8 (d) is obtained by closing the net $|R|$, which in turn is the sequential composition of $repl^b_{\{\alpha,\delta\}}$ with $|Q|$. Notice that the b-labelled transition can fire any number of times, thus generating an unbounded number of tokens in α and δ. Hence also the second a-labelled transition has the opportunity of being fired, in a way which disagree with the semantics of the CSP process.

Roughly speaking, the above problem arises since tokens corresponding to different occurrences of the replicated process are mixed in an improper way. Solving the problem by a different encoding, where each occurrence of a process involved in a replication corresponds to a different subnet in the encoding, would lead to an infinite net for non-bound processes.

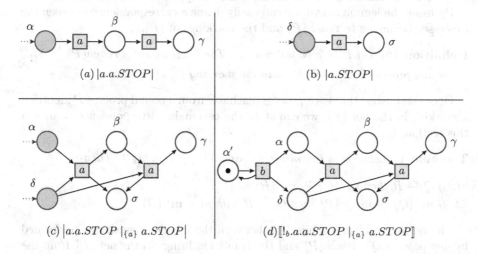

(a) $|a.a.STOP|$

(b) $|a.STOP|$

(c) $|a.a.STOP \mid_{\{a\}} a.STOP|$

(d) $[\![!b.a.a.STOP \mid_{\{a\}} a.STOP]\!]$

Fig. 8. Process encodings

5   Relating CSP and Labelled Nets

In this section we show that any bound CSP process and its net encoding behave essentially in the same way. More precisely, the net encoding of processes preserves and reflects process transitions, and, consequently, the standard behavioural CSP equivalences such as, for instance, trace equivalence.

In order to state these results, we first need to establish a correspondence between the processes reachable from P, hereafter denoted by the set $reach(P) = \{Q : P \to^* Q\}$, and the markings of $[\![P]\!]$.

The encoding of a bound process P is inductively defined as the composition of the encoding of its subprocesses. Note that, by definition of the CSP operational semantics, whenever a process P performs a transition to P', the process P' is obtained from P by replacing a subprocess with its reduct. Then, it is easy to see that the encoding of those processes reachable from P can be mapped to subnets of $[\![P]\!]$.

Lemma 1 (reachable processes as subnets). *Let P be a bound process and let Q be a subprocess of P or a process reachable from P. Let N_P and N_Q be the labelled nets underlying the encodings $[\![P]\!]$ and $[\![Q]\!]$, respectively. Then, a net morphism $f_{Q,P} : N_Q \to N_P$ can by uniquely chosen.*

The proof relies on the fact that given a subprocess Q of a process P, a mapping between the net underlying the encoding $[\![Q]\!]$ into the one underlying $[\![P]\!]$ can be obtained by the inductive definition of the encoding. Hence, each subprocess of P corresponds to a subnet of $[\![P]\!]$. Using this fact, it is not difficult to prove that also the encoding of a process reachable from P can be mapped to a subnet of $[\![P]\!]$. In fact, the processes in $reach(P)$ consist of compositions of reducts of subprocesses of P, where, due to replication, for some reducts we may have several parallel copies. The encodings of these copies, since by definition they do not synchronise on any event, can be mapped to the same subnet.

By using the lemma above, we can easily define a correspondence between the processes belonging to $reach(P)$ and the markings of $[\![P]\!]$.

Definition 16. *Let P be a bound process. The function $\mathbf{m}^P : reach(P) \to S_{[\![P]\!]}^{\oplus}$ maps any process $Q \in reach(P)$ into the marking $f_{Q,P}^{\oplus}(m_{[\![Q]\!]})$.*

Once established that each process reachable from a bound process P identifies a marking in the net $[\![P]\!]$, we can state the two main correspondence results of this section.

Theorem 1. *Let P be a bound process and let $Q \in reach(P)$. Then*

1. *if $Q \xrightarrow{\mu} R$ then $\mathbf{m}^P(Q) \xrightarrow{\mu} \mathbf{m}^P(R)$ in $[\![P]\!]$;*
2. *if $\mathbf{m}^P(Q) \xrightarrow{\mu} m$ in $[\![P]\!]$ then $Q \xrightarrow{\mu} R$ with $m = \mathbf{m}^P(R)$.*

The result establishes a bijection between the labelled transitions performed by any process $Q \in reach(P)$ and the transition firings in the net $[\![P]\!]$ from the marking $\mathbf{m}^P(Q)$.

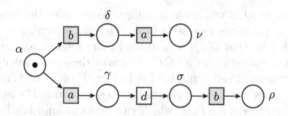

Fig. 9. Net encoding the process $(d.a.b.STOP)\backslash d \oplus b.a.STOP$

Such a bijection can then be lifted to a fundamental correspondence between the trace semantics of processes and of their encodings.

Theorem 2. *Let P, Q be bound processes. Then*

$$P =_T Q \text{ if and only if } [\![P]\!] =_T [\![Q]\!].$$

Example 6. Consider the processes $P = a.(d.b.STOP\backslash d) \oplus b.a.STOP$ and $Q = (c.a.STOP \mid_{\{c\}} c.b.STOP)\backslash c$ of Example 1. The encoding of P is in Fig. 9, while the encoding of Q is the net in Fig. 3 (right), once the interfaces are removed. Note that there is a correspondence between the labelled transitions of each process and those of its encoding. For instance, $P \xrightarrow{a} d.b.STOP\backslash d$ corresponds to $\mathbf{m}^P(P) = \{\alpha\} \xrightarrow{a} \{\gamma\} = \mathbf{m}^P(d.b.STOP\backslash d)$. The transition $d.b.STOP\backslash d \xrightarrow{\tau} b.STOP\backslash d$ corresponds to $\mathbf{m}^P(d.b.STOP\backslash d) = \{\gamma\} \xrightarrow{\tau} \{\sigma\} = \mathbf{m}^P(b.STOP\backslash d)$ and $b.STOP\backslash d \xrightarrow{b} STOP\backslash d$ to $\mathbf{m}^P(b.STOP\backslash d) = \{\sigma\} \xrightarrow{b} \{\rho\} = \mathbf{m}^P(STOP\backslash d)$. Moreover, $P \xrightarrow{b} a.STOP$ corresponds to $\mathbf{m}^P(P) = \{\alpha\} \xrightarrow{b} \{\delta\} = \mathbf{m}^P(a.STOP)$, and finally $a.STOP \xrightarrow{a} STOP$ to $\mathbf{m}^P(a.STOP) = \{\delta\} \xrightarrow{a} \{\nu\} = \mathbf{m}^P(STOP)$.

We have a correspondence also between the transitions of Q and those of its net encoding. Therefore, it is easy to conclude that the nets are trace equivalent.

6 Some Hints about Technology Transfer

The encoding of bound CSP processes into labelled nets enables to transfer results concerning expressiveness and tractability from one formalism to the other, as it was the case for the net encoding of CCS in [1].

Observe that trace equivalence is obviously undecidable for both bound CSP processes and Petri nets (since they include as a fragment the basic parallel processes for which trace equivalence is known to be undecidable [11]). Still, even though this does not give new insights, we note that by using the encoding, the undecidability of trace equivalence for Petri nets can be also deduced directly from the undecidability of trace equivalence for bound CSP.

Reachability, namely the possibility of reaching a given process Q via a sequence of transitions from a start process P, is not a particularly interesting property for CSP. Since during process evolution the number of parallel components can only increase, the property turns out to be decidable. Indeed, in order to establish whether Q is reachable it suffices to consider the fragment of the LTS including the processes reachable from P having a number of parallel sub-processes bounded by that of Q. It is instead more interesting the reachability under the garbage collection of $STOP$: it breaks the monotonicity mentioned above, and the removal itself is not trivial. In fact, $P \mid_X STOP$ is equivalent to P only when X does not include channel names on which P can synchronise. E.g., think of the process $a.STOP$ which can perform an a-labelled transition while $a.STOP \mid_{\{a\}} STOP$ is deadlocked.

Alternatively one can consider control state reachability, i.e., the reachability of a configuration including a given subprocess. In this last case, it is sufficient to consider net coverability. It is folklore that the control state reachability problem is undecidable for full CSP, while the corresponding property of coverability is known to be decidable for Petri nets [8]. By exploiting the encoding, decidability of coverability can be transferred from Petri nets to bound processes.

Corollary 1 (reachability). *Let P, Q be bound processes. The problem of establishing whether there exists bound process R such that $P \to^* R$ and Q is a sub-process of R is decidable.*

Thanks to the correspondence between processes reachable from a process P and reachable markings in the net encoding of P, decidability of boundedness in Petri nets [8] implies that it is possible to determine whether a CSP process has a finite number of states.

Corollary 2 (finite state). *Let P be a bound process. It is decidable whether P has a finite number of reachable states.*

Again, the property of being finite state can be more interesting for CSP processes when working up to garbage collection of useless STOP parallel components. It can be seen that this property is naturally captured by the boundedness of the subset of places of $[\![P]\!]$ not corresponding to STOP processes.

Analogously, it is possible to identify an upper bound to the degree of parallelism of a bound CSP process, i.e., to the number of parallel subcomponents of a process during its evolution. More precisely, define the structural degree of a CSP process P as $sdeg(P \mid_X Q) = sdeg(P) + sdeg(Q)$ and $sdeg(P) = 1$ otherwise. Then the degree of P is $deg(P) = \sup\{sdeg(P') : P \to^* P'\}$. The close correspondence between $deg(P)$ and the maximal total number of tokens in the reachable markings of $[\![P]\!]$ immediately leads to the following result.

Corollary 3 (parallelism). *Let P be a bound process. The problem of determining whether $deg(P)$ is finite is decidable. Moreover, for any given $k \in \mathbb{N}$, it is decidable whether $deg(P) \leq k$.*

A classical property in the analysis of the expressiveness of process calculi is convergence, i.e., the existence of a terminating computation. We recall such notion below, according to [5].

Definition 17 (convergence). *A process P is called convergent if there exists Q such that $P \to^* Q \not\to$.*

Convergence of a bound process can be reduced to the existence of a deadlock in its encoding, a property which is known to be decidable for Petri nets [8].

Corollary 4 (convergence). *Convergence is decidable for bound processes.*

7   Conclusions and Further Works

In this work we have identified a fragment of CSP, consisting of what we called bound processes, that can be encoded into (labelled) Petri nets. The encoding preserves and reflects the (strong) transitions of the process calculus and, consequently, the whole spectrum of (both strong and weak) behavioural equivalences definable on the transition system of CSP processes. Furthermore, the encoding is syntax-driven, hence modular, mapping each process operator into a suitable one for labelled nets with interfaces. As far as we know, this is a main improvement with respect to former proposals.

Interfaces are in fact the key ingredient to achieve modularity: they are needed in defining the net operators upon which our encoding lays its foundations. Reactive extensions of Petri nets, endowed with means for interacting with the environment [3,13,2,4], naturally arise as extensions of nets allowing for compositional reasoning. This feature plays a key role for modelling various brands of process calculi. Indeed, in [1] they were pivotal in the encoding of an asynchronous fragment of CCS into open nets. Interestingly enough, asynchronous interactions are captured by a form of composition where net components interact only over places, while in this paper the synchronous interaction is realised by letting net components interact over an interface consisting of transitions. This should have been intuitively expected, since in Petri nets the token flow is eminently asynchronous, while transitions synchronise different token flows.

Therefore, our results confirm that (open) Petri nets can accommodate both asynchronous message passing and barrier synchronisation. In principle, this leaves space for a calculus combining both characteristics, endowed with a direct encoding into nets. This would take us back in full circle, since this calculus would trace its roots on some early proposals for net encoding of processes [16].

Acknowledgements. We are grateful to the referees for their insightful suggestions on the submitted version of the paper, and, in particular, for pointing out the relevance of control state reachability in the analysis of CSP processes.

References

1. Baldan, P., Bonchi, F., Gadducci, F.: Encoding asynchronous interactions using open Petri nets. In: Bravetti, M., Zavattaro, G. (eds.) CONCUR 2009. LNCS, vol. 5710, pp. 99–114. Springer, Heidelberg (2009)
2. Baldan, P., Corradini, A., Ehrig, H., Heckel, R., König, B.: Bisimilarity and behaviour-preserving reconfigurations of open Petri nets. In: Mossakowski, T., Montanari, U., Haveraaen, M. (eds.) CALCO 2007. LNCS, vol. 4624, pp. 126–142. Springer, Heidelberg (2007)

3. Best, E., Devillers, R., Hall, J.G.: The Petri box calculus: a new causal algebra with multi-label communication. In: Rozenberg, G. (ed.) APN 1992. LNCS, vol. 609, pp. 21–69. Springer, Heidelberg (1992)
4. Bruni, R., Melgratti, H.C., Montanari, U., Sobocinski, P.: Connector algebras for C/E and P/T nets' interactions. Logical Methods in Computer Science 9(3), 1–65 (2013)
5. Busi, N., Gabbrielli, M., Zavattaro, G.: Comparing recursion, replication, and iteration in process calculi. In: Díaz, J., Karhumäki, J., Lepistö, A., Sannella, D. (eds.) ICALP 2004. LNCS, vol. 3142, pp. 307–319. Springer, Heidelberg (2004)
6. Degano, P., Gorrieri, R., Marchetti, S.: An exercise in concurrency: a CSP process as a condition/event system. In: Rozenberg, G. (ed.) APN 1988. LNCS, vol. 340, pp. 85–105. Springer, Heidelberg (1988)
7. Devillers, R., Klaudel, H., Koutny, M.: A compositional Petri net translation of general pi-calculus terms. Formal Aspects of Computing 20(4-5), 429–450 (2008)
8. Esparza, J., Nielsen, M.: Decidability issues for Petri nets - a survey. Elektronische Informationsverarbeitung und Kybernetik 30(3), 143–160 (1994)
9. Goltz, U., Reisig, W.: CSP-programs with individual tokens. In: Rozenberg, G. (ed.) APN 1984. LNCS, vol. 188, pp. 169–196. Springer, Heidelberg (1985)
10. Gorrieri, R., Montanari, U.: SCONE: A simple calculus of nets. In: Baeten, J.C.M., Klop, J.W. (eds.) CONCUR 1990. LNCS, vol. 458, pp. 2–30. Springer, Heidelberg (1990)
11. Hirshfeld, Y.: Petri nets and the equivalence problem. In: Börger, E., Gurevich, Y., Meinke, K. (eds.) CSL 1993. LNCS, vol. 832, pp. 165–174. Springer, Heidelberg (1994)
12. Hoare, C.A.R.: Communicating Sequential Processes. Prentice Hall, Upper Saddle River (1985)
13. Kindler, E.: A compositional partial order semantics for Petri net components. In: Azéma, P., Balbo, G. (eds.) ICATPN 1997. LNCS, vol. 1248, pp. 235–252. Springer, Heidelberg (1997)
14. Llorens, M., Oliver, J., Silva, J., Tamarit, S.: Generating a Petri net from a CSP specification: A semantics-based method. Advances in Engineering Software 50, 110–130 (2012)
15. Nielsen, M., Priese, L., Sassone, V.: Characterizing behavioural congruences for Petri nets. In: Lee, I., Smolka, S.A. (eds.) CONCUR 1995. LNCS, vol. 962, pp. 175–189. Springer, Heidelberg (1995)
16. Olderog, E.R.: Operational Petri net semantics for CCSP. In: Rozenberg, G. (ed.) APN 1987. LNCS, vol. 266, pp. 196–223. Springer, Heidelberg (1987)
17. Reisig, W.: Understanding Petri Nets. Springer (2013)
18. Roscoe, A.W.: The Theory and Practice of Concurrency. Prentice Hall, Upper Saddle River (1998)

Verifiable Decisions in Autonomous Concurrent Systems*

Lenz Belzner

LMU Munich, PST Chair, Germany
belzner@pst.ifi.lmu.de

Abstract. Being able to take decisions at runtime is a crucial ability for any system that is designed to act autonomously in uncertain or even unknown environments. This autonomy necessitates to formally check system properties at design time to ensure avoidance of problems or even harm caused by the system at runtime. This paper is about the formal specification of concurrent systems that are capable of reasoning about the consequences of their actions, enabling them to coordinate and decide on what to do autonomously. A non-deterministic procedural action programming language is defined to constrain system behaviour at design time. Rewriting logic is employed to construct and evaluate possible traces of programs in a decision-theoretic manner, allowing agents to perform goal-based actions autonomously at runtime as well as providing possibilities to model-check system properties at design time.

1 Introduction

Concurrent multiagent systems designed to act autonomously in highly dynamic, non-deterministic environments expose a number of requirements that have to be addressed by modelling and specification approaches. In fact, their design has to enable a system to reason about possibly uncertain outcomes of its actions in order to decide what behaviour to perform at runtime. This kind of cognitive ability requires specification of knowledge about actions' preconditions and effects. Algorithms have to be provided to enable a system to evaluate and decide on particular behavioural alternatives. Also, in the presence of multiple agents that share the same environment, the issues of concurrency and synchronization have to be accounted for by any specification approach.

Along with the specification of knowledge about actions and uncertainty, it should be possible to constrain the behaviour of an autonomous system at design time. To this end, non-deterministic action programming languages [1] allow for specification of behavioural constraints. In fact, non-deterministic programs allow to specify plan sketches that can be seen as behavioural alternatives provided to a system. These alternatives can then be evaluated in the context of a situation that a system finds itself in at runtime.

For systems that act autonomously, formal verification of properties at design time, e.g. by model checking, is a valuable source of information for design

---

* This work has been partially funded by the EU project ASCENS, 257414.

E. Kühn and R. Pugliese (Eds.): COORDINATION 2014, LNCS 8459, pp. 17–32, 2014.

choices and error detection. In this paper, the formalization of knowledge and behavioural constraints for ensembles is realized in rewriting logic [2,3,4]. Domain knowledge is represented as a relational Markov Decision Process [5,6]; a non-deterministic action programming language is defined to allow for specification of behavioural constraints. The rewriting logic concepts of matching and rewriting are employed to provide to a system the ability to reason about the consequences of its behaviour. A number of problems that are typical for cognitive systems are addressed in this paper:

- *Specification of knowledge about actions.* Besides providing to a system information about pre- and postconditions of actions, it is necessary that the system knows what properties of the environment remain unchanged. In static logics like first-order logic, this is a non-trivial issue known as the frame problem [7].
- *Legality & projection.* If a system is provided with the ability to choose from various behavioural alternatives, this may lead to action choices that cannot be executed at runtime due to precondition violations. To decide whether a certain behavioural trace is legal (i.e. executable w.r.t. action preconditions), a cognitive agent has to be capable of deciding whether certain properties of the environment hold as consequences of its actions; an ability that is known as projection [8].
- *Trace evaluation & system property verification.* Non-deterministic action programs are employed to constrain system behaviour, giving raise to various execution traces, thus enabling a system to evaluate behavioural alternatives w.r.t. its goals. Also, the consequences arising from the execution of traces can be used to verify properties of the given action program at design time.
- *Concurrency.* When multiple agents interact dynamically at runtime, the issues of concurrency, synchronization and coordination arise, especially in the presence of sharing. Reasoning about concurrent execution should be possible with specified knowledge about a domain; also, the legality and projection problems have to be dealt with in the presence of concurrency.

This paper extends previous work on action programming in rewriting logic [9] by decision-theoretic concepts, and discusses in more detail the integration of concurrency and coordination. Also, an approach towards probabilistic model-checking for action programs is discussed. The paper is outlined as follows. Section 2 introduces rewriting logic and action programming. Section 3 discusses the specification of knowledge and behaviour for autonomous concurrent systems in terms of a rewrite theory, and defines how the concepts of matching and rewriting are employed to interpret and reason about the specification. Section 4 discusses how to perform model checking of action programs for typical desirable system properties. A short example illustrating the approach is given in section 5. In section 6, related work is compared with the presented specification approach. Finally, section 7 summarizes the results and gives a brief outlook on further research venues.

2   Preliminaries

This section gives a brief introduction to rewriting logic (section 2.1) and action programming (section 2.2).

2.1   Rewriting Logic

The core concept of rewriting logic are rewrite theories $(\Sigma, A \cup E, R, \phi)$ [2,3,4]. Σ is a signature defining sorts, sort-orders and operations to build terms from sorts in the signature. A are axiomatic definitions for operations in Σ like associativity, commutativity, idempotency or identity, and E specifies a set of equations for terms in Σ. $A \cup E$ defines equivalence classes for terms, representing the static structure of the rewrite theory. R is a set of possibly conditional rewrite rules that specify the theory's dynamics. Finally, ϕ is a function from operations to natural numbers that defines which arguments of an operation are frozen, meaning that no rewriting will take place on this argument.

Term rewriting with rewrite theories is performed by matching terms with rules. In rewriting logic, matching is performed *modulo axioms with extensions* (called *Ax-matching*). For example, consider an operation $\circ$ that is associative and commutative. Then, the term $a \circ b \circ c$ would Ax-match the term $c \circ a$, because $a \circ b \circ c =_A c \circ a \circ b$ due to axioms for $\circ$, and obviously $c \circ a$ is a subterm of the given term. If terms contain variables, matching applies if there is a substitution that renders a subterm of a given subject term equal to a term to be matched; thus, a more concrete term matches a more general one.

Rewrite rules are of the form $l \rightarrow r$ **if** *Conditions*, where l and r are terms in Σ that have an equal least sort, and *Conditions* can either be boolean expressions, matching conditions (true if a term t Ax-matches a term t', denoted $t := t'$) and rewriting conditions (true if a term t rewrites to a term t' according to rules in R, denoted $t \rightarrow t'$). Rewriting of a subject term t is performed if a non-variable subterm of t matches a rule's left-hand side, and the conditions of the rule hold for the particular matching substitution. The matched subterm is then replaced by the rules right-hand side. Rewriting of a term to its normal form, where no more rewrite rules can be applied, is denoted by $t \rightarrow_! t'$.

As Ax-matching a term with rules may result in different matched subterms and substitutions, rewriting can naturally express non-determinism. Also, as multiple rules may be applied to different subterms in parallel, rewriting logic is considered an intuitive way to deal with concurrency [4].

As long as some admissibility requirements are satisfied (e.g. if there are no fresh variables in a rule's right-hand side), the process of rewriting can be performed computationally. This fact has led to the development of the term-rewriting language MAUDE [2,3]. Rewrite theories can straightforwardly be implemented as MAUDE modules. The language provides a built-in breadth-first search command to compute all possible rewrites of a term, where search depth and the number of desired solutions are parametrized. This approach can for example be used to perform automated state-space search on rewrite theories in order to model-check a given specification (see section 4).

2.2   Action Programming

Action programming is "the art and science of devising high-level control strategies for autonomous systems which employ a mental model of their environment and which reason about their actions as a means to achieve their goals" [1].

Action programming allows to specify non-deterministic programs that can be considered as a plan sketch, roughly outlining desired behaviour of a system without committing to a certain trace of actions. In other words, an action program defines a constrained space of behavioural alternatives. To allow a system to reason about these alternatives at runtime, a domain specification is provided that contains definitions of *fluents* (i.e. state properties) that are subject to change (e.g. due to action execution) as well as *actions* in terms of their preconditions and effects, which may also be non-deterministic. This knowledge can then be employed by the system to decide what to do at runtime.

For example, consider fluents x, y and z, and actions α and β. Informally, assume $x, y \rightarrow_\alpha z$, $x \rightarrow_\beta y$ and $y \rightarrow_\beta z$, denoting an action's precondition and (non-deterministic) effects. Then, given the action program $\alpha \,\#\, \beta$ where # is a non-deterministic choice operator and a current situation where x and y hold, an agent can derive that executing α will lead to a situation where z holds, and that execution of β could result in a state where either y holds (as $x, y \rightarrow_\beta y, y$) or where x and z hold (according to the latter specification of β).

Influential action programming formalisms are the situation calculus with its language GOLOG [8] and the fluent calculus and its language FLUX [10]. The situation calculus employs a fluent-wise regressive specification of action effects known as *successor state axioms*, where the frame problem is explicitly handled by also stating under what conditions some fluent does not change. States are not explicitly managed, but rather the notion of a *situation* is used to test whether a fluent holds after execution of an action program. On the other hand, the fluent calculus uses a progressive, action-wise specification of domain dynamics by defining modifications of an associative-commutative representation of a state that arise due to action execution.

3   Decisions in Autonomous Concurrent Systems

As mentioned in section 2.2, to provide to a system the ability to reason in terms of action programming, specification of domain dynamics as well as a language to define behavioural alternatives are necessary. In section 3.1, the encoding of domain knowledge in terms of a rewrite theory encoding a relational MDP is discussed. Section 3.2 defines a non-deterministic, procedural action programming language that employs the specified rewrite theory to construct trace consequences through Ax-matching and rewriting (see section 2.1), and introduces the notion of a trace's value, thus enabling systems to reason about action preferences. Section 3.3 deals with the explicit treatment of projection, and provides definitions for branching and loops. Section 3.4 discusses action programming with concurrency in the presence of sharing, allowing for agent synchronization and coordination.

3.1   RMDPs as Rewrite Theories

For specification of non-deterministic domain dynamics, the proposed approach employs the notion of a relational MDP. A relational MDP is a tuple (S, A, T, R), where S is a set of relational states, A a set of actions, $T : S \times A \times S \to [0; 1]$ is a transition function specifying the probability that execution of a particular action in a state results in another one, and $R : S \to \mathbb{R}$ is a reward function. To encode such a relational MDP as a rewrite theory, a set of fluents F is defined (see section 2.2), from which the set of states Σ is built by means of the following syntax. Both $\wedge$ and $\vee$ are associative and commutative with identity element ϵ_σ. The equivalence classes of terms in Σ can be considered the set of states S of a relational MDP.

$$\Sigma := \epsilon_\sigma \mid f \in F \mid \neg\Sigma \mid \Sigma \wedge \Sigma \mid \Sigma \vee \Sigma$$

States annotated with probability are denoted by $\sigma_p := (\sigma \wedge prob(p)) \in \Sigma$, with a fluent $prob : [0; 1] \to F$ encoding the probability of a system being in state σ. The set of states annotated with a probability fluent is denoted by Σ_P.

The transition function T is encoded in terms of rewrite rules. If there are n non-deterministic transitions in T that define the effects of executing action α in state σ each leading to a state σ^i with probability $p^i, i \in \{1, ..., n\}$, a rule is defined for each of them in the form $\Sigma_P \times A \to \Sigma_P$ as follows (with $\sum_{i=1}^{n} p_i = 1$).

$$\sigma_{p^i} \times \alpha \to \sigma^i_{p*T(\sigma, \alpha, \sigma^i)} \ . \tag{1}$$

The states σ and the σ^i can be considered as pre- and postconditions of action α. Note that this notation of transitions provides a solution to the frame problem [7], as subject terms are matched with extension when applying rules. Thus, there is no necessity to explicitly specify state properties that remain unchanged by application of a rule.

Example 1. (Action rules) A rule for defining an action *move* that moves a robot R at position P (denoted by a fluent $pos : Robot \times Position \to F$) to a desired position P' with a probability of 0.9 and has no effect otherwise is specified by the following rules.

$$pos(R, P)_p \times move(R, P') \to pos(R, P')_{p*0.9} \ .$$
$$pos(R, P)_p \times move(R, P') \to pos(R, P)_{p*0.1} \ .$$

Finally, a MDP's reward function R can simply be encoded in terms of an operation together with corresponding equations. For example, considering a variable S of sort state[1], the equations $R(pos(r, p) \wedge S) = 1, R(S) = 0$ *[otherwise]* specify a reward of 1 for states where robot r is at position p and zero reward for all other states.

---

[1] Throughout the paper, variables are denoted by uppercase letters.

3.2   Progressive Action Programming

This section describes how to constrain system behaviour in terms of an action program, and how a system can construct and evaluate behavioural alternatives according to these constraints when given a rewrite theory as domain specification as outlined in section 3.1. To this end, a procedural non-deterministic action programming language is defined with syntax Π.

$$\Pi := \epsilon_\pi \mid \alpha \in A \mid \Pi ; \Pi \mid \Pi \# \Pi$$

Here, ϵ_π denotes the empty program, α is an action from the domain specification, ; is an associative sequential operator, and # is an associative-commutative non-deterministic choice operator, offering behavioural alternatives to a system executing the program. Both operators have ϵ_π as identity element.

To allow for numerical evaluation of states, these are annotated with a value (i.e. gathered reward), denoted by $\sigma_{p \times v} := (\sigma_p \wedge value(v)) \in \Sigma$ with a fluent $value : \mathbb{R} \to F$ encoding the value v gathered in a state σ. The corresponding set of states annotated with probability and value is denoted by $\Sigma_{P \times V}$.

Program interpretation and trace evaluation is then performed by rewriting *configurations* $\Sigma_{P \times V} \times \Pi \times \Pi \times \mathbb{N}$ that consist of a current state, an action program to be evaluated, an action trace leading to the current state and a planning horizon. The set of configurations is denoted as Ξ. For ease of notation, functions $\sigma_\xi, p_\xi, v_\xi, \pi_\xi, \tau_\xi, h_\xi$ are defined, taking as parameter a configuration $\xi := \sigma_{p \times v} \times \pi \times \tau \times h$, returning its respective values, e.g. $\sigma_\xi(\xi) = \sigma$.

To compute possible consequences of executing for h steps an action program π in a particular state σ, an initial configuration $\xi_{\text{init}} := \sigma_{1.0 \times 0.0} \times \pi \times \epsilon_\pi \times h$ is rewritten according to the following rules, resulting in a set of configurations $\{\xi \mid \xi_{\text{init}} \to_! \xi \in \Xi\}$.[2]

$$\sigma_{p \times v} \vee \left(\bigvee_i \sigma^i_{p_i \times v_i} \right) \to \sigma_{p \times v} \, . \tag{2}$$

$$\sigma_{p \times v} \times \alpha \times \tau \times h \to \sigma'_{p' \times v'} \times \epsilon_\pi \times (\tau ; \alpha) \times (h-1)$$
$$\text{if } h > 0 \wedge \sigma_p \times \alpha \to \sigma'_{p'} \wedge v' := v + R(\sigma') \, . \tag{3}$$

$$\sigma_{p \times v} \times (\pi_1 ; \pi_2) \times \tau \times h \to \sigma'_{p' \times v'} \times \pi_2 \times \tau' \times h'$$
$$\text{if } \sigma_{p \times v} \times \pi_1 \times \tau \times h \to \sigma'_{p' \times v'} \times \epsilon_\pi \times \tau' \times h' \, . \tag{4}$$

$$\sigma_{p \times v} \times (\pi_1 \# \pi_2) \times \tau \times h \to \sigma_{p \times v} \times \pi_1 \times \tau \times h \, . \tag{5}$$

As state disjunction is associative and commutative, rule (2) rewrites a state in disjunctive normal form to all its conjunctive subterms, leading to subsequent rewriting of configurations only containing conjunctive states. Note that disjunctive normal form for states can easily be assured by specifying according equations for state-terms.

---

[2] MAUDE's built-in search operator performs a breadth-first search; a depth-first strategy can be defined using MAUDE's internal strategies [3] or a dedicated strategy language [11], e.g. by assigning rule application preferences.

Rule (3) rewrites a configuration containing a single action α as program if the planning horizon has not yet been reached and the action's preconditions are satisfied by the current state. Satisfaction of preconditions is tested by rewriting the current state σ_p with the given action according to the transition rules for actions in the domain. If $\sigma_p \times \alpha$ can be rewritten, the preconditions are satisfied, and any rewards of the reached state are added to v[3]. Otherwise rewriting terminates, thus solving the legality problem by Ax-matching left-hand sides of rewrite rules encoding the transition function of a relational MDP with $\sigma_p \times \alpha$.[4] Note that Ax-matching is highly efficient; for ac-terms typically met in practice, its complexity does not exceed $O(\log n)$, where n is term size [12]. Ax-matching also results in a non-deterministic argument pick if a parameter of the action that is to be processed is a variable.

Rewriting of sequential programs determines all configurations that can result by executing the sequence's head, which are then further rewritten according to the sequence's tail (rule (4)). Choice programs are rewritten according to rule (5), that will rewrite a configuration according to all possible program choices as the choice operator is associative and commutative.

In contrast to configurations for which rewriting terminated due to precondition violation, rewriting also terminates for a configuration ξ exposing $h_\xi(\xi) = 0$ (due to rule (3)) or $\pi_\xi(\xi) = \epsilon_\pi$ (because there is no rule for interpreting ϵ_π). Thus, these properties can be used to define the set of *legally terminating configurations* $\Xi_\downarrow$ arising from rewriting an initial configuration $\xi_{\text{init}} \in \Xi$ according to program traces where no action precondition is violated.

$$\Xi_\downarrow(\xi_{\text{init}}) := \{\xi \mid \xi_{\text{init}} \to_! \xi \wedge (\pi_\xi(\xi) = \epsilon_\pi \vee h_\xi(\xi) = 0)\}$$

The set of *legally terminating program traces* $T_\downarrow$ for an initial configuration $\xi_{\text{init}} \in \Xi$ is defined as follows.

$$T_\downarrow(\xi_{\text{init}}) := \{\tau \mid \xi \in \Xi_\downarrow(\xi_{\text{init}}) \wedge \tau_\xi(\xi) = \tau\}$$

Similarly, the set of *configurations yielding a particular, legally terminating trace* $\Xi_{\tau_\downarrow}$ is defined.

$$\Xi_{\tau_\downarrow}(\xi_{\text{init}}) := \{\xi \mid \xi \in \Xi_\downarrow(\xi_{\text{init}}) \wedge \tau_\xi(\xi) = \tau\}$$

The *expected value of a legally terminating trace* V_e is the sum of expected values (which is the product of probability and value) of its non-deterministic outcomes.

$$V_e(\tau, \xi_{\text{init}}) := \sum_{\xi \in \Xi_{\tau_\downarrow}(\xi_{\text{init}})} (p_\xi(\xi) * v_\xi(\xi)) \qquad (6)$$

---

[3] When rewards are specified action-wise, i.e. $R : \Sigma \times A \times \Sigma$, the computation of v in the condition of rule (3) changes to $v := R(\sigma, \alpha, \sigma')$.

[4] To allow for Ax-matching of states and actions technically, conjunction of fluents and concurrency of actions (see section 3.4) are implemented in terms of a single associative-commutative operation, e.g. $\circ : \text{STATE} \to \text{STATE}$, with sorts FLUENT and ACTION being subsorts of sort STATE. I.e. $\sigma \wedge \sigma' = \sigma \circ \sigma', \sigma \times \alpha = \sigma \circ \alpha, \alpha \parallel \alpha' = \alpha \circ \alpha'$.

The *legal termination probability* $P_\downarrow$ of a particular trace is the sum of all probabilities of configurations that yield the trace.

$$P_\downarrow(\tau, \xi_{\text{init}}) := \sum_{\xi \in \Xi_{\tau_\downarrow}(\xi_{\text{init}})} p_\xi(\xi) \tag{7}$$

Summarizing, given a domain specification and an initial configuration (i.e. a current state[5], an action program and a planning horizon), rules (2) to (5) together with the definitions for V_e and $P_\downarrow$ enable a system to perform the following tasks: (i) Computation of all program traces and their consequences. (ii) Determination of expected values for traces. (iii) Determination of legal termination probability of a particular trace.

Example 2. (Expected trace values and legal termination probability) Consider the rule for action move from example 1. Let S be a variable of sort Σ and $r(\text{pos}(R, sa) \wedge S) = 1.0$ (0 otherwise). Consider $\xi_{\text{init}} = \text{pos}(r, pos)_{1.0 \times 0.0} \times \text{move}(r, sa) \times \epsilon_\pi \times 1$. Then, expected value and legal termination probability of a possible trace of the program $\text{move}(r, sa)$ that tries to move a robot r to the safety area sa compute as follows when executing it in a state where r is at position pos (with $pos \neq sa$).

$$\xi_{\text{init}} \rightarrow \text{pos}(r, sa)_{0.9 \times 1.0} \times \epsilon_\pi \times \text{move}(r, sa) \times 0 \ .$$
$$\xi_{\text{init}} \rightarrow \text{pos}(r, pos)_{0.1 \times 0.0} \times \epsilon_\pi \times \text{move}(r, sa) \times 0 \ .$$
$$V_e(\text{move}(r, sa), \xi_{\text{init}}) = 0.9 * 1.0 + 0.1 * 0.0 = 0.9 \ .$$
$$P_\downarrow(\text{move}(r, sa), \xi_{\text{init}}) = 0.9 + 0.1 = 1.0 \ .$$

3.3 Projection, Branching and Loops

The projection problem is to decide whether a certain property holds in a state or not (e.g. after a number of actions have been executed). As discussed in section 3.2, when interpreting action execution a state term is updated to yield the information about the resulting state. Thus, the projection problem reduces to deciding whether a property holds in a given state term. This is easily solved in rewriting logic: It suffices to check whether a given condition term in Σ Ax-matches a particular state term for a substitution of variables θ. To this end, *state subsumption* (denoted by $\sqsupseteq$) is defined as follows.

$$\sigma_? \sqsupseteq \sigma \rightarrow \theta \text{ if } \sigma_? / \theta := \sigma \ .$$
$$\sigma_? \sqsupseteq \sigma \Leftrightarrow \exists \theta : \sigma_? \sqsupseteq \sigma \rightarrow \theta \ .$$
$$\sigma_? \not\sqsupseteq \sigma \Leftrightarrow \not\exists \theta : \sigma_? \sqsupseteq \sigma \rightarrow \theta \ .$$

A state $\sigma_? \in \Sigma$ thus subsumes another state $\sigma \in \Sigma$ if its corresponding state term is more general than the state term of σ, which is checked by Ax-matching the two terms. With this definition of state subsumption, operations

---

[5] Note that partial observable domains can be accounted for by rewriting an initial configuration $\bigvee_i (\sigma^i_{p^i \times v^i}) \times \pi \times \epsilon_\pi \times h$ with $\sum_i p^i = 1$, where the σ^i represent different possible states an agent considers, each with probability p^i.

are introduced for action programs that check whether a condition holds (or does not hold, respectively) at a particular stage of execution. The syntax for action programs is extended as follows.

$$\Pi_? := \Pi \mid ?(\Sigma)\{\Pi_?\} \mid \neg?(\Sigma)\{\Pi_?\}$$
$$\mid \textbf{if } \Sigma \textbf{ then } \Pi_? \textbf{ else } \Pi_? \textbf{ end}_{\text{if}}$$
$$\mid \textbf{while } \Sigma \textbf{ do } \Pi_? \textbf{ end}_{\text{while}}$$

Interpretation of $?(\sigma_?)\{\pi\}$ succeeds if there is a substitution θ for which a condition $\sigma_?$ subsumes the state of the current configuration to be rewritten. If so, the variable substitutions for which the condition hold are applied to the argument action program π (rule (8)). Similarly, rewriting $\neg?(\sigma_?)\{\pi\}$ succeeds if there is no such substitution (rule (9)).

$$\sigma_{p\times v}\times ?(\sigma_?)\{\pi\} \times \tau \times h \to \sigma_{p\times v} \times \pi/\theta \times \tau \times h \text{ if } \sigma_? \sqsupseteq \sigma \to \theta . \tag{8}$$
$$\sigma_{p\times v} \times \neg?(\sigma_?)\{\pi\} \times \tau \times h \to \sigma_{p\times v} \times \pi \times \tau \times h \text{ if } \sigma_? \not\sqsupseteq \sigma . \tag{9}$$

With these operations, conditional branching can be defined as a macro.

$$\textbf{if } \sigma_? \textbf{ then } \pi_1 \textbf{ else } \pi_2 \textbf{ end}_{\text{if}} = ?(\sigma_?)\{\pi_1\}\#\neg?(\sigma_?)\{\pi_2\} . \tag{10}$$

Testing whether a condition $\sigma_?$ holds in (i.e. subsumes) a particular state σ also allows for interpretation of loops. If $\sigma_?$ subsumes σ for a substitution θ, the loop body will be executed with θ applied, followed by the loop itself; otherwise, the loop reduces to the empty program.

$$\sigma_{p\times v} \times \textbf{while } \sigma_? \textbf{ do } \pi \textbf{ end}_{\text{while}} \times \tau \times h \to$$
$$\sigma_{p\times v} \times \pi/\theta; \textbf{while } \sigma_? \textbf{ do } \pi \textbf{ end}_{\text{while}} \times \tau \times h \text{ if } \sigma_? \sqsupseteq \sigma \to \theta . \tag{11}$$
$$\sigma_{p\times v} \times \textbf{while } \sigma_? \textbf{ do } \pi \textbf{ end}_{\text{while}} \times \tau \times h \to$$
$$\sigma_{p\times v} \times \pi_\epsilon \times \tau \times h \text{ if } \sigma_? \not\sqsupseteq \sigma . \tag{12}$$

3.4   Concurrency

To allow for specification of action programs for agents that act concurrently, the set of actions is extended to $A_{\shortparallel} := \epsilon_\alpha \mid A \mid A_{\shortparallel} \parallel A_{\shortparallel}$ where $\parallel$ is associative-commutative with identity ϵ_α and denotes parallel execution of actions. Programs are allowed to be executed in parallel as well: $\Pi_{\shortparallel} := \Pi_?(A/A_{\shortparallel}) \mid \Pi_{\shortparallel} \parallel \Pi_{\shortparallel}$, where the syntax of programs in $\Pi_?$ is extended to allow for parallel actions.

As action rules are applied sequentially to the current state term when rewriting, it is necessary to *lock* changing subterms of the state term to model true concurrency, disallowing interleaving application of actions that would result in race conditions. To this end, action dynamics as in rule (1) (see section 3.1) are *automatically* compiled to rules of form (13), explicitly denoting which fluents of the precondition σ are changed by action execution and which ones are left unchanged. Changed fluents are locked by an operation $\phi : \Sigma \to \Sigma, \phi(\sigma) \wedge \phi(\sigma') =$

$\phi(\sigma \wedge \sigma')$, keeping them from being further matched with parallel actions' preconditions.

$$\sigma_p \times \alpha_{||} \to \sigma^i_{p*T(\sigma,\alpha_{||},\sigma^i)} \text{ where } \sigma^i = \phi(\sigma^i_{\text{changed}}) \wedge \sigma^i_{\text{unchanged}} . \tag{13}$$

Example 3. (Action Rules for Concurrent Domains) Consider the specification of actions *grab* and *drop* in a domain with concurrency. Note how state properties changed by the actions are locked.

$$(\text{pos}(R,P) \wedge \text{pos}(O,P))_p \times \text{grab}(R,O) \to (\text{pos}(R,P) \wedge \phi(\text{on}(R,O)))_{p*0.9} .$$
$$(\text{pos}(R,P) \wedge \text{pos}(O,P))_p \times \text{grab}(R,O) \to (\text{pos}(R,P) \wedge \text{pos}(O,P))_{p*0.1} .$$
$$(\text{pos}(R,P) \wedge \text{on}(R,O))_p \times \text{drop}(R,O) \to (\text{pos}(R,P) \wedge \phi(\text{pos}(O,P)))_{p*1.0} .$$

For instance, $\text{grab}(r1,o) \parallel \text{drop}(r2,o)$ should always be considered illegal, as at least one precondition is violated in any case before applying any of the actions; if interleaving rewriting was performed without locking state changes, the application of *drop* would in turn render *grab* executable (and vice versa), which is something that should not occur when the actions are considered truly concurrent. I.e., locking of changed properties resembles a precondition check before *any* action is applied and a check of postconditions after application of *all* actions. Note that, if *interleaving concurrency* is to be modelled, locking of changing state properties can simply be dropped. Interleaving is then achieved by the non-deterministic application of rewrite rules for action dynamics from the domain specification.

Concurrent action programs are normalized to sequential and choice terms as shown in equations (14) and (15) (for $\alpha_i \in A_{||}, \pi_i \in \Pi_{||}$). Due to this normalization, interpretation of sequences and choices (rules (4) and (5), see section 3.2) can be performed without rule modification by rewriting configurations with concurrent action programs.

$$(\pi_1 \# \pi_2) \parallel \pi_3 = (\pi_1 \parallel \pi_3) \# (\pi_2 \parallel \pi_3) . \tag{14}$$
$$(\alpha_1 ; \pi_1) \parallel (\alpha_2 ; \pi_2) = (\alpha_1 \parallel \alpha_2) ; (\pi_1 \parallel \pi_2) . \tag{15}$$

Rewriting (i.e. interpretation) of a parallel action (rule (3) for domains without concurrency, see section 3.2) resulting from transformation of a concurrent action program according to equation (15) is changed to account for resolution of locked state properties arising from rewriting according to rules of form (13) that specify action dynamics for concurrent domains. [6]

$$\sigma_{p \times v} \times \alpha_{||} \times \tau \times h \to$$
$$(\sigma_1 \wedge \sigma_2)_{p' \times v'} \times \epsilon_\pi \times (\tau ; \alpha_{||}) \times (h-1)$$
$$\text{if } h > 0 \wedge \sigma_p \times \alpha_{||} \to (\phi(\sigma_1) \wedge \sigma_2)_{p'} \wedge v' := v + R(\sigma_1 \wedge \sigma_2) . \tag{16}$$

---

[6] For action-wise rewards, it is $v' := v + R(\sigma, \alpha_{||}, \sigma_1 \wedge \sigma_2)$. Then, for parallel actions reward is additive: $R(\sigma, \alpha \parallel \alpha', \sigma') = R(\sigma, \alpha, \sigma') + R(\sigma, \alpha', \sigma')$.

Example 4. (Concurrency) Consider the *move* action from example 1. The example shows rewriting a state according to a concurrent action that tries to move two robots to a position p_3, illustrating the evaluation of the rewrite condition in rule (16). Rewrite results in the following set of states matching the conditions right-hand side (i.e. all actions have been rewritten). Note that depending on the outcome of actions, different state properties are locked.

$$(\text{pos}(r_1, p_1) \land \text{pos}(r_2, p_2))_p \times \text{move}(r_1, p_3) \parallel \text{move}(r_2, p_3) \to$$
$$\phi(\text{pos}(r_1, p_3) \land \text{pos}(r_2, p_3))_{p*0.9*0.9} \lor (\phi(\text{pos}(r_1, p_3)) \land \text{pos}(r_2, p_2))_{p*0.9*0.1}$$
$$\lor (\text{pos}(r_1, p_1) \land \phi(\text{pos}(r_2, p_3)))_{p*0.1*0.9} \lor (\text{pos}(r_1, p_1) \land \text{pos}(r_2, p_2))_{p*0.1*0.1} .$$

If particular actions require *synchronization* of agents, this can be specified by defining a rewrite rule according to rule (13) with an action that is explicitly parallel. A rule specified this way will only rewrite to a legal configuration if concurrent processes manage to synchronize their actions accordingly.

Example 5. (Synchronization) Consider an action t (for *transport*) that moves a victim to a target position when two agents perform it synchronously. A single agent trying to transport a victim has no effect and should be interpreted as a precondition violation. Thus, this action requires synchronization of agents' actions. This fact is specified as follows (considering a deterministic outcome for the sake of simplicity).

$$(\text{pos}(R, P) \land \text{pos}(R', P) \land \text{pos}(V, P))_p \times t(R, V, P') \parallel t(R', V, P') \to$$
$$\phi(\text{pos}(R, P') \land \text{pos}(R', P') \land \text{pos}(V, P'))_{p*1.0} .$$

If there is need for agents to synchronize, it may be valuable for agents to *coordinate* their actions by waiting for others to collaborate, eventually rendering a desired action executable. To this end, if an agent should execute an action α as soon as its precondition $\sigma_{\text{pre}_\alpha}$ is satisfied, waiting for satisfaction of preconditions (e.g. collaborating agents) can be specified in terms of a macro **waitFor**. Note that $\sigma_{\text{pre}_\alpha}$ can be determined from the lefthand side of the domain specification rule that specifies the dynamics of α.

$$\textbf{waitFor}(\alpha) = \textbf{while } \neg\sigma_{\text{pre}_\alpha} \textbf{ do noop end}_{\text{while}}; \alpha . \qquad (17)$$

4   Probabilistic Model Checking of Action Programs

This section shows how to perform symbolic probabilistic model checking for action programs, whose interpretation results in configurations containing action traces determined through application of Ax-matching and rewriting as shown in section 3. To this end, this section discusses the relation between typical system properties to be model-checked and rewriting of configurations. System properties are expressed in terms of PCTL formulas. For an in-depth discussion of model-checking in general, and model-checking with PCTL in particular, see e.g. [13]. For the relation of model-checking and classical planning see e.g. [14].

A typical property that can be checked for an action program is whether it contains a legal trace that will reach a particular goal state satisfying[7] a property σ_{goal} within a given number of steps h with at least a desired probability p_{min}. This property can be expressed in terms of a PCTL formula, where $\mathbb{P}_{\geq p_{min}}$ denotes the requirement that its argument is satisfied at least with probability p_{min}, and the *eventually* operator $\Diamond^{\leq h}$ denotes that its argument state is eventually reached within the given horizon h.

$$\mathbb{P}_{\geq p_{min}}(\Diamond^{\leq h} \sigma_{goal}) \tag{18}$$

To check whether a given configuration ξ_{init} satisfies this property, a positive reward is specified for states that satisfy σ_{goal}, i.e. $R(\sigma_{goal}) > 0$; all other states expose a reward of zero. Then, (legally terminating) traces eventually satisfying σ_{goal} expose a positive reward.

$$\Xi_{\tau_\downarrow}^+(\xi_{init}) = \{\xi \,|\, \xi \in \Xi_{\tau_\downarrow}(\xi_{init}) \wedge v_\xi(\xi) > 0\} \tag{19}$$

To determine the probability of a trace eventually satisfying σ_{goal}, the probabilities of terminated configurations with equal traces (arising due to nondeterminism) are summed up. If there is no such trace, the probability is zero.

$$P_\downarrow^+(\tau, \xi_{init}) = \sum_{\xi \in \Xi_{\tau_\downarrow}^+(\xi_{init})} p_\xi(\xi) \tag{20}$$

Property (18) is satisfied if there exists a legally terminating trace with an expected value greater than zero and a probability of eventually reaching a state satisfying σ_{goal} greater than p_{min}.[8]

$$\mathbb{P}_{\geq p_{min}}(\Diamond^{\leq h} \sigma_{goal}) \Leftrightarrow \exists \tau \in T_\downarrow(\xi_{init}) : V_e(\tau, \xi_{init}) > 0 \wedge P_\downarrow^+(\tau, \xi_{init}) \geq p_{min} \tag{21}$$

In general, a PCTL formula of the form $\mathbb{P}_J(\Diamond^{\leq h} \sigma)$, where J is an interval in $[0;1]$ can be checked for any initial configuration $\xi_{init} \in \Xi$ by specifying a reward greater than zero for states subsumed by σ, and zero reward for all other states; then, it is checked by rewriting whether probabilities of legal traces whose expected value is bigger than zero are in the interval J.

$$\mathbb{P}_J(\Diamond^{\leq h} \sigma_{goal}) \Leftrightarrow \exists \tau \in T_\downarrow(\xi_{init}) : V_e(\tau, \xi_{init}) > 0 \wedge P_\downarrow^+(\tau, \xi_{init}) \in J \tag{22}$$

In particular situations, a system may be required to maintain a particular state property $\sigma_{maintain}$. In these cases, it may be valuable to ensure a minimal probability p_{min} that the desired property will sustain with program execution. The PCTL formula $\mathbb{P}_{\geq p_{min}}(\Box^{\leq h} \sigma_{maintain})$ expresses this system property, where the *always*

---

[7] A state σ satisfies a property $\sigma_?$ if $\sigma_? \sqsupseteq \sigma$ (see section 3.3).
[8] Depending on the property to be checked, existential quantification is to be replaced by universal quantification.

operator $\square^{\leq h}$ denotes that its argument state is always satisfied within the given horizon h. This property can be reformulated in terms of an achieve goal that requires an upper bound on the maximal probability that the desired property will be violated by program execution: $\mathbb{P}_{<1-p_{\min}}(\Diamond^{\leq h}\neg\sigma_{\text{maintain}})$. This property can then be checked according to (21). Due to the duality of the always and eventually operators, transformation of maintain to achieve goals can be generalized for probability intervals [13].

$$\mathbb{P}_{]p,p']}(\square^{\leq h}\sigma) = \mathbb{P}_{[1-p',1-p[}(\Diamond^{\leq h}\neg\sigma) \tag{23}$$

5   Example

As a short informal example, consider a rescue scenario. There are two robots r_1 and r_2 at positions p_1 and p_2, respectively. There are also two victims v_1 and v_2, the former at position p_1, the latter at a position p_3. I.e. $\sigma^{\text{init}} := \text{pos}(r_1,p_1) \wedge \text{pos}(r_2,p_2) \wedge \text{pos}(v_1,p_1) \wedge \text{pos}(v_2,p_3)$ (see figure 1). The robots are supposed to transport victims to the safety area; to this end, a reward of one is given if there is any victim at the safety area sa, i.e. $R(\text{pos}(V,sa)) = 1$. Consider the following part of an action program that specifies a behavioural policy for the robots, where actions $move$ and t are defined as in examples 1 and 5. It states that a robot R either moves to the position P of a victim V if there is any, or, if the robot is already at a position of a victim, it waits until it can transport the victim to the safety area in collaboration with another robot.[9]

$$policy(R) := \textbf{while } \sigma_\epsilon \textbf{ do}$$
$$?(\text{pos}(V,P))\{move(R,P)\}\#$$
$$?(\text{pos}(V,P) \wedge \text{pos}(R,P))\{\textbf{waitFor}(t(R,V,sa))\}$$
$$\textbf{end}_{\text{while}}$$

The robots can interpret the action program $\pi := policy(r_1) \parallel policy(r_2)$ for a σ^{init}, for example for a planning horizon of 2 (because, for example, their energy resources suffice only for this horizon). Interpretation of the program leads to various traces due to the choice operator and due to the non-deterministic effect of $move$. Rewriting of an initial configuration $\xi_{\text{init}} := \sigma^{\text{init}}_{1.0\times0.0} \times \pi \times \pi_\epsilon \times 2$ will result in a number of configurations, two of which are considered in more detail.

$$\xi_{\text{init}} \rightarrow_! (\text{pos}(r_1,sa) \wedge \text{pos}(r_2,sa) \wedge \text{pos}(v_1,sa))_{0.9\times1.0} \times \pi \times \tau_1 \times 0$$
$$\vee (\text{pos}(r_1,sa) \wedge \text{pos}(r_2,sa) \wedge \text{pos}(v_2,sa))_{0.81\times1.0} \times \pi \times \tau_2 \times 0$$
$$\vee ...$$

where $\tau_1 = \text{noop} \parallel move(r_2,p_1); t(r_1,v_1,sa) \parallel t(r_2,v_1,sa)$
$\tau_2 = move(r_1,p_3) \parallel move(r_2,p_3); t(r_1,v_2,sa) \parallel t(r_2,v_2,sa)$

---

[9] The loop condition σ_ϵ will always subsume any state, as it is the identity element for states and subsumption is performed through Ax-matching.

τ_1 is arising from r_1 waiting and r_2 moving successfully to p_1 before they transport v_1 to the safety area, τ_2 represents the trace where both robots successfully move to p_3 and subsequently transport v_2 to the safety area. Figure 1 informally illustrates σ_{init} and the two traces τ_1 and τ_2.

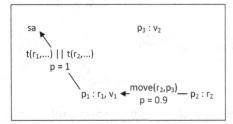 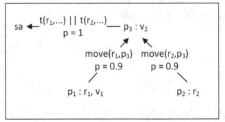

Fig. 1. Two traces τ_1 and τ_2 of executing $policy(r_1) \parallel policy(r_2)$ in state σ_{init}

For the robots to decide which choice is more valuable according to reward specification, the traces' expected values can be determined: $V_e(\tau_1, \xi_{\text{init}}) = 0.9$ and $V_e(\tau_2, \xi_{\text{init}}) = 0.81$. Therefore, deciding on τ_1 is the preferable choice of actions in the state σ_{init}.

Expected values and legal termination probabilities can also be used to prove that executing π in σ_{init} satisfies the PCTL property $\mathbb{P}_{\geq 0.9}(\Diamond^{\leq 2}\text{pos}(V, sa))$, as $\tau_1 \in T_\downarrow(\xi_{\text{init}})$ and $V_e(\tau_1, \xi_{\text{init}}) > 0 \wedge P_\downarrow^+(\tau_1, \xi_{\text{init}}) = 0.9$ (see section 4).

6 Related Work

As mentioned in section 2.2, prominent action programming formalisms have been developed: the situation calculus with its language GOLOG [8] and the fluent calculus with its language FLUX [10]. As already outlined, the situation calculus uses regressive fluent-wise specification of dynamics, which contrasts strongly with modern software design where dynamics are typically progressively defined operation-wise. Regarding this issue, the fluent calculus is more close to modern software design paradigms, as is the approach presented in this paper. While there is a decision-theoretic variant of GOLOG called DT-GOLOG employing the situation calculus [15], and there is a decision-theoretic extension to the fluent calculus (the *probabilistic fluent calculus* [16]), there is no procedural language exploiting decision-theoretic evaluation for a progressive action calculus, as FLUX is purely declarative. The relationship of classical planning and model checking has been investigated thoroughly [14], but, to the best of the author's knowledge, symbolic PCTL model checking approaches have not been investigated in the context of action programming in particular.

Both GOLOG and FLUX have been implemented in the PROLOG language, where specification of domain theories and action programs is done in terms of a logic program. While this is a reasonable approach for the reasoning tasks tackled by these formalisms, PROLOG does not explicitly provide support for formal, algebraic software engineering like MAUDE [2,3]. Thus, MAUDE's features like modularization, explicit sort-hierarchies and polymorphism as well as meta-language operations and user-definable syntax provide additional properties to an action language specified in rewriting logic, as rewrite theories can be implemented in terms of MAUDE modules straightforwardly. Also, model checking as shown in section 4 is quite naturally supported by a MAUDE implementation due to its built-in *search* operator.

7 Conclusion and Further Work

7.1 Conclusion

This paper reports on efforts to integrate various aspects of action programming, algebraic software engineering and model checking to ease the specification of concurrent autonomous systems which expose formally verifiable behaviour and are able to evaluate action alternatives in a decision-theoretic manner, allowing them to autonomously take decisions at runtime that are sensible w.r.t. specified system goals. Domain knowledge (i.e. a relational MDP) is specified as a rewrite theory; system behaviour in terms of a procedural action program. Decision-theoretic evaluation and model-checking of action programs are performed by matching and rewriting modulo the given rewrite theory. Solutions have been provided for typical problems of symbolically reasoning systems like the frame, projection and legality problems. The approach supports true concurrency in the presence of sharing, and provides facilities to specify synchronization and coordination of actions. Symbolic PCTL model checking of typical system properties has been discussed. Action programming in rewriting logic without support for decision-theoretic concepts has been implemented in the MAUDE language [9].[10]

7.2 Further Work

Some directions for further work remain. It would be interesting to provide support for situations with incomplete knowledge, where properties of the environment have to be actively sensed. To this end, sensing actions have to be induced to plans, possibly considering sensing costs and expected rewards.

While explicit specification of concurrency has been discussed in this paper, evaluation of concurrent programs is performed centralized. In large-scale multi-agent domains it is valuable to decentralize the decision making process by localizing and distributing knowledge. In order to coordinate behaviour, sophisticated communication and interaction models (e.g. SCEL [17]) should be integrated with reasoning abilities of agents.

Finally, the relation of action programming and model checking discussed in section 4 only treated a particular class of PCTL formulae. Generalizing this approach as done for classical planning [14] could allow for specification of more complex goals and model checking of more complex system properties.

---

[10] http://www.pst.ifi.lmu.de/~belzner/action-programming/

References

1. Thielscher, M.: Action Programming Languages. Synthesis Lectures on Artificial Intelligence and Machine Learning. Morgan & Claypool Publishers (2008)
2. Clavel, M., Durán, F., Eker, S., Lincoln, P., Martí-Oliet, N., Meseguer, J., Quesada, J.F.: Maude: specification and programming in rewriting logic. Theor. Comput. Sci. 285(2), 187–243 (2002)
3. Clavel, M., Durán, F., Eker, S., Lincoln, P., Martí-Oliet, N., Meseguer, J., Talcott, C.: All About Maude - A High-Performance Logical Framework. LNCS, vol. 4350. Springer, Heidelberg (2007)
4. Meseguer, J.: Conditional rewriting logic as a unified model of concurrency. Theor. Comput. Sci. 96(1), 73–155 (1992)
5. Puterman, M.L.: Markov Decision Processes: Discrete Stochastic Dynamic Programming, 1st edn. John Wiley & Sons, Inc., New York (1994)
6. Boutilier, C., Reiter, R., Price, B.: Symbolic dynamic programming for first-order mdps. In: Nebel, B. (ed.) IJCAI, pp. 690–700. Morgan Kaufmann (2001)
7. Mccarthy, J., Hayes, P.J.: Some philosophical problems from the standpoint of artificial intelligence. Machine Intelligence 4, 463–502 (1969)
8. Reiter, R.: Knowledge in Action: Logical Foundations for Specifying and Implementing Dynamical Systems, illustrated edn. The MIT Press, Massachusetts (2001)
9. Belzner, L.: Action programming in rewriting logic. TPLP 13(4-5-online-suppl.) (2013)
10. Thielscher, M.: Flux: A logic programming method for reasoning agents. TPLP 5(4-5), 533–565 (2005)
11. Eker, S., Martí-Oliet, N., Meseguer, J., Verdejo, A.: Deduction, strategies, and rewriting. Electronic Notes in Theoretical Computer Science 174(11), 3–25 (2007)
12. Eker, S.: Associative-commutative rewriting on large terms. In: Nieuwenhuis, R. (ed.) RTA 2003. LNCS, vol. 2706, pp. 14–29. Springer, Heidelberg (2003)
13. Baier, C., Katoen, J.P., et al.: Principles of model checking, vol. 26202649. MIT Press, Cambridge (2008)
14. Giunchiglia, F., Traverso, P.: Planning as model checking. In: Biundo, S., Fox, M. (eds.) ECP 1999. LNCS (LNAI), vol. 1809, pp. 1–20. Springer, Heidelberg (2000)
15. Boutilier, C., Reiter, R., Soutchanski, M., Thrun, S., et al.: Decision-theoretic, high-level agent programming in the situation calculus. In: AAAI/IAAI, pp. 355–362 (2000)
16. Hölldobler, S., Skvortsova, O.: A logic-based approach to dynamic programming. In: Proceedings of the Workshop on Learning and Planning in Markov Processes–Advances and Challenges at the Nineteenth National Conference on Artificial Intelligence (AAAI 2004), pp. 31–36 (2004)
17. De Nicola, R., Ferrari, G., Loreti, M., Pugliese, R.: A language-based approach to autonomic computing. In: Beckert, B., Bonsangue, M.M. (eds.) FMCO 2011. LNCS, vol. 7542, pp. 25–48. Springer, Heidelberg (2012)

Coordination of ECA Rules
by Verification and Control

Julio Cano[1], Gwenaël Delaval[2], and Eric Rutten[1]

[1] INRIA, Grenoble, France
{julio-angel.cano-romero,eric.rutten}@inria.fr
[2] LIG / UJF, Grenoble, France
gwenael.delaval@inria.fr

Abstract. Event-Condition-Action (ECA) rules are a widely used language for the high level specification of controllers in adaptive systems, such as Cyber-Physical Systems and smart environments, where devices equipped with sensors and actuators are controlled according to a set of rules. The evaluation and execution of every ECA rule is considered to be independent from the others, but interactions of rule actions can cause the system behaviors to be unpredictable or unsafe. Typical problems are in redundancy of rules, inconsistencies, circularity, or application-dependent safety issues. Hence, there is a need for coordination of ECA rule-based systems in order to ensure safety objectives. We propose a tool-supported method for verifying and controlling the correct interactions of rules, relying on formal models related to reactive systems, and Discrete Controller Synthesis (DCS) to generate correct rule controllers.

1 Coordination Problems in ECA Rules

Event-Condition-Action (ECA) rules are defined [13] as a set of rules where each of them *'autonomously reacts to actively or passively detected simple or complex events by evaluating a condition or a set of conditions and by executing a reaction whenever the event happens and the condition is true'*. The form of the rule is: **ON** *Event* **IF** *Condition* **DO** *Action*. Some characteristics are that:

- a rule is activated only by events;
- its execution is autonomous and independent of other rules in the system;
- it implements a reaction to the incoming event;
- it contains a guarding condition to execute such actions.

Research on ECA rules is often related to active database management systems (ADBMS) [3,14], where events represent modifications produced in the database, and ECA rules are used to control the integrity. But they have also been used in different control environments [8] or adaptation frameworks [10], and there are many different implementations of ECA rule-based systems. ECA rules are a language derived from practice, and not constructed from a formal definition in the beginning. This is comparable to other cases like StateCharts and its multiple variants and implementations (e.g. in UML, or in the StateMate tools of

E. Kühn and R. Pugliese (Eds.): COORDINATION 2014, LNCS 8459, pp. 33–48, 2014.
© IFIP International Federation for Information Processing 2014

iLogix [1], or in Stateflow/Simulink), or like works on the verification of implementation languages like Java or C. Therefore, there is no unique reference or formal semantics, and they can not be submitted to formal analysis as such.

Coordination Problems. The nature of ECA rule-based systems shows different problems in their execution, the most extended [18] being as follows.

Redundancy means that there are two (or more) rules in the system whose functionality is replicated. This can happen in large rule systems where rules are written by different persons. An example in a smart home automated system is to have two similar rules: one detects the presence of a person in a room and, if temperature is lower than 15 degrees, then turns on room heaters. The other rule does the same, but also closes the room door. This can be described in ECA syntax as follows (a concrete grammar is described later in Section 3):

```
ON presence IF (temperature_get < 15) DO heater_on
ON presence IF (temperature_get < 15) DO heater_on, door_close
```

This represents an overload in the rules system in the best of cases, and an undesired repetitive activation of orders on environment devices.

Inconsistency occurs when contradictory actions are sent to devices. This can occur if multiple rules are activated at the same time, and their execution order may render different final states in the system. An example is: upon the presence of a person in the room lights are activated, and TV will also be activated. A third rule will turn off the lights then the TV is turned on.

```
ON presence IF true DO lights_on
ON presence IF true DO TV_on
ON TV_light IF TV_on DO lights_off
```

Depending on the order of execution of rules, the final state of the system will be different. If rules 2 and 3 are activated before rule 1 is executed then the final state of lights will be different than executing rule 1 before rule 3. So the result of the execution of these rules is not predictable.

Circularity occurs when rules get activated continuously without reaching a stable system state that makes them finish their execution. For example, the first two rules will try to change the second light to a state different from the first light ; the third and fourth rules will try to maintain both in the same state.

```
ON light1_change IF light1_on DO light2_off
ON light1_change IF light1_off DO light2_on
ON light2_change IF light2_on DO light1_on
ON light2_change IF light2_off DO light1_off
```

Application-specific issues can be considered additionally in an environment. An example is ordering to open a windows and to turn on the room heaters. It can be considered as a contradiction by the user. In order to know which actions are contradictory, specific information must be provided about the environment. In this paper we will consider that multiple actions sent to the same device are contradictory. Only one action can be requested to every device at every instant.

Coordinating ECA rules is therefore necessary in order to enforce safety properties. One of the problems of ECA rules is that they are considered to be executed independently or autonomously. This means that possible interactions between rules and their effects are not controlled. In contrast, synchronous reactive languages, used to design and program control systems, provide some characteristics, such as determinism and verifiability [9]. This is useful for the safe execution of control systems. The objective of this work is to provide validation of the ECA rule system before and during the execution of the system, by relating them to synchronous languages. Here, safety is meant for the control system and people in the environment controlled by this control system. The system should not go into undesired states, and controlled devices are considered part this state.

Our approach proposed in this paper consists of a model transformation from an ECA rules description to a synchronous programming language, which will be used to validate the set of rules. ECA rule systems are validated, detecting the described issues. Our proposal constitutes a formal semantics of ECA rules, covering variants of rule engines, and defined concretely by translation into a formally defined language, for which formal tools are available. Rules execution is also controlled and coordinated to avoid the described problems at run-time. We will concentrate on small or home environment as target systems, although our results are generic enough to be applied in any ECA rule-based system.

The Heptagon/BZR programming language [2] is used here because of its capability to express behavioral invariants in the system in the form of contracts, which allows verifying the application by model checking as well as controlling or coordinating the execution according to the described invariants.

In the following, Section 3 formalizes the ECA rules used in this paper. Section 4 shows their translation to a synchronous program, on which Section 5 shows how we perform verification and control. Section 6 concludes.

2   State of the Art

2.1   ECA Rule Based Control Systems and Their Validation

ECA rule systems are widely used to control the environment as well as to control reconfiguration of software systems. Here are described the closest proposals to our approach and ECA rule-based systems verification and validation. In [10], an adaptation framework is proposed. It detects the state of the system in the form of events. When these events are detected the associated rules can be applied. These rules will perform the required actions according to the detected state, to adapt the behavior of the system to the changes of the environment. In [16,17], a method is proposed to design applications with reconfiguration capabilities. At design time, invariants can be described for every state and transitions between states. These invariants are used in the design of Petri Nets representing the desired behavior of the application. Designed Petri Nets can be used to check the previously defined invariants and to create prototypes of the system. The system is supposed to be safe by design, if the design is correctly translated to the implementation. No control is performed at run-time about the specified invariants. A mixture of rule based system and utility functions is proposed in [5]. Rules are mainly used to change the priorities for the utility functions when a state change is detected. The number of possible available configurations can grow exponentially, so calculation of the utility functions at run-time is costly.

The following work cover basic aspects in verification and validation of ECA rule systems. In [15], a way to validate a set of rules in a knowledge based systems is proposed. It defines different types of rules to create a *rule net* consisting of chained rules, which explicitly invoke other rules. In the rule net, it checks if different paths contain *inconsistencies* according to the constraints defined in the system or other rules. In [11], an infrastructure is described to detect and solve static (compilation time) and dynamic (execution time) conflicts for a framework of WS-ECA. This framework is based in the use of ECA rules for Web Services. The existence of distributed devices with their own rules may lead to conflicting rules. No implementation is described for this infrastructure.

In [18], a more complete proposal is described to verify an ECA rule based system. It starts formalizing the system to be able to define the problems of *redundancy, inconsistency* and *circularity*. Three levels are described regarding the verification and validation of these problems. Level 1 refers only to rule set level, where no information about run-time execution is considered. Level 2 takes into account direct results of the execution of actions on the environment. This means actions that will directly provoke new events activating rules. Level 3 takes into account all the possible responses of the environment, which cannot be previously known because they are completely random or unpredictable. Certain problems can only be verified at some levels because of the required information to perform such verifications. In [4], a method is provided to verify ECA rule systems with formal methods, transforming the ECA rules set into a set of different kinds of automata for every part of the process, and using the automata verification tool Uppaal. This verification is limited to performing model checking of timed automata and their correspondence to the provided ECA rule set.

Every ECA rule-based system implementation imposes different execution semantics. These semantics can vary from parallel synchronized execution of rules to execution in depth first and discard of previously activated rules. So the result of the execution of a rule set differs depending on the execution policy of the implementation. All the proposals described above are centered in one kind of ECA rule system execution policy, or they do not take into account that results depend on the execution policy used by every different implementations. In this paper, we propose a solution that takes into account the desired execution policy of the target implementation to verify an ECA rules set.

2.2   Synchronous Reactive Programming and Heptagon/BZR

Reactive systems are interactive systems that constantly communicate with their environment taking into account the timing needs of this environment [9]. These systems will work reacting to received events or by sampling incoming signals. Synchronous programming languages allow programming of reactive systems using automata, where reactions will correspond to the automata transitions. Computations and transitions performed by composed automata are considered to occur in parallel at the same time instant. This intrinsic synchronism makes it easier to preserve the determinism, and allows these programming languages to be based on sound formal semantics. Thus, these languages are provided with tools for the verification (e.g., by automated test or model-checking) or control (e.g., by controller synthesis) of programs.

Heptagon/BZR [2] is a synchronous dataflow programming language with support for equations and automata. This language also provides a contract mechanism allowing the use of discrete controller synthesis (DCS) within the compilation, using the Sigali synthesis tool [12]. The discrete controller synthesis method is based in partitioning input variables into controllable and uncontrollable ones. For a given objective, such as staying in a subset of states, its DCS algorithm will automatically compute, by symbolic exploration of the state space, the constraint on controllable variables, so that the behavior satisfies the objective, whatever be the values of the inputs from the environment. Figure 1(a) represents the control loop. The automata-based program is in charge of controlling the environment. The behavior of the automata is constrained by the synthesized controller, which is in charge of maintaining the system in the desired subset of states. The main elements of a Heptagon/BZR program are:

- Nodes: blocks of equations or automata with input and output signals
- Equations: determining the value of node outputs. A set of equations in parallel are separated by semicolons.
- Automata: mode automata using states, input and output signals.
- Contracts: describing invariants to be enforced by control at execution.

The compiler generates executable code in C or Java. Figure 1(b) shows an example of Heptagon/BZR code. It contains a `delay` node, with an automaton which makes use of a controlled variable to delay the emission of a received signal. A `main` node makes use of this automaton. It includes a contract to enforce that both signals are not emitted at the same time. Heptagon/BZR makes use of Sigali at compilation time to synthesize the needed controller that will provide the correct value for every controlled variable (`c1` and `c2`), and hence forcing the delay of one of the signals. The control variable (`c`) in Figure 1(b) determines when the signal has to be delayed. When a `new_sig` is received, depending on the value of the controlled variable, the `new_sig` value is emitted (staying in the `Idle` state) or delayed (performing a transition to the `Waiting` state) until the controlled variable indicates that it can be released. The value of the `out` variable is described in function of `new_sig` and the controlled variable. Automata transitions will be effective in the next step of its execution. To avoid delays in the desired automaton output, the value of the `out` variable is described in function of `new_sig` and the controlled variable. This allows emitting the desired value in the same execution step.

Heptagon/BZR has been used by some work in smart home / environment context, to design safe control systems. In [19], Heptagon/BZR is proposed for the autonomic management of small environments. The behavior of devices is

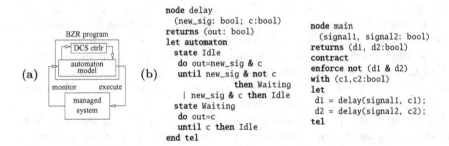

```
                                node delay
                                  (new_sig: bool; c:bool)      node main
       BZR program              returns (out: bool)             (signal1, signal2: bool)
      ┌─ DCS ctrlr ─┐          let automaton                   returns (d1, d2:bool)
      │ ┌─────────┐ │            state Idle                    contract
(a)   │ │automaton│ │  (b)         do out=new_sig & c           enforce not (d1 & d2)
      │ │ model   │ │              until new_sig & not c        with (c1,c2:bool)
      │ └─────────┘ │                       then Waiting       let
  monitor    execute              | new_sig & c then Idle        d1 = delay(signal1, c1);
      │ ┌─────────┐ │            state Waiting                    d2 = delay(signal2, c2);
      │ │ managed │ │              do out=c                     tel
      │ │ system  │ │              until c then Idle
        └─────────┘             end tel
```

Fig. 1. Discrete control: (a) control model; (b) controlled automaton example

represented using automata and control objectives are described as *contracts*. For instance, it can avoid the request to turn on a device if it can generate an energy consumption higher than the specified. In [7], a similar approach is proposed to provide safe environment for disabled people. However, none of these works featured ECA rules as a high-level description language. In another domain, the coordination of multiple autonomic loops in adaptive computing systems has been approached with a discrete control approach [6].

3   Modeling ECA Rules

Here we describe a formalization of an ECA rule-based system to be able to translate it into a Heptagon/BZR program. The ECA rule-based system is assumed to be connected to the physical world through devices that may work as sensors or actuators. The control system loop is generated providing devices information about the environment to the rules and then sending the result of rules again to devices. A rule based system $S = (R, E, D)$ is composed of a set of rules R, a set of events E and a set of devices D. We consider that rules, events, devices and signals are identified by unique names, taken in a name set N. Thus, events are names, i.e., $E \subset N$. Devices $d \in D$ are a virtual representation of physical devices in the system as sensors and actuators. A device $d = (n, I, O)$, named n, is composed of a set of input signals $I \subset N$ and a set of output signals $O \subset N$. In the following, we will denote by Expr(O) the set of Boolean expressions defined on the set of output signals O. The function EventExpr $\in E \to$ Expr(O) maps events to boolean expressions based on output signals received from devices. The event $e \in E$ is activated whenever the expression EventExpr(e) is true. Rules $r \in R$ are defined by a tuple $r = (n, e, c, A)$, where $n \in N$ is the name of the rule, $e \in E$ the activating event, $c \in$ Expr(O) the condition, and $A \subset I$ a set of actions to perform. The condition is a boolean expression based on the output of devices. If the event occurs and the condition is true, the corresponding actions will be performed.

Figure 2 shows the concrete grammar used by the implemented tool to translate a ECA rule-based system into a Heptagon/BZR program. The descriptions

```
<ECA-system> ::= <events_list> <rules_list> <devices_list>
<event_lists> ::= <event> | <event> <event_lists>
<event> ::= EVENT <event_name> IF <expression> | EVENT <event_name> IS INTERNAL
<rules_list> ::= <rule> | <rule> <rule_list>
<rule> ::= ON <event_name> IF <condition> DO <action_list>
<action_list> ::= <action_name> | <action_name>, <action_list>
<device_list> ::= <device> | <device> <device_list>
<device> ::= DEVICE <device_name> [ SIMULTANEOUS ( DISCARD | DELAY )]
                    [INPUTS (<input_list>)] [OUTPUTS (<outputs_list>)]
```

Fig. 2. ECA rule-based system description grammar

contains lists of events, rules and devices. Events can be internal (generated by rules as an action, indicated by the **INTERNAL** term) or be generated if the described expression becomes true (when the term **IF** is used in its description). Rules contain the event name that activates them (preceded by term **ON**), a boolean expression to determine if certain conditions apply (preceded by term **IF**), and the list of actions that have to be performed if event and condition are true (preceded by term **DO**). The device contains the device name, a specification of the policy to be used in the device when multiple simultaneous actions are sent to this device, a list of inputs and a list of outputs of the device. The term **SIMULTANEOUS** allows specifying the policy used when multiple signals are sent to the same device. **DISCARD** allows discarding all the signals but one. **DELAY** allows delaying all the signals but one. Delayed signals will be emitted later, in following executions of the controller, in order of priority. The priority in all cases is given by the order in which input and output signals are declared. Inputs and outputs are optional in the description of the device. At least one should be indicated. If the device policy is not specified, the default value is **DISCARD**.

Figure 3 shows an example including rules from Section 1: **light1_change** will be activated if light1 is turned on or off. The needed events and devices are also described: **presence** and **temperature** sensors are used, with only outputs.

```
EVENT presence:BOOL IF presence_get
EVENT TV_lights:BOOL IF TV_on
EVENT light1_change IF light1_on or light1_off
EVENT light2_change IF light2_on or light2_off

ON presence IF (temperature_get < 15) DO heater_on
ON presence IF (temperature_get < 15) DO heater_on, door_close
ON presence IF true DO light1_on
ON presence IF true DO TV_on
ON TV_lights IF TV_on DO light1_off
ON light1_change IF light1_on DO light2_off
ON light1_change IF light1_off DO light2_on
ON light2_change IF light2_on DO light1_on
ON light2_change IF light2_off DO light1_off

DEVICE presence OUTPUTS (get:BOOL)
DEVICE temperature OUTPUTS (get:BOOL)
DEVICE light1 SIMULTANEOUS DISCARD INPUTS (on:BOOL, off:BOOL) OUTPUTS (on:BOOL, off:BOOL)
DEVICE light2 SIMULTANEOUS DISCARD INPUTS (on:BOOL, off:BOOL) OUTPUTS (on:BOOL, off:BOOL)
DEVICE TV SIMULTANEOUS DELAY INPUTS (on:BOOL, off:BOOL) OUTPUTS (on:BOOL, off:BOOL)
```

Fig. 3. ECA rule-based system description example

4   Transformation to Synchronous Language

We propose a transformation to Heptagon/BZR code from the described ECA rule-based system. As shown in Figure 4, the generated Heptagon/BZR program will be defined in the body of a **main** node. This node is structured into three sub-nodes named **events**, **rules** and **devices**. The **main** node will receive all the sensor signals from the devices. The **events** node will use them to determine if events occur according to their definition. Events and devices signals are then passed to the **rules** node, where rules are activated according to their firing event and condition. Actions corresponding to activated rules are then used in the **devices** node, to be processed before being sent to devices, according to the corresponding device policy. The Rule Engine contains the execution policy to be simulated, determining the behavior of the rule-based system. Its output is the activated internal events, according to the specified policy.

4.1   Code Transformations

Figure 5 shows the skeleton for the code generated from a textual representation of an ECA rule-based system according to the grammar of Figure 2, with terms that are defined in the following. The order of the program is that nodes are defined before being used as sub-nodes in later nodes. The **main** node (e) invokes the sub-nodes **events** (defined in (a)), **rules** (c) and **devices** (d) nodes. The **rules** node (c) invokes the sub-node **rule_engine** (b), which models the execution policy, as described in 4.2. Event detectors, rules and devices are translated as lists of equations inside of the indicated nodes.

The developed tool implements several transformation schemes to translate events, rules and devices descriptions into Heptagon/BZR code, which are described for every element. We consider an ECA system $S = (R, E, D)$. The function *name* is used to define Heptagon/BZR variable names from the set

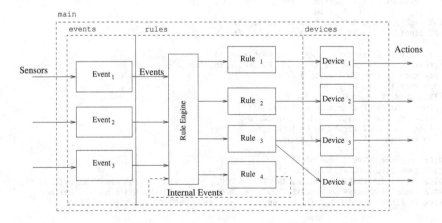

Fig. 4. Heptagon/BZR code detailed model

(a)

```
node events(<devices_ outputs>)
  returns (<event_ names>)
let <event_ detections>
tel
```

(b)

```
node rule_engine(<event_ names>)
  returns (<final_ event_ names>)
  <execution_ policy_ contracts>
let <execution_ policy>
tel
```

(c)

```
node rules(<event_ names>,
           <devices_ outputs>)
  returns (<request_ devices_ inputs>)
var <temp_ event_ names>:bool;
  <rule_ names>:bool;
let (<temp_ event_ names>)
    = rule_engine (<event_ names>) ;
  <rules_ activations> ;
  <signals_ activation>
tel
```

(d)

```
node devices(<request_ devices_ inputs>)
  returns (<final_ devices_ inputs>)
  contract
    enforce <device_ policy_ contracts>
    with <device_ policy_ controllables>
  let
    <devices_ policies>
  tel
```

(e)

```
node main(<devices_ outputs>)
returns (<final_ devices_ inputs>)
var <event_ names> ;
    <request_ devices_ inputs> ;
let
  (<event_ names>)
     = events(<devices_ outputs>) ;
  (<request_ devices_ inputs>)
     = rules(<event_ names>,
             <devices_ outputs>);
  (<devices_ inputs>)
     = devices(<request_ devices_ inputs>);
tel
```

Fig. 5. Program structure in Heptagon/BZR

N of rules, events and devices names. We consider for the sake of clarity and simplicity that Boolean expressions in the ECA language corresponds to the Heptagon/BZR ones, and thus they can be used as they are.

Figure 6 gives transformations to Heptagon/BZR for several terms. The <device_ outputs> list is generated over all the devices and their corresponding outputs. Similarly, we can generate <device_ inputs>. The <final_ event_ names> list is build similarly to <event_ names>, but adding the "final_" prefix, to differentiate inputs and outputs of the **rule_engine** node. Other lists are created similarly, <request_ devices_ inputs> and <temp_ event_ names>, but adding "req_" or "temp_" prefixes respectively to the names in their counterpart lists.

The <rules_ activation> defines the Boolean corresponding to activation of a rule if the corresponding event and its condition are true at the same time.

<device_ outputs> = { name(n)_ name(o) | $(n, I, O) \in D, o \in O$ }

<event_ names> = { name(e) | $e \in E$ }

<event_ detection> = { name(e) = EventExpr(e) | $e \in E$ }

<rule_ names> = { name(n) | $(n, e, c, A) \in R$ }

<rules_ activation> = { name(n) = final_name(e) & c | $(n, e, c, A) \in R$ }

<signals_ activation> = { name(a) = $\bigvee_{(n,e,c,A) \in R | a \in A}$ name(n) | $\exists(n, I, O) \in D, a \in I$ }

Fig. 6. Transformations for various sets

$<device_policy_contracts> = $ true

$<device\_policy\_controllables> = \emptyset$

$$<device\_policy> = \Big\{ \text{ final\_name}(n)\_\text{name}(o) = \text{req\_name}(n)\_\text{name}(o)$$

$$\text{\& not} \bigvee_{o' \in O, o \prec o'} \text{final\_name}(n)\_\text{name}(o') \mid (n, I, O) \in D, o \in O \Big\}$$

Fig. 7. Transformation for devices (discarding policy)

$<device_policy_contracts> = $

$$\bigwedge_{(n,I,O) \in D, o_1, o_2 \in O, o_1 \neq o_2} \text{not (final\_name}(n)\_\text{name}(o_1) \text{ \& final\_name}(n)\_\text{name}(o_2) \text{)}$$

$<device\_policy\_controllables> = \{ \text{ name}(n)\_\text{name}(o)\_\text{c} \mid (n, I, O) \in D, o \in O \}$

$<device\_policy> = \{\text{final\_}m = \text{delay}(\text{req\_}m, m\_\text{c}) \mid (n, I, O) \in D, o \in O, m = \text{name}(n)\_\text{name}(o)\}$

Fig. 8. Transformation for devices (delaying policy)

Then, $<signals\_activation>$ allows activating every device input if it has been requested by any of the rules. Given that multiple rules could activate the same signal, a disjunction is used to fuse them.

Transformation for devices differs depending on the specified execution policy to apply on signals sent to the device. Actions from rules correspond to devices inputs. The two specified strategies are *discarding* or *delaying* contradictory signals sent to a device. Equations are used in the first case, shown in Figure 7, to discard contradictory signals: the total order $\prec$ is used to give priorities. Once a signal with higher priority has already been activated, the rest are discarded. The $<device\_policy>$ equations are composed for every device in the system. In the second case, shown in Figures 8, a contract is used to delay signals. Only one of them is sent to the device. The `delay` automaton from Figure 1 will store the input signal until it can be released and sent to the device. The generated controller will be in charge of selecting the right values for the controlled variables to send only one signal at a time and delay the others.

```
node rule_engine(<event_names>) returns (<final_event_names>)
  contract enforce ⋀_{e1,e2 ∈ E, e1 ≠ e2} not (final_name(e1) & final_name(e2))
    with { name(e)_c | e ∈ E }
let { final_name(e) = delay(name(e), name(e)_c) | e ∈ E }
tel
```

Fig. 9. Delayed execution model

```
node rule_engine(<event_names>) returns (<final_event_names>)
let { final_name(e) = name(e) | e ∈ E }
tel
```

Fig. 10. Parallel execution model

4.2 Execution Models

As said before, the transformation is designed to support different execution policies in ECA rule-based systems. We currently support transformations for *parallel* and *delayed* execution. The code generation for the `rule_engine` node will differ for every case. For the delaying of events, as shown in Figure 9, the `delay` automaton is used as for the device node code generation. Only one event will be sent to the `rules` node for every execution of the controller. For the parallel execution model, as shown in Figure 10, all the events are allowed to be activated in the same execution step without restrictions. Other execution policies can be added in this node to simulate any ECA execution model.

5 ECA Rule Set Verification and Control

The previous transformation makes it possible to handle the problems described in Section 1 and to validate, verify or control the execution of the ECA rule set. Different kinds of verifications can be performed on the ECA rule based system, depending on the available information, as described in [18]. Verifications can be static (performed at compilation time) or dynamic (performed at run-time). They can also be classified as generic ECA rule verifications or domain specific issues that can verified. Diagnosis information about the detection of static errors can be extracted in the form of rule identifiers or line position, as well as identifiers of involved signals, by instrumenting the generated code.

5.1 Verifications at Compilation Time

The first verification to be performed is the detection of *syntax errors*. The use of undeclared events or unavailable device actions are examples of such errors in the declaration of rules. Syntax errors are easily detected by any compiler or interpreter when recognizing the ECA rules source code.

Redundancy of rules is detected when the condition and actions of one rule represent a subset of conditions and actions of the other rule. This means that having two rules $r_1 = (n_1, e_1, c_1, A_1)$ and $r_2 = (n_2, e_2, c_2, A_2)$ where $e_1 = e_2$, $c_1 \Rightarrow c_2$ and $A_1 \subseteq A_2$.

Redundant rules are not directly detected by Heptagon/BZR. Duplicated rules will be compiled and executed at run-time without problems. Rule actions will be activated using the **or** operator, so the results will not result in redundancy. Here is a simple example of redundancy:

```
ON presence IF true DO Tv_on
ON presence IF true DO Tv_on
```

This example generates the following Heptagon/BZR code:

```
rule6 = (presence) & (true);
rule7 = (presence) & (true);
req_tv_on = rule6 or rule7;
```

The Sigali tool is used to solve this problem. The redundancy can be better checked using this tool. The capability of working with equations [12] in Sigali is used to detect the situation where the condition of one rule is included in the condition of another rule, thus making them redundant. For Sigali this means that the solutions for the equation $c_1 = $ true is a subset of the solutions of $c_2 = $ true. Sigali code performing this check is generated for every couple of rules that fulfills the following conditions:

- Rules are activated by the same event
- The set of actions of one rule is a subset of actions of the other one.
- The set of variables used in the conditions of both rules are not disjoint.

This filtering also helps reducing the quantity of operations in Sigali.

Inconsistency is also detected at compilation time. It can be defined as the result of contradictory actions, provided as result of activation of different rules. It can be formalized as having two rules $r_1 = (n_1, e_1, c_1, A_1)$ and $r_2 = (n_2, e_2, c_2, A_2)$ where $e_1 = e_2$ and $c_1 = c_2$, but A_1 and A_2 are contradictory. As previously defined in Section 1, we consider as contradictory actions sending more than one signal to the same device at the same step of the rule system. Due to having the same event and condition to be activated, they will always be activated together, generating contradictory actions, even if not executed simultaneously. This verification is performed by compiling the corresponding Heptagon/BZR contracts on the device node, but not discarding or delaying signals. The Sigali tool will detect inconsistencies failing to generate the controller, indicating that the program it not executable regarding the contracts.

Circularity generated by internal events can be detected by Heptagon/BZR, for the case of the parallel execution model, as a causality error at compilation time. The following code generates a circularity problem:

```
ON internal1 IF true DO internal2
ON internal2 IF true DO internal3
ON internal3 IF true DO internal1
```

A dependency cycle occurs in the definition of rules in a way that these rules are always activating themselves. The circularity is detected independently of the number of involved events. The generated code is as follows:

```
rule0 = (internal3) & (true);
rule1 = (internal2) & (true);
rule2 = (internal1) & (true);
internal2 = rule2;
internal1 = rule0;
internal3 = rule1;
```

The dependency cycle will be detected by Heptagon/BZR as a causality error. Detection is conservative, so even if conditions in rules may avoid this dependency for some values, it is detected as a possible violation.

5.2   Control at Run-Time

It can not be foreseen at compilation time if two different rules with different events and contradictory actions will be activated at the same time instant at run-time. Coordination or control techniques have to applied in that case. Heptagon/BZR is designed to provide this kind of run-time control.

Inconsistency at run-time is controlled with the already described code generated for the devices. Contradictory signals can be discarded or delayed depending on the chosen policy. This provides more control on the execution of rules than avoiding the rules. In case that one rule has more than one action, only the inconsistent actions will be discarded or delayed, allowing the rest of actions to be performed. In this case, inconsistency is not only detected, as in the compilation time, but solved using the order priority to discard or delay signals.

Circularity is detected using automata and model checking capabilities of Heptagon/BZR, for two different circular behaviors. Automata are used to represent the behavior of devices. The actual state of the device and possible transitions are represented. Automata are designed to send the required signals to a device only if it represents a change of state in the signal. In this case the action of the corresponding rule is avoided, interrupting an endless chained execution of rules. Figure 11(a) represents an automaton for a devices with two states. The automaton receives requests to change the state. The outputs are the actual state of the device (st_On or st_Off become true or false respectively), and the signal to change the state of the device (On or Off). These signals are only emitted if the devices is not already in this state.

The other possibility is that rules continuously modify the state of a device. This represents an *oscillation* in the state of the device. An observer automaton is used to detect undesired oscillations. Oscillations can be considered undesired if they have not been generated by external events, this means not directly generated by the execution of rules. For instance, user actions are considered external events, while a light turned on by a rule is not an external event. In

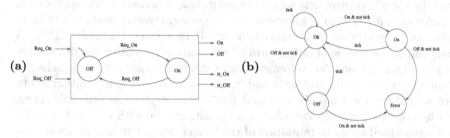

Fig. 11. (a) Two states device behavior **(b)** Observer for oscillation detection

Figure 11(b) an automaton is represented. This is an observer automaton able to detect if the state of a two states devices is oscillating. A `tick` signal is used to represent the activation of an external event. In case that the oscillation is produced by the presence of external events, then it is considered as a desired oscillation. In case of the absence of the `tick` signal, the oscillation is considered as undesired. To avoid this situation, besides the automaton, a contract is included in the Heptagon/BZR code. This contract indicates that the **Error** state must not be reached. The use DCS in Heptagon/BZR can control the avoidance of this oscillation at run-time using the delaying automata.

```
node device1(on, off: bool; c:bool) returns (st_on, st_off: bool; power:int)
let
  automaton
    state Off do st_off = true; st_on = false; power = 0;
      until on & c then On
    state On do st_on = true; st_off = false; power = CONSUMPTION;
      until off & c then Off
  end
tel

node devices(req_d1_on, req_d1_off: bool; req_d2_on, req_d2_off: bool)
  returns (st1_on, st1_off: bool; ... ; power:int)
  contract
    enforce (power ≤ LIMIT)
    with (dev1_c, dev2_c:bool)
  var power1, power2:bool
let
  power = power1 + power2;
  (st1_on, st1_off, power1) = device1(req_d1_on, req_d1_off, dev1_c);
  (st2_on, st2_off, power2) = device1(req_d2_on, req_d2_off, dev2_c);
  ...
tel
```

Fig. 12. Application-specific scenario behavior control

Application-specific issues can be considered additionally to the above generic ECA rule-based system issues, for specific scenarios with specific requirements. These requirements can also be expressed in Heptagon/BZR, to provide more control on the ECA rule set execution. These requirements are also difficult to express in ECA rules, because of the lack of language support to describe them, but their violation would cause inconsistencies during the execution.

Additional information is required about the environment to be able to perform the specific control actions on the environment, following the approach in [19]. An example of such application-specific scenario requirements would be to forbid an energy power consumption higher than a given threshold LIMIT. A model should be provided in the form of automata representing the devices behaviors. Figure 12 shows an automaton called **device1**, representing the behavior of one device type, with states On and Off, associated with consumption levels, here valued for the example at 0 and CONSUMPTION. A node called **devices**, shown here only partially, describes a composite system with two such devices, each represented by an instantiation of the former node. The overall power consumption is defined as the sum of local power consumptions. A contract is then declaratively specified, as defined in Section 2.2, such that the global power is lower than the given limit. DCS is applied during the compilation of this program, to automatically solve the control problem. The generated controller will avoid entering the On state of a device if it makes the total power consumption to overcome the threshold. An ECA rule would be able to detect the situation when it is already occurring, whereas DCS performs an analysis predicting possible problems, and the controller generated by Heptagon/BZR will directly avoid reaching the undesired state.

6   Conclusions

We propose a novel method for coordination in ECA rule-based systems, by verification and control based on behavioral models, in order to avoid problems of redundancy, inconsistency, and circularity, as well as application-specific issues. This method is based on the use of model checking and a control technique (DCS) which provides safe control during the execution of the system. Verifications are performed at compilation time with simple transformations and model checking, ensuring that the desired system defined invariants apply. So, for the execution of the ECA rule set, the generated controller ensures that the desired properties will always apply. Our method also takes into account different possible execution models for the ECA rule-based system. These execution models can be modeled, ensuring that the final implementation of the system is correctly verified. Our work offers users with a combination of a high-level ECA rules language with the compiler and formal tool support of Heptagon/BZR, which can seen in both ways: formal support of ECA rules, and user-friendly language above Heptagon/BZR.

We are presently working on the integration of the generated controller, using the executable code in C or Java, in an experimental embedded platform for small or home environments where users could introduce ECA rules in the system to control home sensors and actuators using the automatically generated safe controller. We are also working on the possibility to automatically provide device models representing their behavior. This allows specifying, at the same level as ECA rules rather than in Heptagon/BZR, safety properties for application-specific scenarios as the one described in last section. Other perspective involves modular compilation and DCS, which can improve scalability of the approach, as well as distribution of the executable code, to design distributed controllers.

References

1. Beauvais, J.-R., Rutten, E., Gautier, T., Houdebine, R., Le Guernic, P., Tang, Y.-M.: Modeling statecharts and activitycharts as signal equations. ACM Transactions on Software Engineering and Methodology 10(4), 397–451 (2001)
2. Delaval, G., Rutten, É., Marchand, H.: Integrating discrete controller synthesis into a reactive programming language compiler. Discrete Event Dynamic Systems 23(4), 385–418 (2013)

3. Dittrich, K., Gatziu, S., Geppert, A.: The Active Database Management System Manifesto: A Rulebase of ADBMS Features. In: Sellis, T.K. (ed.) RIDS 1995. LNCS, vol. 985, pp. 1–17. Springer, Heidelberg (1995)
4. Ericsson, A.: Enabling Tool Support for Formal Analysis of ECA Rules. Phd thesis, University of Skövde (2009)
5. Fleurey, F., Solberg, A.: A Domain Specific Modeling Language Supporting Specification, Simulation and Execution of Dynamic Adaptive Systems. In: Schürr, A., Selic, B. (eds.) MODELS 2009. LNCS, vol. 5795, pp. 606–621. Springer, Heidelberg (2009)
6. Gueye, S.M.K., de Palma, N., Rutten, E.: Component-based autonomic managers for coordination control. In: De Nicola, R., Julien, C. (eds.) COORDINATION 2013. LNCS, vol. 7890, pp. 75–89. Springer, Heidelberg (2013)
7. Guillet, S., Bouchard, B., Bouzouane, A.: Correct by construction security approach to design fault tolerant smart homes for disabled people. Procedia Computer Science 21, 257–264 (2013)
8. Gürgen, L., Cherbal, A., Sharrock, R., Honiden, S.: Autonomic management of heterogeneous sensing devices with ECA rules. In: 2011 IEEE International Conference on Communications Workshops (ICC), pp. 1–5 (2011)
9. Halbwachs, N.: Synchronous Programming of Reactive Systems. Springer (2010)
10. Keeney, J., Cahill, V.: Chisel: a policy-driven, context-aware, dynamic adaptation framework. In: Proceedings POLICY 2003. IEEE 4th International Workshop on Policies for Distributed Systems and Networks, pp. 3–14 (2003)
11. Lee, W., Lee, S., Lee, K.: Conflict Detection and Resolution method in WS-ECA framework. In: The 9th International Conference on Advanced Communication Technology, pp. 786–791 (February 2007)
12. Marchand, H., Bournai, P., Borgne, M., Guernic, P.: Synthesis of discrete-event controllers based on the signal environment. Discrete Event Dynamic System: Theory and Applications, 1–26 (2000)
13. Paschke, A.: ECA-RuleML: An approach combining ECA rules with temporal interval-based KR event/action logics and transactional update logics. Computer Research Repository, abs/cs/061 (2006)
14. Turker, C., Gertz, M.: Semantic Integrity Support in SQL-99 and Commercial Object- Relational Database Management Systems. The International Journal on Very Large Data Bases 10(4), 241–269 (2001)
15. Yoon, J.P.: Techniques for data and rule validation in knowledge based systems. In: Proceedings of the Fourth Annual Conference on Computer Assurance, 'Systems Integrity, Software Safety and Process Security, pp. 62–70 (1989)
16. Zhang, J., Cheng, B.: Specifying adaptation semantics. ACM SIGSOFT Software Engineering Notes, 1–7 (2005)
17. Zhang, J., Cheng, B.: Model-based development of dynamically adaptive software. In: Proc. of the 28th International Conference on Software Engineering (2006)
18. Zhang, J., Moyne, J., Tilbury, D.: Verification of ECA rule based management and control systems. In: IEEE Int. Conf. Automation Science and Engineering (2008)
19. Zhao, M., Privat, G., Rutten, E., Alla, H.: Discrete Control for the Internet of Things and Smart Environments. In: Int. Workshop on Feedback Computing (2013)

Progress as Compositional Lock-Freedom

Marco Carbone[1],[*], Ornela Dardha[2], and Fabrizio Montesi[1]

[1] IT University of Copenhagen, Denmark
{carbonem,fmontesi}@itu.dk
[2] University of Glasgow, United Kingdom
Ornela.Dardha@glasgow.ac.uk

Abstract. A session-based process satisfies the *progress* property if its
sessions never get stuck when it is executed in an adequate context. Previous work studied how to define progress by introducing the notion of
catalysers, execution contexts generated from the type of a process. In
this paper, we refine such definition to capture a more intuitive notion
of context adequacy for checking progress. Interestingly, our new catalysers lead to a novel characterisation of progress in terms of the standard notion of lock-freedom. Guided by this discovery, we also develop a
conservative extension of catalysers that does not depend on types, gen-
eralising the notion of progress to untyped session-based processes. We
combine our results with existing techniques for lock-freedom, obtaining
a new methodology for proving progress. Our methodology captures new
processes wrt previous progress analysis based on session types.

1 Introduction

Progress is a fundamental property of safe programs in a language model. Intuitively, a program with the progress property should never get "stuck", i.e., reach
a state that is not designated as a final value and that the language semantics
does not tell how to evaluate further [23]. Progress is well-understood in models such as the λ-calculus, and typically analysed in closed terms through type
systems. On the other hand, we have only recently begun to scratch the surface
of its meaning in models for concurrency. A basic property related to progress
in concurrency is deadlock-freedom: a process is deadlock-free if it can always
reduce unless it terminates [16]. In a deadlock-free process, some subprocesses
can get stuck. For instance, consider the following process in the π-calculus [18]:

$$P \ = \ (\nu x)(x?(y).\mathbf{0} \mid \Omega)$$

where Ω is a diverging process executing an infinite series of internal actions.
Although the subterm $x?(y).\mathbf{0}$ will never reduce, process P is deadlock-free. Following this observation, lock-freedom has been proposed as a stronger property
that requires every input/output action to be eventually executed under fair
process scheduling [15]: all communications must be reduced even if the whole
process diverges. Various static analyses, in particular many type systems, have
been proposed for ensuring deadlock- or lock-freedom [5, 6, 15–17].

---

[*] Research supported by the Danish Agency for Science, Technology and Innovation.

E. Kühn and R. Pugliese (Eds.): COORDINATION 2014, LNCS 8459, pp. 49–64, 2014.

The aforementioned analyses are applied to closed processes, i.e., processes that do not communicate with the environment. However, process models are often used to capture open-ended systems where participants can join the system dynamically [10, 19–21]. A recent line of work has begun investigating a *compositional* formulation of progress for such systems, which are captured by open processes missing some participants. An open process has then the progress property if it can reduce within all adequate execution contexts, called *catalysers*, that provide the missing participants [4, 8]. Interestingly, this compositionality seems to lead back to the notion of lock-freedom, in that both notions inspect the behaviour of subprocesses in a system. Thus, we ask:

What is the relationship between the notions of lock-freedom and progress for open-ended systems?

Answering the question above would lead to a better understanding of the progress property for concurrent systems. Ideally, it would allow techniques and results obtained for one property to be applied to the other.

1.1   Contributions

We list our major contributions. Full proofs and definitions can be found in [3].

Progress through Typed Closure. We study progress and lock-freedom in the π-calculus with sessions [25], by conservatively extending the notion of catalysers based on session types [13, 25] (§ 3). We show that progress and lock-freedom coincide for well-typed closed processes (§ 3, Theorem 2). Building on this result we construct a procedure, called *typed closure*, that wraps an open process in a special catalyser to transform it into a closed process. Typed closure allows us to relate the progress and lock-freedom properties for well-typed processes: a well-typed process has progress if and only if its typed closure is lock-free (§ 3, Theorem 4), i.e., *progress is a compositional form of the notion of lock-freedom*.

Progress through Untyped Closure. We explore an alternative procedure for closing a process that is not based on session types, but rather on the structure of the process itself, called *untyped closure* (§ 4). Interestingly, we can show that a process has progress if and only if its untyped closure is lock-free, yielding a new characterisation of progress that can capture also untyped processes.

Progress through Lock-Freedom. We combine our results with existing techniques for guaranteeing lock-freedom, obtaining a new methodology for proving progress in the π-calculus with sessions (§ 5). Specifically, we present how Kobayashi's type system for lock-freedom, from [15], can be reused for establishing whether a process has progress. Our methodology captures new processes wrt previous progress analysis based on session types (§ 5, Comparison).

2   The Model

In this section we introduce the π-calculus with sessions and its typing discipline, from [25], which we will use as reference model for our investigation of progress.

2.1   The π-Calculus with Sessions

Syntax. The syntax of the π-calculus with sessions is given in Fig.1.

$P, Q, \ldots ::= $	$x!\langle v\rangle.P$	(output)	$\mid$	$x?(y).P$	(input)
$\mid$	$x \triangleleft \{l_i.P_i\}_{i \in I}$	(selection)	$\mid$	$x \triangleright \{l_i : P_i\}_{i \in I}$	(branching)
$\mid$	$P \mid Q$	(parallel)	$\mid$	$(\nu xy)P$	(restriction)
$\mid$	$\mathbf{rec} X.P$	(rec)	$\mid$	X	(call)
$\mid$	$\mathbf{0}$	(inaction)			
$v ::= $	x	(var)	$\mid$	unit	(unit)

Fig. 1. π-calculus with sessions, syntax

P, Q range over processes, x, y over variables, and v over values. Values can be either variables or the unit value unit, which abstracts basic values. An output process $x!\langle v\rangle.P$ sends a value v on channel x and proceeds as process P; the input process $x?(y).P$ receives a value on channel x, stores it in variable y and proceeds as P. Process $x \triangleleft \{l_i.P_i\}_{i \in I}$ is a generalisation of the standard selection $x \triangleleft l_j.P_j$ found in [13, 25]: it sends on channel x the selection of a label l_j among the labels in $\{l_i\}_{i \in I}$, and then proceeds as the corresponding process P_j. This generalised selection will be important for our characterisation of progress, in § 3. A label selection is received by a branching process $x \triangleright \{l_i : P_i\}_{i \in I}$, which offers a range of labelled alternatives on channel x followed by their respective process continuations. Term $(\nu xy)P$ binds two variables x and y in P as the two respective endpoints of a session; when restricted together as in $(\nu xy)P$, we say that x and y are co-variables. All the other terms are standard.

Semantics. We give semantics to the π-calculus with sessions in terms of the reduction relation $\rightarrow$, a binary relation over processes, defined by the rules in Fig. 2. Rule (R-COM) is the rule for communication: the process on the left sends a value v on x, while the process on the right receives the value on y and substitutes the placeholder z with it. A key difference wrt the standard π-calculus is that the subject of the output, x, and the subject of the input, y, are required to be co-variables of each other, formalised by the external restriction (νxy). A consequence of this is that communication happens only on bound variables. Rule (R-CHOICE) models an internal choice, in which a process $x \triangleleft \{l_i.P_i\}_{i \in I}$ non-deterministically chooses one of its possible labelled continuations. Rule (R-SEL) is similar to rule (R-COM), but in this case captures the communication of a label selection. We require the label selected by the process on the left to be among the labels offered by the process on the right. Rule (R-REC) models the recursion process reduction. The remaining rules and the structural congruence $\equiv$ are standard (see [25] for a more complete explanation).

2.2   Typing the π-Calculus with Sessions

We report a typing discipline for typing sessions in processes, from [25].

(R-COM) $(\boldsymbol{\nu}xy)(x!\langle v\rangle.P \mid y?(z).Q \mid R) \rightarrow (\boldsymbol{\nu}xy)(P \mid Q[v/z] \mid R)$

(R-CHOICE) $x \triangleleft \{l_i.P_i\}_{i\in I} \rightarrow x \triangleleft l_j.P_j$ if $j \in I$

(R-SEL) $(\boldsymbol{\nu}xy)(x \triangleleft l_j.P \mid y \triangleright \{l_i : P_i\}_{i\in I} \mid R) \rightarrow (\boldsymbol{\nu}xy)(P \mid P_j \mid R)$ if $j \in I$

(R-REC) $P[\text{rec}X.P/X] \rightarrow P' \quad \Rightarrow \quad \text{rec}X.P \rightarrow P'$

(R-RES) $P \rightarrow Q \quad \Rightarrow \quad (\boldsymbol{\nu}xy)P \rightarrow (\boldsymbol{\nu}xy)Q$

(R-PAR) $P \rightarrow P' \quad \Rightarrow \quad P \mid Q \rightarrow P' \mid Q$

(R-STRUCT) $P \equiv P', \ P' \rightarrow Q', \ Q' \equiv Q \quad \Rightarrow \quad P \rightarrow Q$

Fig. 2. π-calculus with sessions, semantics

Types. The syntax of types is given in Fig. 3.

$q ::=$ lin	*(linear)*		$\mid$ un		*(unrestricted)*
$p ::=$ $!T.U$	*(send)*		$\mid$ $?T.U$		*(receive)*
$\mid$ $\oplus\{l_i : T_i\}_{i\in I}$	*(select)*		$\mid$ $\&\{l_i : T_i\}_{i\in I}$	*(branch)*	
$T, U ::=$ $q\,p$	*(qualified pretype)*				
$\mid$ end	*(termination)*		$\mid$ 1		*(unit type)*
$\mid$ $\mu t.T$	*(recursive type)*		$\mid$ t		*(rec var)*

Fig. 3. Session types, syntax

Let q range over type qualifiers, p over pretypes, $q\,p$ over qualified pretypes, and T, U over types. Qualifiers are lin (for linear) or un (for unrestricted) and are used respectively to distinguish between types for sessions, i.e., channels whose pretype is executed exactly once, and standard channel types that can be used any number of times in parallel. In the pretypes, $!T.U$ and $?T.U$ are, respectively, the types of a sending and receiving of a value of type T with continuation of type U. Select and branch are sets of labelled session types indicating, respectively, internal and external choice. A type T can be a qualified pretype $q\,p$; end, the type of a terminated session; the unit type unit; a recursive type $\mu t.T$; or, finally, a type variable t. Recursive types are required to be *contractive*. Type equality in recursive types is based on the regular infinite trees and we consider a recursive type and its unfolding to be equal. In the rest of the paper, we implicitly assume that the qualifier lin is used in every qualified pretype unless it is explicitly stated otherwise. Also, we refer to types with a lin qualifier as session types.

Session Typing. We present now the session typing discipline for the π-calculus with sessions, which avoids communication errors such as type mismatches and race conditions. The syntax of typing environments is defined as:

$$\Gamma ::= \emptyset \mid \Gamma, x : T$$
$$\Theta ::= \emptyset \mid \Theta, X : \Gamma$$

$$\frac{un(\Gamma)}{\Theta;\Gamma \vdash \mathbf{0}} \text{(T-Inact)} \qquad \frac{\Theta;\Gamma_1 \vdash P \quad \Theta;\Gamma_2 \vdash Q}{\Theta;\Gamma_1 \circ \Gamma_2 \vdash P \mid Q} \text{(T-Par)}$$

$$\frac{un(\Gamma)}{\Theta;\Gamma, x:T \vdash x:T} \text{(T-Var)} \qquad \frac{\Theta;\Gamma, x:T, y:T' \vdash P \quad T \bot T'}{\Theta;\Gamma \vdash (\nu xy)P} \text{(T-Res)}$$

$$\frac{\Theta;\Gamma_1 \vdash x:q?T.U \quad \Theta;(\Gamma_2 + x:U), y:T \vdash P}{\Theta;\Gamma_1 \circ \Gamma_2 \vdash x?(y).P} \text{(T-In)}$$

$$\frac{\Theta;\Gamma_1 \vdash x:q!T.U \quad \Theta;\Gamma_2 \vdash v:T \quad \Theta;\Gamma_3 + x:U \vdash P}{\Theta;\Gamma_1 \circ \Gamma_2 \circ \Gamma_3 \vdash x!\langle v\rangle.P} \text{(T-Out)}$$

$$\frac{\Theta;\Gamma_1 \vdash x:q\&\{l_i:T_i\}_{i\in I} \quad \Theta;\Gamma_2 + x:T_i \vdash P_i \quad \forall i \in I}{\Theta;\Gamma_1 \circ \Gamma_2 \vdash x \triangleright \{l_i:P_i\}_{i\in I}} \text{(T-Brch)}$$

$$\frac{\Theta;\Gamma_1 \vdash x:q \oplus \{l_i:T_i\}_{i\in I} \quad \Theta;\Gamma_2 + x:T_i \vdash P_i \quad J \subseteq I}{\Theta;\Gamma_1 \circ \Gamma_2 \vdash x \triangleleft \{l_j.P_j\}_{j\in J}} \text{(T-Sel)}$$

$$\frac{\Theta, X:\Gamma;\Gamma \vdash P}{\Theta;\Gamma \vdash \mathbf{rec}X.P} \text{(T-RecP)} \qquad \frac{\Theta(X) = \Gamma}{\Theta;\Gamma \vdash X} \text{(T-RecV)}$$

Fig. 4. π-calculus with sessions, typing rules

We adopt the standard convention that we can write Γ, $x:T$ only if x does not appear in Γ, and Θ, $X:\Gamma$ only if X does not appear in Θ. Therefore, we can write Γ, Γ' (or Θ, Θ') only if the two environments have disjoint domains. Typing judgements have the form $\Theta;\Gamma \vdash P$, reading "process P is well-typed using variables according to Γ and recursion variables according to Θ". With an abuse of notation, we also write $\Theta;\Gamma \vdash x:T$ for "x has type T in Γ". We report the typing rules in Fig. 4. Rule (T-Inact) states that the terminated process $\mathbf{0}$ is well-typed under an unrestricted Γ, i.e., a Γ containing only types qualified with un, and any Θ. Rule (T-Par) types the parallel composition of two processes; it uses the split operator for typing environments $\circ$, which is defined by the following equations, and is undefined otherwise.

$$\emptyset \circ \emptyset = \emptyset$$
$$\Gamma \circ x:T = \Gamma, x:T \qquad\qquad\qquad \text{if } x \notin \mathsf{dom}(\Gamma)$$
$$(\Gamma, x:T) \circ x:T = \Gamma, x:T \qquad\quad \text{if } T \text{ is not a session type,}$$

The operator $\circ$ ensures that each linearly-typed channel x occurs either in P or in Q but never in both, to avoid races. Rule (T-Var) says that a variable x has type T if the pair $x:T$ is in the environment Γ. Rule (T-Res) states that $(\nu xy)P$ is well-typed if P is well-typed and the co-variables have dual types. Type duality $\perp$ is standard, as $\perp_c$ in [12], and relates two types that describe compatible behaviours (for example, inputs are matched with outputs and selections are matched with compatible branchings). Rules (T-IN) and (T-OUT) type, respectively, the receiving and the sending of a value; these rules deal with both linear and unrestricted types. Rule (T-BRCH) types an external choice on channel x, checking that each branch continuation P_i follows the respective type continuation in the type of x. Similarly, rule (T-SEL) types an internal choice communicated on channel x by checking the possible continuations. The operator $+$ is used to update the type of a variable with the continuation type in order to enable typing after an input (or branch) or an output (or select) operation has occurred. Rules (T-RECP) and (T-RECV) are standard, and type respectively a recursive process and a recursive process variable.

The type system above guarantees type preservation.

Theorem 1 (Preservation [25]). *If $\Theta; \Gamma \vdash P$ and $P \to Q$ then $\Theta; \Gamma \vdash Q$.*

Remark 1 (Type Safety and Well-Formedness). In [25], type safety is defined using an auxiliary definition of well-formedness. Intuitively, all enabled actions in a well-formed process must be such that (i) guards of conditionals are boolean values; (ii) unrestricted channels are used in the same way; (iii) actions on co-variables form a redex. Well-formedness is then guaranteed to follow from well-typedness, but only in the case of closed processes due to a technicality with condition (i). In our setting without conditionals, condition (i) does not apply and therefore well-typed processes are always well-formed.

3   Lock-Freedom and Progress

3.1   Definitions

Lock-Freedom. Intuitively, a process is lock-free if any communication action that becomes active during execution is eventually consumed. Below, we assume that reduction sequences are fair, as formalised in [15].

Definition 1 (Lock-Freedom for Sessions). *A process P_0 is lock-free if for any fair reduction sequence $P_0 \to P_1 \to P_2 \to \dots$, we have that*

1. *$P_i \equiv (\nu \widetilde{xy})(x!\langle v \rangle.Q \mid R)$, for $i \geq 0$, implies that there exists $n \geq i$ such that $P_n \equiv (\nu \widetilde{x'y'})(x!\langle v \rangle.Q \mid y?(z).R_1 \mid R_2)$ and $P_{n+1} \equiv (\nu \widetilde{x'y'})(Q \mid R_1[v/z] \mid R_2)$;*
2. *$P_i \equiv (\nu \widetilde{xy})(x \triangleleft l_j.Q \mid R)$, for some $i \geq 0$, implies that there exists $n \geq i$ such that $P_n \equiv (\nu \widetilde{x'y'})(x \triangleleft l_j.Q \mid y \triangleright \{l_k : R_k\}_{k \in I \cup \{j\}} \mid S)$ and $P_{n+1} \equiv (\nu \widetilde{x'y'})(Q \mid R_j \mid S)$.*

For simplicity, above we have omitted the dual cases for input and branching.

Progress. Before giving the formal definition of progress, we first need to introduce some auxiliary definitions. We start with the definition of characteristic process, which is the simplest process that can inhabit a type:

Definition 2 (Characteristic Process). *Given a type T, its characteristic process $(\!|T|\!)_g^x$ is inductively defined on the structure of T as:*

$$
\begin{array}{ll}
(\textsc{InVal}) & (\!|q?\mathbf{1}.U|\!)_g^x = x?(y).(\!|U|\!)_g^x \\[4pt]
(\textsc{OutVal}) & (\!|q!\mathbf{1}.U|\!)_g^x = x!\langle\mathsf{unit}\rangle.(\!|U|\!)_g^x \\[4pt]
(\textsc{InSess}) & (\!|q'?(qp).U|\!)_g^x = x?(y).((\!|U|\!)_g^x \mid (\!|qp|\!)_g^y) \\[4pt]
(\textsc{OutSess}) & (\!|q'!(qp).U|\!)_g^x = (\boldsymbol{\nu}zw)(x!\langle z\rangle.((\!|U|\!)_g^x \mid (\!|\overline{qp}|\!)_g^w)) \\[4pt]
(\textsc{InSum}) & (\!|q\&\{l_i : (q_i p_i)_i\}_{i\in I}|\!)_g^x = x \triangleright \{l_i : (\!|q_i p_i|\!)_g^x\}_{i\in I} \\[4pt]
(\textsc{OutSum}) & (\!|q \oplus \{l_i : (q_i p_i)_i\}_{i\in I}|\!)_g^x = x \triangleleft \{l_i : (\!|q_i p_i|\!)_g^x\}_{i\in I} \\[4pt]
(\textsc{End}) & (\!|\mathsf{end}|\!)_g^x = \mathbf{0} \\[4pt]
(\textsc{RecVar}) & (\!|\mathbf{t}|\!)_g^x = g(\mathbf{t}) \\[4pt]
(\textsc{Rec}) & (\!|\mu t.T|\!)_g^x = \mathbf{rec}X.(\!|T|\!)_{g,\{t\mapsto X\}}^x
\end{array}
$$

Above, the characteristic process $(\!|T|\!)_g^x$ is a process that implements type T on session channel x; function g maps type variables for recursion in T to the recursion variables in the process that implements them. The definition above is a refinement of that in [4, 8], with two modifications. The first is an extension to recursive processes. The second is that our rule (\textsc{OutSum}) produces a process that may select any label among those reported in the selection type. Previous work, instead, limited the characteristic process to selecting only the first label. We will show that this difference directly refines our definition of progress.

We now define *catalysers*, execution contexts that contain only restrictions and characteristic processes:

Definition 3 (Catalyser). *A catalyser $\mathcal{C}[\cdot]$ is a context such that:*

$$\mathcal{C}[\cdot] ::= [\cdot] \mid (\boldsymbol{\nu}xy)\mathcal{C}[\cdot] \mid \mathcal{C}[\cdot] \mid (\!|qp|\!)_g^x$$

Example 1. The following context $\mathcal{C}[\cdot]$ is a catalyser obtained by composing the characteristic processes P_1 and P_2 respectively of the types $T_1 = \mathsf{un}\,?(!\mathbf{1}.\mathsf{end}).\mathsf{un}\,\mathsf{end}$ and $T_2 = \mathsf{lin} \oplus \{l_1 : \mathsf{end}, l_2 : !\mathbf{1}.\mathsf{end}\}$:

$$
\begin{aligned}
\mathcal{C}[\cdot] &= (\boldsymbol{\nu}wx)(\boldsymbol{\nu}uy)([\cdot] \mid P_1 \mid P_2) \\
P_1 &= x?(z).(z!\langle\mathsf{unit}\rangle.\mathbf{0} \mid \mathbf{0}) \\
P_2 &= y \triangleleft \{l_1.\mathbf{0},\ l_2.y!\langle\mathsf{unit}\rangle.\mathbf{0}\}
\end{aligned}
$$
$\hspace{1cm}\square$

The duality operator $\bowtie$ is a relation over processes with respective co-actions.

Definition 4 ($\bowtie$). *The duality $\bowtie_{\{x,y\}}$ is defined as follows:*

$$
\begin{aligned}
x!\langle v\rangle.P &\bowtie_{\{x,y\}} y?(z).Q \\
x \triangleleft \{l_i.P_i\}_{i\in I} &\bowtie_{\{x,y\}} y \triangleright \{l_i : Q_i\}_{i\in I}
\end{aligned}
$$

As last auxiliary definition for progress, we define evaluation contexts. An *evaluation context* (or context, for short) $\mathcal{E}[\cdot]$ is a process with holes such that:

$$\mathcal{E}[\cdot] ::= [\cdot] \mid P \mid (\boldsymbol{\nu}xy)\mathcal{E}[\cdot] \mid \mathcal{E}[\cdot] \mid \mathcal{E}[\cdot] \mid \mathbf{rec}X.\mathcal{E}[\cdot]$$

We are now ready to give the formal definition of progress.

Definition 5 (Progress). *A process P has* progress *if for all catalysers $C[\cdot]$ such that $C[P]$ is well-typed, $C[P] \to^* \mathcal{E}[R]$ (where R is an input or an output) implies that there exist $C'[\cdot]$, $\mathcal{E}'[\cdot][\cdot]$ and R' such that $C'[\mathcal{E}[R]] \to^* \mathcal{E}'[R][R']$ and $R \bowtie_{\{x,y\}} R'$ for some x and y such that $(\boldsymbol{\nu} xy)$ is a restriction in $C'[\mathcal{E}[R]]$.*

Remark 2. Our formulation of progress is inspired by [4, 8]. However, our catalysers are different when it comes to selection. Consider the following example:

$$P = \quad x \triangleright \left\{ \begin{array}{l} l_1 : \mathbf{0}, \\ l_2 : (\boldsymbol{\nu} y_1 y_2)(y_1!\langle \mathsf{unit} \rangle . y_2?(z).\mathbf{0}) \end{array} \right\}$$

Process P above offers branches l_1 and l_2 on x. If l_2 is chosen, then P gets stuck into a deadlock. In previous works, P has progress since only the first branch is checked (l_1 in our example). This is unsatisfactory, because P may be composed with other systems that select branch l_2, and then get stuck. Instead, process P does not satisfy Definition 5 since all branches are checked by our characteristic processes (Definition 2, rule (OUTSUM)).

3.2   Properties

We now move to presenting the relationship between progress and lock-freedom. For well-typed closed terms, i.e., well-typed processes with no free variables, the properties of lock-freedom and progress coincide. Intuitively, this is because closed processes cannot interact with catalysers and the latter are always lock-free by construction. We formalise this aspect in the theorem below.

Theorem 2 (Lock-freedom $\Leftrightarrow$ Closed Progress). *Let P be a well-typed closed process. Then, P is lock-free if and only if P has progress.*

We now switch to a more general setting, i.e., processes that can be open. Differently than in the case of closed terms, the definitions of lock-freedom and progress do not coincide for open terms. For example, consider the process:

$$P = x!\langle \mathsf{unit} \rangle . x?(z).\mathbf{0} \tag{1}$$

Process P above has progress, since we can find a catalyser for reducing it, but it is not lock-free as it does not respect Definition 1.

Even if progress and lock-freedom do not coincide for open terms, we can still formally relate the two properties. The key idea for reaching this objective is to wrap an open term using catalysers until all sessions are closed, a procedure we call *typed closure*. We formally define typed closure below.

Definition 6 (Typed Closure). *Let $\Gamma \vdash P$. Then, the typed closure of P, denoted by $\mathsf{tclose}(P)$, is the process $C[P]$ where*

$$C[\cdot] = (\boldsymbol{\nu} \widetilde{xy})\left([\cdot] \mid \prod_{\forall x_i : T_i \in \Gamma} (\!|T_i|\!)_\emptyset^{y_i} \right)$$

Above, all x_i in $\widetilde{xy}$ correspond exactly to the domain of Γ. Typed closure is the identity for closed processes, since those are typed with empty environments.

Example 2. Consider the previous open process P in (1):

$$P = x!\langle \text{unit}\rangle.x?(z).\mathbf{0}$$

P can be typed with environment $\Gamma = x : !\mathbf{1}.?\mathbf{1}.\text{end}$. Its typed closure is then:

$$\text{tclose}(P) = (\boldsymbol{\nu}xy)(P \mid y?(w).y!\langle\text{unit}\rangle.\mathbf{0})$$

$\square$

Typed closure preserves typability:

Proposition 1 (Closure preserves typability). *If $\Gamma \vdash P$ then $\emptyset \vdash \text{tclose}(P)$.*

We are now going to present one of the major properties in our technical development, which will be crucial in establishing our main results: a process has progress if and only if its typed closure reduces to terms where actions at the top level can always be matched with their respective co-actions in a parallel subterm. Intuitively, this is because the catalysers in the typed closure of a process are exactly all those ones needed for further reducing the process as required by the definition of progress (Definition 5).

Lemma 1 (From Closure to Progress). *Let P be well-typed. Then, P has progress if and only if $\text{tclose}(P) \rightarrow^* \mathcal{E}[R]$ (where R is an input or an output process) implies that there exist $\mathcal{E}'[\cdot][\cdot]$ and R' such that $\mathcal{E}[R] \rightarrow^* \mathcal{E}'[R][R']$ and $R \bowtie_{\{x,y\}} R'$ for some x and y such that $(\boldsymbol{\nu}xy)$ is a restriction in $\mathcal{E}[R]$.*

Thanks to Lemma 1, we are able to establish that checking progress for a process P is equivalent to checking the progress property for its closure:

Theorem 3 (Closure Progress $\Leftrightarrow$ Progress). *If P is well-typed then $\text{tclose}(P)$ has progress if and only if P has progress.*

We are finally able to link progress and lock-freedom in the general case of open processes: a well-typed process has progress if and only if its typed closure is lock-free. This is an immediate consequence of Theorem 2 and Theorem 3.

Theorem 4 (Progress $\Leftrightarrow$ Closed Lock-Free). *If P is well-typed then P has progress if and only if $\text{tclose}(P)$ is lock-free.*

4 Untyped Closure

4.1 Definitions

So far, we have investigated the notion of progress and its connection with lock-freedom by building on top of the typing discipline for the π-calculus with sessions. Typing is useful for defining the adequate contexts for checking progress, namely our catalysers. In this section, we show that adequate contexts can be defined without the need for a typing discipline. Such contexts are based solely on the structure of processes, and lead to a more general notion of progress. Below, we introduce the notion of *co-process*:

Definition 7 (Co-Process). *Given a process P, its co-process $\mathsf{co}[P]_f$ is inductively defined as:*

$$\mathsf{co}[x?(y).P]_f = \begin{cases} \mathsf{co}[P]_f & \textit{if } x \notin \mathsf{dom}(f) \\ (\nu zw)(f_x!\langle z\rangle.\mathsf{co}[P]_{f,y\mapsto w}) & \textit{if } x \in \mathsf{dom}(f), \ y \textit{ is a channel}, \ z,w \textit{ fresh} \\ f_x!\langle\mathsf{unit}\rangle.\mathsf{co}[P]_f & \textit{otherwise} \end{cases}$$

$$\mathsf{co}[x!\langle v\rangle.P]_f = \begin{cases} \mathsf{co}[P]_f & \textit{if } x \notin \mathsf{dom}(f) \\ f_x?(y).\mathsf{co}[P]_f & \textit{otherwise} \end{cases}$$

$$\mathsf{co}[(\nu xy)P]_f = \mathsf{co}[P]_f \quad (\textit{if } x,y \notin \mathsf{dom}(f)) \qquad\qquad \mathsf{co}[X]_f = X$$

$$\mathsf{co}[\mathbf{rec}X.P]_f = \mathbf{rec}X.\mathsf{co}[P]_f \qquad \mathsf{co}[P \mid Q]_f = \mathsf{co}[P]_f \mid \mathsf{co}[Q]_f \qquad \mathsf{co}[0]_f = 0$$

$$\mathsf{co}[x \triangleright \{l_i : P_i\}_{i\in I}]_f = \begin{cases} f_x \triangleleft \{l_i : \mathsf{co}[P_i]_f\}_{i\in I} & \textit{if } x \in \mathsf{dom}(f) \\ \sqcup\, \mathsf{co}[P_i]_f & \textit{otherwise} \end{cases}$$

$$\mathsf{co}[x \triangleleft \{l_i.P_i\}_{i\in I}]_f = \begin{cases} f_x \triangleright \{l_i : \mathsf{co}[P_i]_f\}_{i\in I} & \textit{if } x \in \mathsf{dom}(f) \\ \sqcup\, \mathsf{co}[P_i]_f & \textit{otherwise} \end{cases}$$

Roughly, the co-process $\mathsf{co}[P]_f$ of a process P is P with all its actions replaced with respective compatible co-actions. The function f is a renaming for variables. Intuitively, we use it for mapping free variables in P, which identify the open communication endpoints in P, to their respective co-variables in $\mathsf{co}[P]_f$. For an input $x?(y).P$, its co-process is: the co-process of the continuation P if x is not in f; the output of a fresh variable z if y is used as a channel in P (we distinguish channels in inputs using standard sorting from the π-calculus, omitted here); the output of a unit value otherwise. The rule for outputs is similar. For a restriction $(\nu xy)P$, we check that the restricted names are not in f since their actions are already matched inside P. The cases of recursion, parallel, and the terminated process are simply homomorphisms. We assume that in $\mathsf{co}[P]_f$, any occurrence of recursion calls not guarded by actions, e.g., $\mathbf{rec}X.X$, are replaced with 0. Branching and selection are defined similarly to inputs and outputs whenever the subject of the communication is in f. Otherwise, since we cannot predict which choice will be made at run-time, we make use of the auxiliary operator $\sqcup$ to *merge* the behaviours in the different branches. We formally define $\sqcup$ below.

Definition 8 (Merge). *The merge operator $\sqcup$ is defined by the equations below.*

$$x \triangleright \{\widetilde{l : P}, \widetilde{l' : P'}\} \sqcup x \triangleright \{\widetilde{l : Q}, \widetilde{l'' : P''}\} = x \triangleright \{\widetilde{l : P \sqcup Q}, \widetilde{l' : P'}, \widetilde{l'' : P''}\}$$

$$x \triangleleft \{\widetilde{l : P}, \widetilde{l' : P'}\} \sqcup x \triangleleft \{\widetilde{l : Q}, \widetilde{l'' : P''}\} = x \triangleleft \{\widetilde{l : P \sqcup Q}\}$$

$$P \sqcup Q = P \quad \textit{if } P \equiv Q$$

We say that P and Q are mergeable, written $P \clubsuit Q$, whenever $P \sqcup Q$ is defined.

Using co-processes, we can define a new closure independent from types.

Definition 9 (Untyped Closure). *The untyped closure of P, uclose(P), is:*

$$(\boldsymbol{\nu}\widetilde{xf_x})(P \mid \mathrm{co}[P]_f)$$

where $\mathrm{dom}(f) = \mathrm{fn}(P)$.

Example 3. Untyped closure is not always defined. For example,

$$P = (\boldsymbol{\nu}xx')\big(x \triangleright \{l_1 : y \triangleleft l_3, l_2 : y!\langle v\rangle\} \mid x' \triangleleft \{l_1 : y' \triangleright l_3, l_2 : y'?(z)\}\big)$$

cannot be expressed as $P \equiv (\boldsymbol{\nu}\widetilde{x}y)(Q \mid \mathrm{co}[Q]_f)$ because the merge operation given in Definition 8 cannot be defined. This is because y and y' perform once a selection and once an output, which cannot be merged together.   □

For well-typed processes, untyped closure preserves typability:

Proposition 2. *If P is well-typed, then* uclose(P) *is well-typed.*

4.2 Adequacy of Untyped Closure

We conclude this section by showing that untyped closure is a conservative extension of typed closure, i.e., it preserves the same connection between lock-freedom and progress for well-typed processes. Technically, for well-typed processes, untyped closure and typed closure have equivalent behaviours. First, we show that for a typed process, the reductions of its untyped closure can mimic the reductions of its typed closure and vice versa. Below, we denote with $\mathrm{tclose}_0(P)$ the typed closure of P generated using the simplest output typing of P, namely if $\Gamma \vdash_0 P$ then all carried types in the output types of Γ are equal to end.

Lemma 2. *Let P be well-typed. Then,* uclose(P) $\rightarrow$ ♣uclose(P') *iff* $\mathrm{tclose}_0(P) \rightarrow \mathrm{tclose}_0(P')$.

As a consequence of Lemma 2, we obtain that the untyped closure of a well-typed process is lock-free if and only if its typed closure is lock-free.

Theorem 5. *Let P be well-typed.* uclose(P) *is lock-free iff* tclose(P) *is lock-free.*

Proof (Sketch). By Lemma 2, we observe that if two processes can be merged then they are related by a strong typed bisimulation (cf. [5]). Then, the thesis follows by observing that $\mathrm{tclose}(P)$ is closed under reductions, and uclose(P) is closed under reductions up-to strong bisimulation (merging).   □

From Theorem 4 in § 3.2, and Theorem 5 we conclude:

Corollary 1. *Let P be well-typed. If* uclose(P) *is lock-free, then P has progress.*

5   Progress through Static Analysis for Lock-Freedom

Our technical development reduced the problem of checking whether a process has progress to the problem of checking whether its closure (typed or untyped) is lock-free. A direct consequence of this result is that static analysis for lock-freedom can be lifted to static analysis for progress. In this section we show an example of how to apply this methodology, by using the typing discipline for lock-freedom in the standard π-calculus by Kobayashi [15].

The π-Calculus. We report the syntax of the standard π-calculus [18] where standard choice is replaced by the **case** v **of** $\{l_{i\_}(x_i) \triangleright P_i\}_{i\in I}$ constructor:

$$P, Q ::= \quad x!\langle \tilde{v}\rangle.P \quad | \quad x?(\tilde{y}).P \quad | \quad P \mid Q \quad | \quad \mathbf{0} \quad | \quad (\nu x)P$$
$$| \quad \mathbf{case}\, v\, \mathbf{of}\, \{l_{i\_}(x_i) \triangleright P_i\}_{i\in I} \quad | \quad X \quad | \quad \mathbf{rec} X.P$$
$$v ::= \quad x \quad | \quad \mathsf{unit} \quad | \quad l\_v$$

The differences wrt to the syntax of the π-calculus with sessions are that restriction is now on a single variable and that there are no constructs for branching and selection. Values include variables and the unit value, as in the π-calculus with sessions, and also the labelled values l_v, used in the **case** process.

We report below the main reduction rules:

$$(\text{R}\pi\text{- Com}) \qquad x!\langle \tilde{v}\rangle.P \mid x?(\tilde{z}).Q \rightarrow P \mid Q[\tilde{v}/\tilde{z}]$$

$$(\text{R}\pi\text{- Case})\ \mathbf{case}\, l_{j\_}v\, \mathbf{of}\, \{l_{i\_}(x_i) \triangleright P_i\}_{i\in I} \rightarrow P_j[v/x_j] \quad j \in I$$

The main difference wrt the π-calculus with sessions is that communications happen when sending and receiving actions have the same subject (the variable used as a channel for sending or receiving a value), and not when the two actions in question have different subjects that were linked by a shared restriction. Moreover, the communicating channels need not be restricted. For simplicity, we omit all the other rules, as well as the definition of the structural congruence relation $\equiv$ between standard π-calculus processes.

Kobayashi's Typing for Lock-Freedom. We briefly introduce Kobayashi's type system for checking lock-freedom in the standard π-calculus, from [15]. The syntax of types is defined as.

(actions)	$\alpha ::= \ ? \mid !$
(usage types)	$U ::= \mathbf{0} \mid \alpha_c^o.U \mid U_1 \mid U_2 \mid U_1 \& U_2 \mid t \mid \mu t.U$
(channel types)	$T ::= [\tilde{T}]\, U \quad | \quad \langle l_i : T_i \rangle_{i\in I} \quad\quad | \quad \mathbf{1}$

Types T include channel types $[\tilde{T}]\, U$, the variant type $\langle l_i : T_i \rangle_{i\in I}$, and the unit type $\mathbf{1}$. In a channel type $[\tilde{T}]\, U$, $\tilde{T}$ are the types of the values transmitted over the channel and U is a usage type, describing how the channel is used. Usage types are similar to session types. Usage $\mathbf{0}$ describes a channel that cannot be used anymore (we will often omit it when not necessary); usage $\alpha_c^o.U$ describes a channel used for an input action (when $\alpha = ?$) or output action (when $\alpha = !$), and then used according to U. The annotations o and c, called tags, are natural numbers that indicate respectively the *obligation* and *capability* of an action, described below. Usage $U_1 \mid U_2$ describes a channel used according to U_1 and U_2 in parallel. Usage $U_1 \& U_2$ describes a channel used according to either U_1 or U_2. Usages $\mu t.U$ and t indicate standard recursive types.

We describe the intuition behind reasoning with tags in usage types (see [15] for a full description). The tags o and c are abstract representations of time steps and describe dependencies between the usage of channels, corresponding to how actions on channels are interleaved in processes. Intuitively, an obligation o denotes a guarantee that its action will become available at most in time o, while a capability c denotes a requirement that a compatible co-action becomes available at most in time c. This information is crucial to ensure that processes do not get stuck, and it is checked to be consistent by Kobayashi's typing rules. As an example, we consider the rules for typing input and restriction:

$$\frac{\Gamma, \tilde{y} : \tilde{T} \vdash_{\text{LF}} P}{x : [\tilde{T}] \ ?^0_c \ ; \Gamma \vdash_{\text{LF}} x?(\tilde{y}).P} \ (\text{LF-In}) \qquad \frac{\Gamma, x : [\tilde{T}] \ U \vdash_{\text{LF}} P \quad rel(U)}{\Gamma \vdash_{\text{LF}} (\nu x)P} \ (\text{LF-Res})$$

Rule (LF-In) states that the $x?(\tilde{y}).P$ is well-typed if x is a channel used in input with obligation 0. Moreover, the operator ; raises (increases by one) the obligations of the other channels in Γ in the conclusion of the rule, in order to reflect that actions inside process P are prefixed by an input action and will thus become available later. Rule (LF-Res) is the key rule for establishing lock-freedom; it states that the restriction of a name x in process P is well-typed if x is used *reliably* in P. The notion of reliability of a usage is as follows. A usage U is said to be reliable, denoted with $rel(U)$, if after any step, whenever it contains an action (input or output) having capability tag c, it also contains the co-action with an obligation tag *at most c*. This means that the guarantee that the action will become available is at most the requirement for its availability (we refer the reader to [15] for the formal definition of $rel(U)$).

Kobayashi's type system guarantees lock-freedom:

Theorem 6 (Lock-Freedom [15]). *If $\Gamma \vdash_{\text{LF}} P$ and $rel(\Gamma)$, then P is lock-free.*

Above, $rel(\Gamma)$ checks $rel(U)$ for all the usage types in Γ.

From the above theorem, we immediately get the following corollary:

Corollary 2. $\emptyset \vdash_{\text{LF}} P$ *implies that P is lock-free.*

Encoding. Processes in the π-calculus with sessions can be translated to equivalent processes in the standard π-calculus, using the encoding $[\![-]\!]_f$ presented in [9]. Intuitively, such encoding transforms each action on sessions in the original process into an action on a linear channel in the standard π-calculus. We report a selection of the rules defining $[\![-]\!]_f$ in Fig. 5.

The parameter f renames the variables involved in a communication in order to simulate the structure of sessions using linear channels that are used exactly once. For example, in (E-Output) a new channel c is created and sent along

$$\begin{aligned}
[\![x!\langle v\rangle.P]\!]_f &= (\boldsymbol{\nu} c) f_x!\langle v, c\rangle.[\![P]\!]_{f,x\mapsto c} & \text{(E-Output)} \\
[\![x?(y).P]\!]_f &= f_x?(y, c).[\![P]\!]_{f,x\mapsto c} & \text{(E-Input)} \\
[\![x \triangleright \{l_i : P_i\}_{i\in I}]\!]_f &= f_x?(y).\ \mathbf{case}\, y\, \mathbf{of}\, \{l_{i\_}(c) \triangleright [\![P_i]\!]_{f,x\mapsto c}\}_{i\in I} & \text{(E-Branching)} \\
[\![(\boldsymbol{\nu} xy)P]\!]_f &= (\boldsymbol{\nu} c)[\![P]\!]_{f,x\mapsto c,y\mapsto c} & \text{(E-Res)}
\end{aligned}$$

Fig. 5. π-calculus with sessions, encoding to standard π-calculus

with the original value v. The function f is then updated by mapping x to the new channel c, which is used in the continuation process. On the other hand, the process produced by rule (E-Input) performs the dual action by receiving the value of the communication and the new channel. (E-Branching) encodes the branching process by using the **case** process, after the guard of the **case** is received in input. Rule (E-Res) encodes the restriction $(\boldsymbol{\nu} xy)$ as $(\boldsymbol{\nu} c)$.

The encoding $[\![-]\!]_f$ is semantically correct:

Theorem 7 (Operational Correspondence [9]). *Let P be a process in the π-calculus with sessions. Then:*

- *If $P \to P'$ then $\exists Q$ such that $[\![P]\!]_f \to Q$ and $Q \hookrightarrow [\![P']\!]_f$, where $\hookrightarrow$ denotes a structural congruence extended with a case normalisation;*
- *If $[\![P]\!]_f \to\equiv Q$ then, $\exists\, P'$ such that $(\boldsymbol{\nu} xy)P \to (\boldsymbol{\nu} xy)P'$ and $Q \to^n\equiv [\![P']\!]_{f'}$, where $f_x = f_y$, $n \in \{1, 2\}$ and f' is f updated after the reduction.*

From lock-freedom in the π-calculus to progress for sessions. We can finally present how to use our results in combination with Kobayashi's typing system for lock-freedom. First, from Theorem 7 we get that:

Corollary 3. *P in the π-calculus with sessions is lock-free iff $[\![P]\!]_f$ is lock-free.*

From our Corollaries 1 and 3, we can lift Kobayashi's analysis to progress in the π-calculus with sessions:

Theorem 8 (Typing Progress). *Let P be a well-typed process in the π-calculus with sessions. If $\emptyset \vdash_{LF} [\![\text{uclose}(P)]\!]_f$, then P has progress.*

Comparison. We conclude this section by comparing our approach with other static analysis for guaranteeing the progress property for session-based calculi in the literature [4, 11, 22]. For readability reasons, we omit some empty processes and restrictions of unused channels.

Example 4. The following process is lock-free and has progress:

$$(\boldsymbol{\nu} a_1 a_2)\Big(a_1!\langle\text{unit}\rangle \mid (\boldsymbol{\nu} b_1 b_2)\big(b_1!\langle\text{unit}\rangle \mid b_2?(y).a_2?(z) \big) \Big)$$

However, it is rejected by [22], since the type system presented therein does not distinguish between obligation and capability tags, but uses a single tag instead. If we consider its encoding in the π-calculus, we obtain the following process

$$(\boldsymbol{\nu} a)\Big(a!\langle\text{unit}\rangle \mid (\boldsymbol{\nu} b)\big(b!\langle\text{unit}\rangle \mid b?(y).a?(z) \big) \Big)$$

This process is accepted by Kobayashi's type system with types $a :!^0_1 \mid ?^1_0$ and $b :!^0_0 \mid ?^0_0$ and therefore our initial process has progress. $\square$

Example 5. Consider the session process

$$(\nu a_1 a_2)(\nu b_1 b_2)\left(a_1?(x).\ b_1!\langle x\rangle.\ b_1?(y).\ a_1!\langle y\rangle \mid a_2!\langle \mathsf{unit}\rangle.\ b_2?(z).\ b_2!\langle \mathsf{unit}\rangle.\ a_2?(z)\right)$$

This process satisfies the progress property, but it is rejected by the type systems in [1] and [4]. This is because, in the two processes in parallel, there is a circular dependency between channels that such type systems cannot handle. Let us now consider its encoding in the π-calculus, given as the process:

$$(\nu a)(\nu b)\begin{pmatrix} a?(x,c_1).\ (\nu c_2)\Big(\ b!\langle x,c_2\rangle.\ c_2?(y).\ c_1!\langle y\rangle\ \Big)\ \mid \\ (\nu c_1)\Big(a!\langle \mathsf{unit},c_1\rangle.\ b?(z,c_2).\ c_2!\langle \mathsf{unit}\rangle.\ c_1?(z)\Big)\end{pmatrix}$$

This process is correctly recognised as having progress by our technique, since it is well-typed in Kobayashi's type system. □

6   Conclusions and Future Work

In this paper we studied the relationship between the notions of progress and lock-freedom in the π-calculus with sessions, proving that they are strongly linked: progress can be thought of as a generalisation of lock-freedom to open processes. We have shown how to characterise progress using session types (typed closure) or the structure of processes (untyped closure). Our results can be used to lift static analyses for lock-freedom to the progress property. For example, we showed that reusing Kobayashi's type system [15] captures new interesting cases of processes that have progress that could not be recognised by previous work.

Future Work. As future work, we plan to extend our approach to multiparty sessions [7, 14]. For the multiparty setting, we need to investigate an extension of the encoding in [9] to a setting where sessions are established between more than two peers and messaging is asynchronous. It is not clear whether Kobayashi's usage types are expressive enough for handling such situations.

The works in [2, 26] use linear logic to type processes in the π-calculus with sessions. While these works guarantee lock-freedom, we conjecture that their techniques can be reused for progress, similarly to what we have done with Kobayashi's type system. We leave such an investigation as future work.

Kobayashi's type system comes with the reference implementation TyPi-Cal [24]. We are currently implementing a tool that allows to write processes in the π-calculus with sessions, checks that they are well-typed, and then uses the encoding in [9] for generating π-calculus code that can be analysed in TyPiCal.

References

1. Bettini, L., Coppo, M., D'Antoni, L., De Luca, M., Dezani-Ciancaglini, M., Yoshida, N.: Global progress in dynamically interleaved multiparty sessions. In: van Breugel, F., Chechik, M. (eds.) CONCUR 2008. LNCS, vol. 5201, pp. 418–433. Springer, Heidelberg (2008)
2. Caires, L., Pfenning, F.: Session types as intuitionistic linear propositions. In: Gastin, P., Laroussinie, F. (eds.) CONCUR 2010. LNCS, vol. 6269, pp. 222–236. Springer, Heidelberg (2010)

3. Carbone, M., Dardha, O., Montesi, F.: Progress as compositional lock-freedom (2014), http://www.dcs.gla.ac.uk/~ornela/my_papers/CDM-Extended.pdf
4. Carbone, M., Debois, S.: A graphical approach to progress for structured communication in web services. In: Proc. of ICE 2010, pp. 13–27 (2010)
5. Carbone, M., Honda, K., Yoshida, N.: Structured communication-centered programming for web services. ACM Trans. Program. Lang. Syst. 34(2), 8 (2012)
6. Carbone, M., Montesi, F.: Deadlock-freedom-by-design: multiparty asynchronous global programming. In: POPL, pp. 263–274 (2013)
7. Coppo, M., Dezani-Ciancaglini, M., Yoshida, N.: Global progress for dynamically interleaved multiparty sessions (long version) (2008), http://www.di.unito.it/~dezani/papers/cdy12.pdf
8. Coppo, M., Dezani-Ciancaglini, M., Yoshida, N., Padovani, L.: Global progress for dynamically interleaved multiparty sessions. Mathematical Structures of Computer Science (to appear)
9. Dardha, O., Giachino, E., Sangiorgi, D.: Session types revisited. In: Schreye, D.D., Janssens, G., King, A. (eds.) PPDP, pp. 139–150. ACM (2012)
10. Deniélou, P.-M., Yoshida, N.: Dynamic multirole session types. In: Proc. of POPL, pp. 435–446. ACM (2011)
11. Dezani-Ciancaglini, M., de'Liguoro, U., Yoshida, N.: On Progress for Structured Communications. In: Barthe, G., Fournet, C. (eds.) TGC 2007. LNCS, vol. 4912, pp. 257–275. Springer, Heidelberg (2008)
12. Gay, S., Hole, M.: Subtyping for session types in the pi calculus. Acta Informatica 42(2-3), 191–225 (2005)
13. Honda, K., Vasconcelos, V.T., Kubo, M.: Language primitives and type disciplines for structured communication-based programming. In: Hankin, C. (ed.) ESOP 1998. LNCS, vol. 1381, pp. 122–138. Springer, Heidelberg (1998)
14. Honda, K., Yoshida, N., Carbone, M.: Multiparty asynchronous session types. In: Proc. of POPL, vol. 43(1), pp. 273–284. ACM (2008)
15. Kobayashi, N.: A type system for lock-free processes. Inf. Comput. 177(2), 122–159 (2002)
16. Kobayashi, N.: A new type system for deadlock-free processes. In: Baier, C., Hermanns, H. (eds.) CONCUR 2006. LNCS, vol. 4137, pp. 233–247. Springer, Heidelberg (2006)
17. Kobayashi, N., Sangiorgi, D.: A hybrid type system for lock-freedom of mobile processes. ACM Trans. Program. Lang. Syst. 32(5) (2010)
18. Milner, R., Parrow, J., Walker, D.: A calculus of mobile processes, I and II. Information and Computation 100(1), 1–40, 41–77 (1992)
19. Montesi, F., Carbone, M.: Programming services with correlation sets. In: Kappel, G., Maamar, Z., Motahari-Nezhad, H.R. (eds.) ICSOC 2011. LNCS, vol. 7084, pp. 125–141. Springer, Heidelberg (2011)
20. Montesi, F., Yoshida, N.: Compositional choreographies. In: D'Argenio, P.R., Melgratti, H. (eds.) CONCUR 2013. LNCS, vol. 8052, pp. 425–439. Springer, Heidelberg (2013)
21. OASIS. Web Services Business Process Execution Language, http://docs.oasis-open.org/wsbpel/2.0/wsbpel-v2.0.html
22. Padovani, L.: From lock freedom to progress using session types. In: Proc. of PLACES (2013)
23. Pierce, B.C.: Types and programming languages. MIT Press (2002)
24. TYPICAL. Type-based static analyzer for the pi-calculus, http://www-kb.is.s.u-tokyo.ac.jp/~koba/typical/
25. Vasconcelos, V.T.: Fundamentals of session types. Inf. Comput. 217, 52–70 (2012)
26. Wadler, P.: Propositions as sessions. In: ICFP, pp. 273–286 (2012)

Automata-Based Optimization of Interaction Protocols for Scalable Multicore Platforms

Sung-Shik T.Q. Jongmans, Sean Halle, and Farhad Arbab

Centrum Wiskunde & Informatica, Amsterdam, The Netherlands
{jongmans,sean,farhad}@cwi.nl

Abstract. Multicore platforms offer the opportunity for utilizing massively parallel resources. However, programming them is challenging. We need good compilers that optimize commonly occurring synchronization/ interaction patterns. To facilitate optimization, a programming language must convey what needs to be done in a form that leaves a considerably large decision space on *how* to do it for the compiler/run-time system.

Reo is a coordination-inspired model of concurrency that allows compositional construction of interaction protocols as declarative specifications. This form of protocol programming specifies only *what* needs to be done and leaves virtually all *how*-decisions involved in obtaining a concrete implementation for the compiler and the run-time system to make, thereby maximizing the potential opportunities for optimization. In contrast, the imperative form of protocol specification in conventional concurrent programming languages, generally, restrict implementation choices (and thereby hamper optimization) due to overspecification.

In this paper, we use the Constraint Automata semantics of Reo protocols as the formal basis for our optimizations. We optimize a generalization of the producer-consumer pattern, by applying CA transformations and prove the correctness of the transforms.

1 Introduction

Context. Coordination languages have emerged for the implementation of protocols among concurrent entities (e.g., threads on multicore hardware). One such language is Reo [1,2], a graphical language for compositional construction of *connectors* (i.e., custom synchronization protocols). Figure 1a shows an example. Briefly, a connector consists of one or more edges (henceforth referred to as *channels*), through which data items flow, and a number of nodes (henceforth referred to as *ports*), on which channel ends coincide. The connector in Figure 1a contains three different channel classes, including standard synchronous channels (normal arrows) and asynchronous channels with a buffer of capacity 1 (arrows decorated with a white rectangle, which represents a buffer). Through connector *composition* (the act of gluing connectors together on their shared ports), programmers can construct arbitrarily complex connectors. As Reo supports both synchronous and asynchronous channels, connector composition enables mixing synchronous and asynchronous communication within the same specification.

E. Kühn and R. Pugliese (Eds.): COORDINATION 2014, LNCS 8459, pp. 65–82, 2014.
© IFIP International Federation for Information Processing 2014

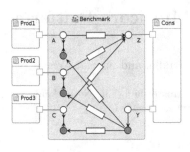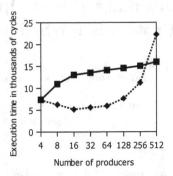

(a) Connector

(b) Per-interaction overhead for the Pthreads-based implementation (continuous line; squares) and the pre-optimized CA-based implementation (dotted line; diamonds)

Fig. 1. Producers–consumer benchmark

Especially when it comes to multicore programming, Reo has a number of advantages over conventional programming languages with a fixed set of low-level synchronization constructs (locks, mutexes, etc.). Programmers using such a conventional language have to translate the synchronization needs of their protocols into the synchronization constructs of that language. Because this translation occurs in the mind of the programmer, invariably some context information either gets irretrievably lost or becomes implicit and difficult to extract in the resulting code. In contrast, Reo allows programmers to compose their own synchronization constructs (i.e., connectors) at a high abstraction level to perfectly fit the protocols of their application. Not only does this reduce the conceptual gap for programmers, which makes it easier to implement and reason about protocols, but by preserving all relevant context information, such user-defined synchronization constructs also offer considerable novel opportunities for compilers to do optimizations on multicore hardware. This paper shows one such occasion.

Additionally, Reo has several software engineering advantages as a domain-specific language for protocols [3]. For instance, Reo forces developers to separate their computation code from their protocol code. Such a separation facilitates verbatim reuse, independent modification, and compositional construction of protocol implementations (i.e., connectors) in a straightforward way. Moreover, Reo has a strong mathematical foundation [4], which enables formal connector analyses (e.g., deadlock detection, model checking [5]).

To use connectors in real programs, developers need tools that automatically generate executable code for connectors. In previous work [6], we therefore developed a Reo-to-C compiler, based on Reo's formal semantics of *constraint automata* (CA) [7]. In its simplest form, this tool works roughly as follows. First, it extracts from an input XML representation of a connector a list of its primitive constituents.[1] Second, it consults a database to find for every constituent in the list a "small" CA that formally describes the behavior of that particular constituent. Third, it computes the product of the CA in the constructed collection to obtain one "big" CA describing the behavior of the whole connector. Fourth, it feeds a data structure representing that big CA to a template. Essentially, this template is an incomplete C file with "holes" that need be "filled". The generated code simulates the big CA by repeatedly computing and firing eligible transitions in an event-driven fashion. It runs on top of Proto-Runtime [8,9], an execution environment for C code on multicore hardware. A key feature of Proto-Runtime is that it provides more direct access to processor cores and control over scheduling than threading libraries based on OS threads, such as Pthreads [10].

Problem. Figure 1a shows a connector for a protocol among $k = 3$ producers and one consumer in a producers–consumer benchmark. Every producer loops through the following steps: (i) it produces, (ii) it blocks until the consumer has signaled ready for processing the next batch of productions, and (iii) it sends its production. Meanwhile, the consumer runs the following loop: (i) it signals ready, and (ii) it receives exactly one production from every producer in arbitrary order. We compared the CA-based implementation generated by our tool with a hand-crafted implementation written by a competent C programmer using Pthreads, investigating the time required for communicating a production from a producer to the consumer as a function of the number of producers.

Figure 1b shows our results. On the positive side, for $k \leq 256$, the CA-based implementation outperforms the hand-crafted implementation. For $k = 512$, however, the Pthreads-based implementation outperforms the generated implementation. Moreover, the dotted curve looks disturbing, because it grows more-than-linearly in k: indeed, the CA-based implementation scales poorly. (We skip many details of this benchmark, including those of the Pthreads-based implementation, and the meaning/implications of these experimental results. The reason is that this paper is *not* about this benchmark, and its details do not matter. We use this benchmark only as a concrete case to better explain problems of our compilation approach and as a source of inspiration for solutions.)

Contribution. In this paper, we report on work at improving the scalability of code generated by our Reo-to-C compiler. First, we identify a cause of poor scalability: briefly, computing eligibility of k transitions in producers–consumer-style protocols (and those generalizations thereof that allow any synchronization involving one party from every one of ℓ groups) takes $\mathcal{O}(k)$ time instead of $\mathcal{O}(1)$, of which the Pthreads-based implementation shows that it is possible. Second, to familiarize the reader with certain essential concepts, we explain a manual solution (in terms of Reo's CA semantics) that achieves $\mathcal{O}(1)$. Third, we propose

---

[1] Programmers can use the ECT plugins for Eclipse (http://reo.project.cwi.nl) to draw connectors such as the one in Figure 1a, internally represented as XML.

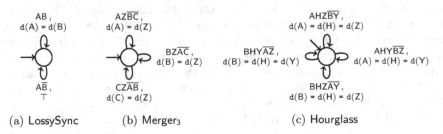

Fig. 2. Example CA, called LossySync, Merger3 and Hourglass

an automated, general solution, built upon the same concepts as the manual solution. We formalize this automated solution and prove it correct. Although inspired by our work on Reo and formulated in terms of CA, we make more general contributions beyond Reo and CA, better explained in our conclusion.

We organized the rest of this paper as follows. In Section 2, we explain CA. In Section 3, we analyze how the Pthreads-based implementation avoids scalability issues and how we can export that to our setting. In Sections 4–6, we automate the solution proposed in Section 3. Section 7 concludes this paper. Definitions and detailed proofs appear in the appendix of a technical report [11].

Although inspired by Reo, we can express our main results in a purely automata-theoretic setting. We therefore skip a primer on Reo [1,2].

2   Constraint Automata

Constraint automata are a general formalism for describing systems behavior and have been used to model not only connectors but also, for instance, actors [12]. Figure 2 shows examples.[2,3] In the context of this paper, a CA specifies *when* during execution of a connector *which* data items flow *where*. Structurally, every CA consists of finite sets of states, transitions between states, and ports. States represent the internal configurations of a connector, while transitions describe its atomic execution steps. Every transition has a label that consists of two elements: a *synchronization constraint* (SC) and a *data constraint* (DC). An SC is a

---

[2] The LossySync CA models a connector with one input port A and one output port B. It repeatedly chooses between two atomic execution steps (constrained by availability of pending I/O operations): synchronous flow of data from A to B or flow of data only on A (after which the data is lost, before reaching B). The Merger3 CA models a connector with three input ports A, B, and C and one output port Z. It repeatedly chooses between three atomic execution steps: synchronous flow of data from A to Z, from B to Z, or from C to Z. Finally, the Hourglass CA models a connector with two input ports A and B, one internal port H, and two output ports Y and Z. It repeatedly chooses between four atomic execution steps: synchronous flow of data from A via H to Y, from A via H to Z, from B via H to Y, or from B via H to Z.

[3] We show only single state CA for simplicity. Generally, a CA can have any finite number of states, and the results in this paper are applicable also to such CA.

p ::= any element from PORT
Ψ ::= any set of SCs
a ::= $0 \mid 1 \mid p$
ψ ::= $a \mid \overline{\psi} \mid \psi + \psi \mid \psi \cdot \psi \mid \bigoplus(\Psi)$

p ::= any element from PORT
P ::= any subset of PORT
b ::= $\bot \mid \top \mid \mathsf{Eq}(P) \mid \mathsf{d}(p) = \mathsf{d}(p)$
ϕ ::= $b \mid \neg\phi \mid \phi \vee \phi \mid \phi \wedge \phi$

(a) Synchronization constraints   (b) Data constraints

Fig. 3. Syntax

propositional formula that specifies which ports synchronize in a firing transition (i.e., where data items flow); a DC is a propositional formula that (under)specifies which particular data items flow where. For instance, in Figure 2a, the DC $\mathsf{d}(\mathsf{A}) = \mathsf{d}(\mathsf{B})$ means that the data item on A equals the data item on B; the DC $\top$ means that it does not matter which data items flow. Let PORT denote the global set of all ports. Formally, an SC is a word ψ generated by the grammar in Figure 3a, while a DC is a word ϕ generated by the grammar in Figure 3b.

Figure 3a generalizes the original definition of SCs as sets of ports interpreted as conjunctions [7] (shortly, we elaborate on the exact correspondence). Operator $\bigoplus$ is a uniqueness quantifier: $\bigoplus(\Psi)$ holds if exactly one SC in Ψ holds. Also, we remark that predicate $\mathsf{Eq}(P)$ is novel. It holds if equal data items are distributed over all ports in P. In many practical cases—but not all—we can replace a DC of the shape $\mathsf{d}(p_1) = \mathsf{d}(p_2)$ with $\mathsf{Eq}(P)$ if $\{p_1, p_2\} \subseteq P$. In the development of our optimization technique, $\mathsf{Eq}(P)$ plays an important role (see also Section 7).

Let DATA denote the set of all data items. Formally, we interpret SCs and DCs over *distributions* of data over ports, $\delta : \text{PORT} \rightharpoonup \text{DATA}$, using relations $\overset{sc}{\models}$ and $\overset{dc}{\models}$ and the corresponding equivalence relations $\equiv_{sc}$ and $\equiv_{dc}$. Their definition for negation, disjunction, and conjunction is standard; for atoms, we have:

$$\delta \overset{sc}{\models} p \text{ iff } p \in \text{Dom}(\delta) \qquad \delta \overset{dc}{\models} \mathsf{Eq}(P) \qquad \text{iff } |\text{Img}(\delta|_P)| = 1$$
$$\delta \overset{dc}{\models} \mathsf{d}(p_1) = \mathsf{d}(p_2) \text{ iff } \delta(p_1) = \delta(p_2)$$

Let $\sum(\{\psi_1, \dots, \psi_k\})$ and $\prod(\{\psi_1, \dots, \psi_k\})$ abbreviate $\psi_1 + \dots + \psi_k$ and $\psi_1 \cdots \psi_k$, let SC denote the sets of all SCs, and let $\mathsf{SC}(P)$ and $\mathsf{DC}(P)$ denote the sets of all SCs and all DCs over ports in P.

A constraint automaton is a tuple $(Q, P, \longrightarrow, \imath)$ with Q a set of states, $P \subseteq \text{PORT}$ a set of ports, $\longrightarrow \subseteq Q \times \mathsf{SC}(P) \times \mathsf{DC}(P) \times Q$ a transition relation labeled with [SC, DC]-pairs of the form (ψ, ϕ), and $\imath \in Q$ an initial state.

A distribution δ represents a single atomic execution step of a connector in which data item $\delta(p)$ flows on port p (for all ports in the domain of δ). A CA α accepts *streams* (i.e., infinite sequences) of such distributions. Every such a stream represents one possible infinite execution of the connector modeled by α. Intuitively, to see if α accepts a stream σ, starting from the initial state, take the first element $\sigma(0)$ from the stream, check if α has a (ψ, ϕ)-labeled transition from the current state such that $\sigma(0) \overset{sc}{\models} \psi$ and $\sigma(0) \overset{dc}{\models} \phi$, and if so, make this transition, remove $\sigma(0)$ from the stream, and repeat.

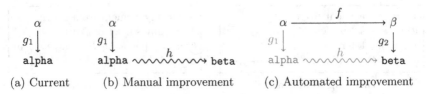

Fig. 4. Code generation diagrams

Our CA definition generalizes the original definition of CA [7], because Figure 3a generalizes the original definition of SCs. However, CA as originally defined still play a role in the development of our optimization technique: all input CA that this technique operates on are original. Therefore, we make more precise what "originality" means. First, let a *P-complete product* be a product of either a positive or a negative literal for every port in P. Intuitively, a P-complete product specifies not only which ports participate in a transition, but it also makes explicit which ports idle in that transition. Let $\mathsf{cp}(P, P_+)$ denote a P-complete product with positive literals $P_+ \subseteq P$. Then, we call an SC ψ original if a set P_+ exists such that $\mathsf{cp}(P, P_+) \equiv \psi$ (originally, set P_+ would be the SC); we call a CA original if it has only original SCs. All CA in Figure 2 are original.

We adopt *bisimilarity* on CA as behavioral congruence, derived from the definition for original CA of Baier et al. [7]. Roughly, if α and β are bisimilar, denoted as $\alpha \sim \beta$, α can simulate every transition of β in every state and vice versa (see Definition 32 in [11, Appendix A]).

3   Enhancing Scalability: Problem and Solution

We study the scalability of code generated by our compiler using Figure 4. We start with Figure 4a, which summarizes the code generation process of our current tool: given an original CA α (computed for the connector to generate code for), it generates a piece of code **alpha** by applying transformation g_1.

Essentially, **alpha** consists of an event-driven *handler*, which simulates α. This handler runs concurrently with the code of its environment (i.e., the code of the entitites under coordination), whose events (i.e., I/O operations performed on ports) it listens and responds to, as follows. Whenever the environment performs an I/O operation on a port p, it assigns a representation of that operation to an **event** variable in a data structure for p (also generated by transformation g_1 and part of **alpha**). This causes the handler to start a new round of simulating α. Based on the state of α that the handler at that point should behave as, the handler knows which transitions of α *may* fire. Which of those transitions actually *can* fire, however, depends also on the pending events that previously occurred (i.e., the pending I/O operations on ports). To investigate this, the handler checks *for every transition* that may fire if the pending events (including the new one) can constitute a distribution δ that satisfies the transition's label. If so, the handler fires the transition: it distributes data over ports according to

δ, and the events involved dissolve. Otherwise, if no transition can fire, all events remain for the next round, and the handler goes dormant.

Now, recall our producers–consumer benchmark in Section 1. Figure 2b shows the CA for the connector in Figure 1a.[4] Generally, for an arbitrary number of producers k, the corresponding CA α_k has k transitions. Consequently, in the worst case, the handler in the generated alpha_k code performs k checks in every event handling round, which takes $\mathcal{O}(k)$ time. Figure 1b shows this as a more-than-linear increase in execution time for the dotted curve.[5] The Pthreads-based implementation, in contrast, uses a queue for lining up available productions. To receive a production, the consumer simply dequeues, which takes only $\mathcal{O}(1)$ time (ignoring, for simplicity, the overhead of synchronizing queue accesses). Figure 1b shows this as a linear increase in execution time for the continuous curve.

Intuitively, by checking all transitions to make the consumer receive, the generated CA-based implementation performs an exhaustive search for a particular producer that sent a production. In contrast, by using a queue, the Pthreads-based implementation avoids such a search: the queue embodies that in this protocol, it does not matter which *particular* producer sent a production as long as *some* producer has done so (in which case the queue is nonempty). The producers are really *indistinguishable* from the perspective of the consumer. Thus, to improve the scalability of code generated by our tool, we want to export the idea of "using queues to leverage indistinguishability" to our setting.

Figure 4b shows a first attempt at achieving this goal: we introduce a manual transformation h that takes alpha as input and hacks together a new piece of code beta, which should (i) behave as alpha, (ii) demonstrate good scalability, and (iii) use queues. For instance, in our producers–consumer example ($k = 3$), h works roughly as follows. First, h replaces the event variable in the data structure for every port $p \in \{A, B, C, Z\}$ with an eventQueue variable that points to a queue of pending events. In this new setup, to perform an I/O operation, the environment enqueues an eventQueue, while handler code tests eventQueues for nonemptiness to check SCs, peeks eventQueues to check DCs, and dequeues eventQueues to fire transitions. Subsequently, h adds initialization code to alpha to ensure that the eventQueue variables of ports A, B, and C all point to the same shared queue, while the eventQueue variable for port Z points to a different queue. Here, h effectively exploits the indistinguishability property of producers

---

[4] To be precise, the CA in Figure 2b describes the behavior of one of the *synchronous regions* of the connector in Figure 1a (i.e., a particular subconnector of the whole). This point is immaterial to our present discussion, however, and ignoring it simplifies our presentation without loss of generality or applicability.

[5] The growth is more-than-linear instead of just linear because of the barrier in the protocol. When producer P is ready to send its $(i + 1)$-th production, the consumer may not yet have received the i-th production from all other producers. Then, P must wait until the consumer signals ready (i.e., the barrier). In the worst case, however, the consumer has received an i-th production only from P such that P has to wait $(k - 1) \cdot \mathcal{O}(k)$ time. Afterward, it takes another $\mathcal{O}(k)$ time for P to send its $(i + 1)$-th production. Consequently, sending the $(i + 1)$-th production takes $k \cdot \mathcal{O}(k)$ time, and the complexity of sending a production lies between $\mathcal{O}(k)$ and $\mathcal{O}(k^2)$.

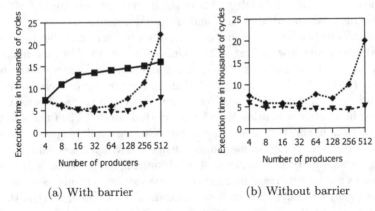

(a) With barrier   (b) Without barrier

Fig. 5. Per-interaction overhead for the Pthreads-based implementation (continuous line; squares), the pre-optimized CA-based implementation (dotted line; diamonds), and the optimized, h-transformed CA-based implementation (dashed line; triangles) of the producers–consumer scenario in Figure 1

by making *the ports* that those producers use indistinguishable in our setting. Finally, h updates the handler code such that it processes the shared queue only once per event handling round instead of thrice (i.e., once for every transition). From an automata-theoretic perspective, h replaces the implementation of the three "physical" transitions with an implementation of one merged "virtual" transition. When the handler fires this virtual transition at run-time, it actually fires one of the three physical transitions.

Property (iii) holds of the piece of code `beta` resulting from applying h to `alpha` as just described. Figure 5 shows that also property (ii) holds. The dashed curve in Figure 5a shows execution times of h-transformed code of the CA-based implementation in the producers–consumer benchmark. The h-transformed code scales much better than the original code. Additionally, Figure 5b shows execution times of the producers–consumer benchmark without a barrier (i.e., producers send productions whenever they want). In this variant, h achieves even better results: it transforms a poorly scalable program into one that scales perfectly.[6]

Establishing property (i), however, is problematic. Although we can informally argue that it holds, proving this—formally showing the equivalence of two concurrent C programs—seems prohibitively complex. That aside, the manual nature of h makes its usage generally impractical, and it seems extremely difficult to automate it: an automated version of h would have to analyze C code

---

[6] Of course, in many cases and for many applications, a purely asynchronous producers–consumer protocol without a barrier, as in Figure 5b, suffices. The reason that we initially focused on a producers–consumer protocol with a barrier, which is also useful yet in other applications, is that its mix of synchrony and asynchrony makes it a harder, and arguably more interesting, protocol to achieve good scalability for. Comparing the results in Figures 5a and 5b also shows this.

to recover relevant context information about the protocol, which is not only hard but often theoretically impossible. Similarly, it seems infeasible to write an optimizing compiler able to transform, for instance, less scalable Pthreads-based implementations of the producers-consumer scenario (without queues) into the Pthreads-based implementation (with queues) used in our benchmark. The inability of compilers for lower-level languages to do such optimizations seems a significant disadvantage of using such languages for multicore programming.

We therefore pursue an alternative approach, outlined in Figure 4c: we introduce a transformation f that takes CA α as input—instead of the low-level C code generated for it—and transforms it into an equivalent automaton β, a variant of α with *merged transitions* (cf. transformation h, which implicitly replaced the implementation of several physical transitions with one virtual transition). Crucially, α still explicitly contains all relevant context information about the protocol, exactly what makes f eligible to automation. In particular, to merge transitions effectively, f carefully inspects transition labels and takes port indistinguishability into account. The resulting merged transitions have an "obvious" and mechanically obtainable implementation using queues. A subsequent transformation g_2, from β to beta, performs this final straightforward step.

We divide transformation $\alpha \xrightarrow{f} \beta$ into a number of constituent transformations $\alpha \xrightarrow{f_1} \beta' \xrightarrow{f_2} (\beta', \Gamma) \xrightarrow{f_3} \beta$, discussed in detail in the following sections.

4   Transformation f_1: Preprocessing

Transformation f_1 aims at merging transitions $t_1, \ldots, t_k$ into one transition $(q, \psi, \text{Eq}(P), q')$, where $\psi = \sum(\{\psi_1, \ldots, \psi_k\})$. It consists of two steps.

In the first step, transformation f_1 replaces DCs on transitions of $\alpha = (Q, P, \longrightarrow, \imath)$ with $\text{Eq}(P)$, as follows. Because α is an original CA (our current code generator can handle only original CA), every SC in α is an original SC: for every transition label (ψ, ϕ), a set of ports P_+ exists such that $\text{cp}(P, P_+) \equiv \psi$. Now, for every product in *disjunctive normal form* (DNF) of ϕ, transformation f_1 constructs a graph with vertices P_+ and an edge (p_1, p_2) for every $\text{d}(p_1) = \text{d}(p_2)$ literal. Because $\text{cp}(P, P_+) \equiv \psi$, if the resulting graph is connected, the product of the $\text{d}(p_1) = \text{d}(p_2)$ literals is equivalent to $\text{Eq}(P)$. Thus, f_1 replaces every transition label (ψ, ϕ) in α with an equivalent label (ψ, ϕ'), where ϕ' denotes the modified DNF of ϕ, with $\text{Eq}(P)$ for every product of $\text{d}(p_1) = \text{d}(p_2)$ literals if those literals induce a connected graph. Let α' denote the resulting CA. We can prove that $\alpha' \sim \alpha$ holds (see Lemma 16 in [11, Appendix A]).

In the second step, transformation f_1 merges, for every pair of states (q, q'), all transitions from q to q' labeled by DC ϕ into one new transition. (The individual transitions differ only in their SC.) Every resulting transition has as its SC the sum of the SCs of the individual transitions. Figure 6 shows examples. We denote the resulting CA by $f_1(\alpha)$. The following proposition holds, because choices between individual transitions in α are encoded in $f_1(\alpha)$ by sum-SCs of merged transitions. Consequently, α and $f_1(\alpha)$ can simulate each other's steps.

Proposition 1. $f_1(\alpha) \sim \alpha'$

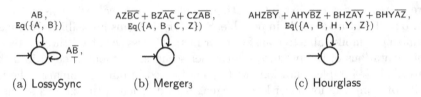

(a) LossySync   (b) Merger₃   (c) Hourglass

Fig. 6. Application of transformations f_1 to the CA in Figure 2

5   Transformation f_2: Constructing Hypergraphs

Every merged transition resulting from the previous preprocessing transformations can *perhaps* be implemented using queues along the same lines as transformation h (see Section 3). In the first place, this depends on the extent to which ports in a merged transition are indistinguishable: no indistinguishable ports means no queues. Second, the SC of a merged transition should make port indistinguishability (i.e., queues), if present, apparent and *mechanically detectable*. The SCs of transitions in $f_1(\alpha)$ fail to do so. For instance, we (hence a computer) cannot directly derive from the syntax of SC $\mathsf{AZ\overline{BC}+BZ\overline{AC}+CZ\overline{AB}}$ in Figure 6b that its transition has a scalable implementation with queues. In contrast, the equivalent SC $\bigoplus(\{\mathsf{A}, \mathsf{B}, \mathsf{C}\}) \cdot \mathsf{Z}$ makes this much more apparent. From this SC, we can "obviously" (and mechanically by transformation g_2 in Figure 4c) conclude that ports A, B, and C may share the same queue, from which exactly one element is dequeued per firing, because they are indistinguishable indeed: intuitively, if $\delta \models^{\mathsf{sc}} \bigoplus(\{\mathsf{A}, \mathsf{B}, \mathsf{C}\}) \cdot \mathsf{Z}$, we cannot know which one of A, B, or C holds, unless we inspect δ. Thus, beside automatically detecting indistinguishable ports in a transition, to actually reveal them as queues, we additionally need an algorithm for syntactically manipulating that transition's SC. We formulate both these aspects in terms of a per-transition *hypergraph* [13]. Working with hypergraph representations simplifies our reasoning about, and manipulation of, SCs modulo associativity and commutativity. We compute hypergraphs as follows.

Let $\alpha = (Q, P, \longrightarrow, \imath)$ be an original CA as before, and let (q, ψ, ϕ, q') be a (merged) transition in $f_1(\alpha)$. Because α is an original CA and by the construction of $f_1(\alpha)$, we know that ψ is a sum of P-complete products of ports (e.g., Figure 6). Because every single port p is equivalent to $\bigoplus(\{p\})$, transformation f_2 can represent ψ as a set $\mathcal{E}$ of sets E of sets V: $\mathcal{E}$ represents the outer sum, every E represents a P-complete product (E includes/excludes every positive/negative port), and every V represents an inner exclusive sum. For instance, $\{\{\{\mathsf{A}\}, \{\mathsf{Z}\}\}, \{\{\mathsf{B}\}, \{\mathsf{Z}\}\}, \{\{\mathsf{C}\}, \{\mathsf{Z}\}\}\}$ represents the SC of the transition in Figure 6b. Transformation f_2 considers $\mathcal{E}$ as the set of hyperedges of a hypergraph over the set of vertices $\wp(\mathsf{Port}(\psi))$, where $\mathsf{Port}(\psi)$ denotes the ports occurring in ψ (i.e., every vertex is a set of ports). Formally, f_2 computes a function graph. Let $\mathbb{GRAPH}$ denote the set of all hypergraphs with sets of ports as vertices.

Definition 1. graph : $\mathbb{SC} \rightharpoonup \text{GRAPH}$ *denotes the partial function from SCs to hypergraphs defined as:*[7]

$$\text{graph}(\psi) = (\wp(\text{Port}(\psi)), \left\{ E \middle| \begin{array}{l} E = \{V \mid V = \{p\} \text{ and } p \in P_+\} \\ \text{and } P_+ \subseteq \text{Port}(\psi) \text{ and } P_+ \in \mathcal{P} \end{array} \right\})$$

$$\text{if } [\psi = \sum(\left\{ \psi' \middle| \begin{array}{l} \psi' \equiv_{\text{sc}} \text{cp}(\text{Port}(\psi), P_+) \text{ and} \\ P_+ \subseteq \text{Port}(\psi) \text{ and } P_+ \in \mathcal{P} \end{array} \right\}) \text{ for some } \mathcal{P}]$$

(The side condition states just that ψ is a sum of P-complete products of ports.)

Figure 7 shows example hypergraphs (without unconnected vertices).

We define the *meaning* of a hypergraph as a sum of products of exclusive sums, where every product corresponds to a hyperedge. Such a product consists of exclusive sums of positive ports (one for each vertex in the hyperedge), and it consists of negative ports (one for every port outside the vertices in the hyperedge). We can show that graph is an isomorphism (i.e., graph(ψ) is a sound and complete representation of ψ).

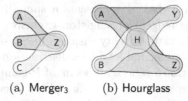

(a) Merger₃   (b) Hourglass

Fig. 7. Hypergraphs for the transitions of the CA in Figure 6

Definition 2. $[\![\cdot]\!] : (\wp(\text{VER}) \times \wp(\text{PORT})) \cup \text{GRAPH} \rightarrow \mathbb{SC}$ *denotes the function from [hyperedge, set of ports]-pairs and hypergraphs to SCs defined as:*

$$[\![E]\!]_P = \prod(\{\psi \mid \psi = \bigoplus(V) \text{ and } V \in E\} \cup \{\psi \mid \psi = \overline{p} \text{ and } p \in P \setminus (\bigcup E)\})$$

$$[\![(\mathcal{V}, \mathcal{E})]\!] = \sum(\{\psi \mid \psi = [\![E]\!]_{\bigcup \mathcal{V}} \text{ and } E \in \mathcal{E}\})$$

Theorem 1. *(Theorem 3 in [11, Appendix A])* $\qquad\qquad \psi \equiv [\![\text{graph}(\psi)]\!]$

In summary, transformation f_2 computes graph for every merged transition in $f_1(\alpha)$ and stores each of those graphs in a set Γ (indexed by transitions).

Hypergraphs as introduced are generic representations of synchronization patterns, isomorphic to but independent of SCs in CA. This reinforces that our optimization approach, transformation f, is not tied CA but a generally applicable technique when relevant context information is available.

6 Transformation f_3: Manipulating SCs

Transformation f_3 aims at making all indistinguishable ports (hence queues) in SCs on (merged) transitions in $f_1(\alpha)$ apparent by analyzing and manipulating the hypergraphs in Γ, computed by transformation f_2. It consists of two steps.

In the first step, transformation f_3 computes the indistinguishable ports under every transition $t = (q, \psi, \phi, q')$ in $f_1(\alpha)$. We call the ports in a set I indistinguishable under t if for every distribution δ such that $\delta \models^{\text{sc}} \psi$ and $|I \cap \text{Dom}($

---

[7] Let $\wp(X)$ denote the power set of X.

$\delta)| = 1$, we cannot deduce from $\delta|_{P \setminus I}$ which particular port in I is satisfied by δ. An example appeared in the first paragraph of Section 5. In an implementation with a queue shared among the ports in I, this means that whenever t fires, we know that exactly one port in I participated in the transition but not which one, even if we know all other participating ports (i.e., those outside I).

By analyzing hypergraph $\gamma_t \in \Gamma$ for the SC ψ of t, transformation f_3 computes maximal sets of indistinguishable ports under t (larger sets of indistinguishable ports means larger queues means better scalability), as follows. Recall from Section 5 that γ_t represents a sum (hyperedge relation) of P-complete products (hyperedges) of singleton exclusive sums (vertices). To understand how port indistinguishability displays in γ_t, suppose that ports p_1, $p_2 \in P$ are indistinguishable, and let δ be a distribution such that $\delta \overset{\text{sc}}{\models} [\![\gamma_t]\!]$. Because γ_t's hyperedge relation $\mathcal{E}$ represents a sum of P-complete products, exactly one hyperedge $E \in \mathcal{E}$ exists such that δ satisfies $[\![E]\!]_P$. Then, because $|\{p_1 , p_2\} \cap \text{Dom}(\delta)| = 1$, a vertex $V \in E$ exists such that $p_1 \in V$ or $p_2 \in V$.[8] In fact, because every hyperedge consists of singleton vertices, either $\{p_1\} \in E$ or $\{p_2\} \in E$. Now, by inspecting $\delta|_{P \setminus \{p_1, p_2\}}$, we can infer the other vertices in E, beside either $\{p_1\}$ or $\{p_2\}$. Let E' denote this set of vertices, and observe that either $E = E_1 = E' \uplus \{\{p_1\}\}$ or $E = E_2 = E' \uplus \{\{p_2\}\}$. Because both options are possible, $\mathcal{E}$ necessarily includes both E_1 and E_2, and importantly, E_1 and E_2 are equal up to p_1 and p_2.

Generalizing this example from $\{p_1 , p_2\}$ to arbitrarily sized sets I, informally, the ports in I are indistinguishable if every port in I is involved in the same hyperedges as every other port in I *up to occurrences of ports in I*. The following definitions make this generalization formally precise. First, we introduce a function Edge that determines for a port p which hyperedges in $\mathcal{E}$ include p. (In fact, Edge$(p, \mathcal{E})$ contains all such hypergedges up to occurrences of vertices with p.) Then, we define a function $\star$ that computes maximal sets of ports with the same set Edge$(p, \mathcal{E})$. Importantly, $\star$ yields a partition of the set of ports in vertices connected by $\mathcal{E}$, denoted by Port$(\mathcal{E})$. Henceforth, we therefore call every maximal set of indistinguishable ports computed by $\star$ a *part*.

Definition 3. Edge $: \mathbb{PORT} \times \wp^2(\text{VER}) \to \wp^2(\text{VER})$ *denotes the function from* [*port, set of hyperedges*] *-pairs to sets of hyperedges defined as:*

$$\text{Edge}(p, \mathcal{E}) = \{W \mid W = E \setminus \{V\} \text{ and } p \in V \in E \in \mathcal{E}\}$$

Definition 4. $\star : \wp^2(\text{VER}) \to \wp^2(\mathbb{PORT})$ *denotes the function from sets of hyperedges to sets of sets of ports defined as:*

$$\star(\mathcal{E}) = \{P \mid P \in \wp^+(\text{Port}(\mathcal{E})) \text{ and } [\![p \in P \text{ iff } \mathcal{T} = \text{Edge}(p, \mathcal{E})]\!] \text{ for all } p]\}$$

Lemma 1. *(Lemma 12 in [11, Appendix A])*

1. $\bigcup \star(\mathcal{E}) = \text{Port}(\mathcal{E})$
2. $[P_1 \neq P_2 \text{ and } P_1, P_2 \in \star(\mathcal{E})]$ **implies** $P_1 \cap P_2 = \emptyset$

---

[8] Otherwise, if p_1, $p_2 \notin V$ for all $V \in E$, the P-complete product represented by E contains $\overline{p}_1$ and $\overline{p}_2$ such that $\delta \not\models p_1$ and $\delta \not\models p_2$. This contradicts the assumption $|\{p_1 , p_2\} \cap \text{Dom}(\delta)| = 1$, which implies either $\delta \overset{\text{sc}}{\models} p_1$ or $\delta \overset{\text{sc}}{\models} p_2$.

```
Edge(A, E) = {{{Z}}}
Edge(B, E) = {{{Z}}}
Edge(C, E) = {{{Z}}}
Edge(Z, E) = {{{A}}, {{B}}, {{C}}}
★(E)       = {{A, B, C}, {Z}}
```

```
Edge(A, E) = {{{H}, {Y}}, {{H}, {Z}}}
Edge(B, E) = {{{H}, {Y}}, {{H}, {Z}}}
Edge(H, E) = {{{A}, {Y}}, {{A}, {Z}}, {{B}, {Y}}, {{B}, {Z}}}
Edge(Y, E) = {{{A}, {H}}, {{B}, {H}}}
Edge(Z, E) = {{{A}, {H}}, {{B}, {H}}}
★(E)       = {{A, B}, {H}, {Y, Z}}
```

(a) Merger$_3$ (b) Hourglass

Fig. 8. Maximal sets of indistinguishable ports of the hypergraphs in Figure 7

In summary, in the first step, transformation f_3 computes maximal sets of indistinguishable ports in every merged transition $t = (q, \psi, \phi, q')$ by applying ★ to hyperedge relation $\mathcal{E}$ in hypergraph γ_t for ψ. Figure 8 shows examples.

In the second step, f_3 manipulates $\mathcal{E}$ of every hypergraph γ_t such that afterward, every vertex in every hyperedge in $\mathcal{E}$ is a part in ★$(\mathcal{E})$. Importantly, every vertex $V \in E \in \mathcal{E}$ such that $V \in$ ★$(\mathcal{E})$ represents not just any $\oplus$-formula but one of indistinguishable ports. Consequently, in the meaning of the manipulated γ_t, indistinguishable ports become apparent as inner $\oplus$-formulas as in the example in the first paragraph of Section 5.

For manipulating hyperedge relation $\mathcal{E}$, we introduce an operation $\sqcup$ that combines two *combinable* hyperedges into one in a semantics-preserving way. Roughly, we call two distinct hyperedges $E_1, E_2 \in \mathcal{E}$ combinable if we can select disjoint vertices $V_1, V_2 \in E_1 \cup E_2$ such that E_1 and E_2 are equal up to inclusion of V_1 and V_2. We denote this property as $(E_1, V_1) \Upsilon_{\mathcal{E}} (E_2, V_2)$. Applied to combinable hyperedges E_1 and E_2, operation $\sqcup$ removes E_1 and E_2 from $\mathcal{E}$ and adds their combination $E_† = \{V_1 \cup V_2\} \cup (E_1 \cap E_2)$ to $\mathcal{E}$. Formally, we have the following. Let VER denote the set of all vertices.

Definition 5. $\Upsilon \subseteq (\wp(\text{VER}) \times \text{VER}) \times (\wp(\text{VER}) \times \text{VER}) \times \wp^2(\text{VER})$ *denotes the relation on tuples consisting of two sets of* [hyperedge, vertex]-*pairs and a set of hyperedges defined as:*

$$(E_1, V_1) \Upsilon_{\mathcal{E}} (E_2, V_2) \text{ iff } \begin{bmatrix} E_1, E_2 \in \mathcal{E} \text{ and } E_1 \neq E_2 \text{ and } V_1 \cap V_2 = \emptyset \\ \text{and } E_1 = (E_2 \setminus \{V_2\}) \cup \{V_1\} \\ \text{and } E_2 = (E_1 \setminus \{V_1\}) \cup \{V_2\} \end{bmatrix}$$

Definition 6. $\sqcup : (\wp(\text{VER}) \times \text{VER}) \times (\wp(\text{VER}) \times \text{VER}) \times \wp^2(\text{VER}) \rightharpoonup \wp^2(\text{VER})$ *denotes the partial function from tuples consisting of two* [hyperedge, vertex]-*pairs and a set of hyperedges to sets of hyperedges defined as:*

$$(E_1, V_1) \sqcup_{\mathcal{E}} (E_2, V_2) = \mathcal{E} \setminus \{E_1, E_2\}) \cup \{\{V_1 \cup V_2\} \cup (E_1 \cap E_2)\}$$

$$\text{if } (E_1, V_1) \Upsilon_{\mathcal{E}} (E_2, V_2)$$

Lemma 2. *(Lemma 8 in [11, Appendix A])*

$$(E_1, V_1) \Upsilon_{\mathcal{E}} (E_2, V_2) \text{ implies } [\![(\mathcal{V}, \mathcal{E})]\!] \equiv_{\text{sc}} [\![(\mathcal{V}, (E_1, V_1) \sqcup_{\mathcal{E}} (E_2, V_2))]\!]$$

Transformation f_3 uses operation $\sqcup$ in the algorithm for combining hyperedges in Figure 9. Essentially, as long as vertices V_1 and V_2 exist such that the ports

$$
\textbf{while } \left[\begin{array}{l} (X, V_1) \; \Upsilon_{\mathcal{E}} \; (Y, V_2) \textbf{ and} \\ V_1 \cup V_2 \subseteq P \textbf{ and } P \in \bigstar(\mathcal{E}) \end{array} \right] \textbf{ for some } X, Y, V_1, V_2, P \; \textbf{do}
$$
$$
\textbf{while } [[(E_1, V_1) \; \Upsilon_{\mathcal{E}} \; (E_2, V_2)] \textbf{ for some } E_1, E_2] \; \textbf{do}
$$
$$
\mathcal{E} := (E_1, V_1) \sqcup_{\mathcal{E}} (E_2, V_2)
$$

Fig. 9. Algorithm for combining hyperedges

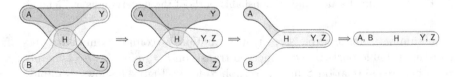

Fig. 10. Evolution of the hypergraphs in Figure 7b

in $V_1 \cup V_2$ are indistinguishable (as computed by $\bigstar$), the algorithm combines all combinable hyperedges that include V_1 and V_2. For instance, Figure 10 shows the evolution of the hypergraph in Figure 7b during the run of the algorithm in which it first selects Y and Z as V_1 and V_2 and afterward A and B. (In another run, the algorithm may change this order to obtain the same result.)

Let $\mathcal{E}_{\text{in}}$ and $\mathcal{E}_{\text{out}}$ denote the sets of hyperedges before and after running the algorithm. To consider the algorithm correct, $\mathcal{E}_{\text{out}}$ must satisfy two properties: it should represent an SC equivalent to the SC represented by $\mathcal{E}_{\text{in}}$ (i.e., the algorithm is semantics-preserving), and every vertex in every hyperedge in $\mathcal{E}_{\text{out}}$ should be a part in $\bigstar(\mathcal{E}_{\text{in}})$ (i.e., the algorithm effectively reveals indistinguishability). We use *Hoare logic* to prove these properties [14,15]. In particular, we can show that the triple {Pre} A {Post} holds, where A denotes the algorithm in Figure 9. Precondition Pre states that $\gamma_t = (\mathcal{V}, \mathcal{E}_{\text{in}})$ is a hypergraph (for the SC of transition t) such that every port in a connected vertex inhabits at most one connected vertex, and such that every connected vertex is nonempty. The definition of graph in Definition 1 implies these conditions. (However, because its precondition is more liberal, the algorithm is more generally applicable.) The postcondition Post states that correctness as previously formulated holds. Formally:

$$
[\![(\mathcal{V}, \mathcal{E}_{\text{out}})]\!] = [\![(\mathcal{V}, \mathcal{E}_{\text{in}})]\!] \textbf{ and } \left[\begin{array}{l} E \in \mathcal{E}_{\text{out}} \textbf{ implies} \\ E \subseteq \bigstar(\mathcal{E}_{\text{in}}) \end{array} \right] \textbf{ for all } E]
$$

Figure 11 shows the algorithm annotated with assertions for total correctness. By the axioms and rules of Hoare logic, this proof is valid if we can prove that for all six pairs of consecutive assertions, the upper assertion implies the lower one. For brevity, below, we discuss some salient aspects.

First, the algorithm terminates, because (i) every iteration of the outer loop consists of at least one iteration of the inner loop, for $X = E_1$ and $Y = E_2$, (ii) in every iteration of the inner loop, $\mathcal{E}$ decreases by one, and (iii) $\mathcal{E}$ is finite. Second, the algorithm is semantics-preserving by Lemma 2. The main challenge is proving that the algorithm is also effective. A notable step in this proof is establishing the property labeled Interm from Inv_2 (the invariant of the inner

$$
\begin{aligned}
&\{\text{Pre}\} \\
&\{\text{Inv}_1\} \\
&\textbf{while } \Big[\begin{matrix} (X,\,V_1)\,\Upsilon_{\mathcal{E}}\,(Y,\,V_2) \textbf{ and} \\ V_1 \cup V_2 \subseteq P \textbf{ and } P \in \bigstar(\mathcal{E}) \end{matrix} \Big] \textbf{ for some } X,\,Y,\,V_1,\,V_2,\,P] \textbf{ do} \\
&\quad \{\text{Inv}_1 \textbf{ and } \text{Cond}_1 \textbf{ and } |\mathcal{E}| = z_1\} \\
&\quad \{\text{Inv}_2\} \\
&\quad \textbf{while } [[(E_1,\,V_1)\,\Upsilon_{\mathcal{E}}\,(E_2,\,V_2)] \textbf{ for some } E_1,\,E_2] \textbf{ do} \\
&\qquad \{\text{Inv}_2 \textbf{ and } \text{Cond}_2 \textbf{ and } |\mathcal{E}| = z_2\} \\
&\qquad \{\text{Inv}_2[\mathcal{E} := (E_1,\,V_1)\,\sqcup_{\mathcal{E}}\,(E_2,\,V_2)] \textbf{ and } (|\mathcal{E}| < z_2)[\mathcal{E} := (E_1,\,V_1)\,\sqcup_{\mathcal{E}}\,(E_2,\,V_2)]\} \\
&\qquad \mathcal{E} := (E_1,\,V_1)\,\sqcup_{\mathcal{E}}\,(E_2,\,V_2) \\
&\qquad \{\text{Inv}_2 \textbf{ and } |\mathcal{E}| < z_2\} \\
&\quad \{\text{Inv}_2 \textbf{ and } [\text{not } \text{Cond}_2]\} \\
&\quad \{\text{Inv}_2 \textbf{ and } \text{Interm} \textbf{ and } |\mathcal{E}| < z_1\} \\
&\quad \{\text{Inv}_1 \textbf{ and } |\mathcal{E}| < z_1\} \\
&\{\text{Inv}_1 \textbf{ and } [\text{not } \text{Cond}_1]\} \\
&\{\text{Post}\}
\end{aligned}
$$

Fig. 11. Algorithm for combining hyperedges with assertions for total correctness

loop) and $[\textbf{not } \text{Cond}_2]$ (the negation of the inner loop's condition). Informally, Interm states that if $\mathcal{F}$ denotes the hyperedge relation *before* running the inner loop, we have $\mathcal{E} = \mathcal{F} \setminus (\mathcal{F}_{1,2} \cup \mathcal{F}_\dagger)$ *after* running the inner loop. Here, $\mathcal{F}_{1,2}$ contains all hyperedges from $\mathcal{F}$ that include V_1 or V_2, while $\mathcal{F}_\dagger$ denotes all new hyperedges added by $\sqcup$ during the loop. This property subsequently enables us to prove Inv_1 (the invariant of the outer loop), which among other properties states $\bigstar(\mathcal{E}_{\text{in}}) = \bigstar(\mathcal{E})$. Consequently, to prove the algorithm's effectiveness, it suffices to show that $E \in \mathcal{E}_{\text{out}}$ implies $E \subseteq \bigstar(\mathcal{E}_{\text{out}})$ (for all E).

Theorem 2. *(Theorem 4 in [11, Appendix A])* $\{\text{Pre}\}\ A\ \{\text{Post}\}$

In summary, in the second step, for every (merged) transition $t = (q,\,\psi,\,\phi,\,q')$ in $f_1(\alpha)$, transformation f_3 manipulates hypergraph γ_t to γ'_t by running the algorithm in Figure 9, given the maximal sets of indistinguishable ports computed in f_3's first step with $\bigstar$. Afterward, f_3 replaces ψ in t with $[\![\gamma'_t]\!]$, which by the correctness of the algorithm is equivalent to $[\![\gamma_t]\!]$ and has made indistinguishable ports (hence queues) apparent. We denote the resulting transition relation by $(f_3 \circ f_1)(\longrightarrow)$ and the resulting CA by $(f_3 \circ f_1)(\alpha)$. Because $\psi \equiv_{\text{sc}} [\![\gamma_t]\!] \equiv_{\text{sc}} [\![\gamma'_t]\!]$ for all transitions t in $f_1(\alpha)$, the following proposition follows from Lemma 16 in [11, Appendix A]. Together, Propositions 1 and 2 imply that transformation f is semantics-preserving.

Proposition 2. $(f_3 \circ f_1)(\alpha) \sim f_1(\alpha)$

We end with some examples in Figure 12. Transformation f_3 has not had any effect on the LossySync CA, so its implementation does not benefit from queues (no indistinguishable ports), as expected. The Merger$_3$ and Hourglass CA, in contrast, have changed significantly. In the SC of Merger$_3$, we can now clearly recognize one queue for ports A, B, and C and one queue for port Z (cf. transformation h in Section 3); similarly, in the SC of Hourglass, we can now clearly recognize one queue for ports A and B and one queue for ports Y and Z.

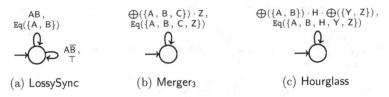

(a) LossySync   (b) Merger₃   (c) Hourglass

Fig. 12. Application of transformation f_3 to the CA in Figure 6

Applied to Merger₃, transformation f optimizes a multiple-producer-single-consumer protocol. More abstractly, in this case, f optimizes a protocol among two groups of processes, X_1 (producers) and X_2 (consumer), such that $|X_1| = 3$ and $|X_2| = 1$ and all processes in X_1 are indistinguishable to all processes in X_2 and vice versa. Generally, f can optimize protocols among n groups of processes $X_1, \ldots, X_n$ such that for all $1 \leq i, j \leq n$, all processes in X_i are indistinguishable to all processes in X_j and vice versa. For instance, applied to Hourglass, f optimizes a protocol among three groups of processes such that $|X_1| = |X_3| = 2$ and $|X_2| = 1$.

After having applied transformation f, the automatic generation of actual implementations is straightforward (i.e., transformation g_2 in Figure 4c). The resulting code is, in fact, exactly the same as the code that results from manually applying transformation h as in Section 3 (and consequently, it has the same performance): instead of checking an **event** structure for every port as pre-optimized code does, optimized code checks one **eventQueue** structure for every maximal set of indistinguishable ports, which transformation f has made explicit as $\oplus$-formulas in SCs (and are thus easy to detect in the f-transformed CA). As such, optimized code checks the SC of all transitions in the pre-transformation CA that differ only in indistinguishable ports (before applying f) at the same time. For k such transitions, consequently, an unscalable exhaustive $\mathcal{O}(k)$ search is optimized to perfectly scalable $\mathcal{O}(1)$ queue operations. Thus, with respect to Figure 4c, the fully mechanical transformation $g_2 \circ f = g_2 \circ f_3 \circ f_2 \circ f_1$ yields the same code and scalability as the partially manual transformation $h \circ g_1$.

7 Concluding Remarks

In this paper, we analyzed scalability issues of the code generated by our Reo-to-C compiler, we explained a manual solution, and we studied the various steps of a mechanical procedure for transforming a CA α to an equivalent CA β, which makes port indistinguishability (hence queues) maximally apparent, using the $\oplus$-operator. Our tool can use this mechanical procedure to generate code for α via β with good scalability. In particular, whereas unoptimized code generated for α requires $\mathcal{O}(k)$ time to compute eligibility of k transitions—essentially an exhaustive search—the optimized code generated for β requires only $\mathcal{O}(1)$ time: all maximal sets of indistinguishable ports (explicit in β as a $\oplus$-formulas in SCs) in the implementation share the same queue, which optimizes the unscalable $\mathcal{O}(k)$ search to perfectly scalable $\mathcal{O}(1)$ queue operations.

Although inspired by our work on a Reo compiler and formulated generally in terms of CA, we make contributions beyond Reo and CA. The synchronization pattern that we identified and optimized is common and occurs in many classes of protocols and their implementation, regardless of the particular language. Therefore, compilers for other high-level languages may use the same approach as explained in this paper to similarly optimize code generated for programs in those languages. In fact, this paper led to adding new features to Proto-Runtime to enable our optimization technique, thereby facilitating efficient implementation of our f-transformed CA. Importantly, these new features in Proto-Runtime can now benefit other languages implemented on top of Proto-Runtime as well.

Automatically performing our optimization directly on low-level code such as C (instead of on CA) is extremely complex, if not impossible. This shows that using higher-level languages (that preserve relevant context information about protocols) for multicore programming can indeed be advantageous for performance, a significant general observation in language and compiler design for multicore platforms. Indeed, the work presented in this paper serves as evidence that it is possible not only to specify interaction protocols at a higher level of abstraction (than locks, mutex, semaphores, message exchanges, etc.) but also automatically compile and optimize such high-level specifications down to executable code. Such higher-level specifications convey more of the intention behind the protocol, which gives more room for a compiler/optimizer to find and apply efficient implementation alternatives. Lower-level, more imperative, specifications of interaction protocols either lose or obscure the intentions behind protocols and seriously constrict the ability of compilers/optimizers to find efficient implementation alternatives. See [11] for related work on high-level approaches to multicore programming.

This paper makes primarily conceptual and theoretical contributions, and we used performance figures only to motivate and explain the development of our optimization technique. An in-depth study of the use of this technique in practice, including more benchmarks and experiments with different kinds of protocols and contexts, is our next objective, now that we know that the technique is correct. As part of this future work, we will also extend our current, limited proof-of-concept implementation (used in obtaining the data for Figure 5) to a full implementation. We end with the following remarks.

Indistinguishability of data. Transformation f effectively merges transitions with labels of the form $(\psi, \text{Eq}(P))$. The reason is that the ports in $\text{Eq}(P)$ are indistinguishable from a data perspective. (Whether those ports are also indistinguishable in ψ is exactly what transformation f_3 investigates.) Detecting port indistinguishability in *arbitrary* DCs so as to improve the applicability of f seems an interesting and important future challenge.

Guarded automata. Our SCs, as arbitrary propositional formulas, seem similar to guards on transitions in the guarded automata used by Bonsangue et al. for modeling connector behavior [16]. The intuitive meaning of such guards, however, significantly differs: guards specify a constraint on the environment, while SCs specify a constraint on an execution step. (In fact, transition labels of guarded automata carry both a guard and an SC.)

Model-based testing. We skipped an explanation of the actual code generation process (i.e., transformation g_2 in Figure 4), dismissing it as "straightforward" and "obviously correct". An interesting line of work to better substantiate the latter statement is to have our tool generate not only executable code but also test cases derived from the input CA. Kokash et al. have already worked on such model-based testing for CA in a different context [17].

References

1. Arbab, F.: Reo: a channel-based coordination model for component composition. MSCS 14(3), 329–366 (2004)
2. Arbab, F.: Puff, The Magic Protocol. In: Agha, G., Danvy, O., Meseguer, J. (eds.) Talcott Festschrift. LNCS, vol. 7000, pp. 169–206. Springer, Heidelberg (2011)
3. Jongmans, S.S., Arbab, F.: Modularizing and Specifying Protocols among Threads. In: Proceedings of PLACES 2012. EPTCS. CoRR, vol. 109, pp. 34–45 (2013)
4. Jongmans, S.S., Arbab, F.: Overview of Thirty Semantic Formalisms for Reo. SACS 22(1), 201–251 (2012)
5. Kokash, N., Krause, C., de Vink, E.: Reo+mCRL2: A framework for model-checking dataflow in service compositions. FAC 24(2), 187–216 (2012)
6. Jongmans, S.S., Halle, S., Arbab, F.: Reo: A Dataflow Inspired Language for Multicore. In: Proceedings of DFM 2013 (2013)
7. Baier, C., Sirjani, M., Arbab, F., Rutten, J.: Modeling component connectors in Reo by constraint automata. SCP 61(2), 75–113 (2006)
8. Halle, S.: A Study of Frameworks for Collectively Meeting the Productivity, Portability, and Adoptability Goals for Parallel Software. PhD thesis, University of California, Santa Cruz (2011)
9. Halle, S., Cohen, A.: A Mutable Hardware Abstraction to Replace Threads. In: Rajopadhye, S., Mills Strout, M. (eds.) LCPC 2011. LNCS, vol. 7146, pp. 185–202. Springer, Heidelberg (2013)
10. Butenhof, D.: Programming with POSIX Threads. Addison-Wesley (1997)
11. Jongmans, S.S., Halle, S., Arbab, F.: Automata-based Optimization of Interaction Protocols for Scalable Multicore Platforms (Technical Report). Technical Report FM-1402, CWI (2014)
12. Sirjani, M., Jaghoori, M.M., Baier, C., Arbab, F.: Compositional Semantics of an Actor-Based Language Using Constraint Automata. In: Ciancarini, P., Wiklicky, H. (eds.) COORDINATION 2006. LNCS, vol. 4038, pp. 281–297. Springer, Heidelberg (2006)
13. Bretto, A.: Hypergraph Theory: An Introduction. Springer (2013)
14. Hoare, T.: An Axiomatic Basis for Computer Programming. CACM 12(10), 576–580 (1969)
15. Apt, K., de Boer, F., Olderog, E.R.: Verification of Sequential and Concurrent Programs. Springer (2009)
16. Bonsangue, M., Clarke, D., Silva, A.: A model of context-dependent component connectors. SCP 77(6), 685–706 (2009)
17. Kokash, N., Arbab, F., Changizi, B., Makhnist, L.: Input-output Conformance Testing for Channel-based Service Connectors. In: Proceedings of PACO 2011. EPTCS. CoRR, vol. 60, pp. 19–35 (2011)

LINC: A Compact Yet Powerful Coordination Environment

Maxime Louvel and François Pacull

Univ. Grenoble Alpes, F-38000 Grenoble, France
CEA, LETI, MINATEC Campus, F-38054 Grenoble, France
17 rue des Martyrs 38000 Grenoble, France
{maxime.louvel,francois.pacull}@cea.fr

Abstract. This paper presents LINC, a coordination programming environment. It is an evolution of earlier middlewares (the Coordination Language Facility (CLF) and Stitch). The aim is to provide a more flexible and expressive language correcting several of their limitations and an improved run-time environment. LINC provides a compact yet powerful coordination language and an optimised run-time which executes rules. This paper describes the intrinsic properties brought by the LINC environment and how it helps the coordination aspects in a distributed system. This paper also emphasises on the reflexivity of LINC and its usage at system level. Finally, it illustrates through several case studies, how LINC can manage a wide range of application domains.

Keywords: Coordination, language, tuplespace, distributed systems.

1 Introduction

Today's systems are not only distributed, they are composed of other systems more or less opaque. They have to interact with real world and thus have to consider on the one hand very small embedded systems and on the other end unbounded resources sprayed in the "cloud". Some pieces of work consider that the traditional approaches based on objects and services cannot hold such complexity [18]. In this context, coordination models and languages [25] are essential to coordinate basic elements as well as systems of systems. The last decades have seen a lot of work in the coordination area [24], starting with Linda [13]. Linda firstly introduced the notion of tuple-space as the ground for coordination. In Linda, components exchange and synchronise through tuples addition and removal in a shared tuple-space. This approach allows the decoupling of processes both in space and time. Indeed to exchange data between two components, the first one simply puts a tuple in the shared tuple-space. It does not have to worry if another component is currently waiting for this information or how this information should be exchanged. The data is exchanged when another component reads the tuple. The read may come before, at the same time or after the put.

Based on Linda, a number of evolutions have been proposed. Starting in the 2000s, researchers have focused on using tuple-spaces for mobile computing

E. Kühn and R. Pugliese (Eds.): COORDINATION 2014, LNCS 8459, pp. 83–98, 2014.

[8, 12, 22, 33]. To support mobile environment, one of the main improvement is the use of several tuple-spaces instead of a single one shared by all the processes. Then, from mobile computing, researchers have focused on making applications context aware by the use of tuple-spaces [5, 7, 15]. To go a step further with the mobility, toward autonomous systems, researchers considered more intelligent tuples [21, 30]. They have shown the interest of relying on tuple-spaces in nowadays systems. However, there is still a gap between what people express and how the developer will implement it. We believe it is essential to provide means for developers to focus on the coordination of the systems. It is also tremendously important to provide them with a simple programming environment powerful enough to handle the system complexity. The response to the management of complex system should not be a complex programming environment.

This paper presents the full set of LINC features with a special focus on how it eases the coordination tasks. It complements partial description in earlier application domain oriented papers [10, 20]. LINC is a compact yet powerful coordination environment which relies on the three basic primitives of Linda to read, add and remove tuples in a tuple-space. It uses distributed tuple-spaces called bags. A bag is responsible for storing the tuples and may provide a special implementation of the three primitives. This is very convenient when communicating with the physical world (e.g. sensors or actuators) or when integrating legacy systems. LINC uses production rules to interact on the tuple-space rather than using imperative code to glue the primitives. Actions on the bags are embedded into distributed transactions which simplifies a lot the job of the developer that does not have to worry about writing code to roll back half of the actions done so far when something goes wrong. Transactions also enforce the consistency between the actual system and the software view. This, once again aims at helping developers to focus only on the coordination.

The paper is structured as follows. Section 2 presents the coordination language of LINC. Then, Section 3 describes its main features. Section 4 sketches several concrete case studies where LINC has been used. Section 5 positions our approach with respect to related works. Finally, Section 6 concludes the paper.

2   LINC Coordination Language

LINC is the natural evolution of the Coordination Language Facility (CLF) [2] and Stitch [1] middlewares initially developed for deploying distributed applications. The three of them share the resource oriented approach manipulated through a high level rule-based language. However, the architecture of LINC has been completely revisited to adapt to the new landscape defined by the combination of the Internet-of-things, the cloud and the Cyber-Physical Systems. The main differences are:

- in LINC, the coordination engine has been improved both in term of CPU usage and memory footprint. It is embedded in every object while CLF/Stitch relied on more complex dedicated objects. This allows to better distribute the coordination by delegating some parts to more modest CPU;

- the rule language has been extended to improve its expressiveness;
- the environment comes with tools: monitoring, rule analysis (memory, time and dependencies) and a replay mechanism allowing post-mortem re-execution preserving causal order to debug the initial run. Tools are not the focus of this paper, details may be found in the LINC wiki (http://linc.middlewares.info).

2.1 LINC Roots

We briefly recall here the basics of LINC to make the paper self contained. LINC, like CLF or Stitch, is rooted in Linda-like tuple-spaces (*Associative Memory*), *Production Rules* and *Distributed Transactions*.

Associative Memory: The global tuple-space is composed of several distributed tuple-spaces called bags. Tuples in bags are accessed with the three operations: rd(), get() and put(). The rd() verifies the presence of resources matching some given criteria: resources corresponding to the requested pattern (partially instantiated tuple) passed as parameter. The get() (in in Linda) removes a tuple while the put() (out in Linda) inserts a new tuple in a bag.

Production Rules: In LINC, the rd(), get() and put() primitives are invoked through production rules [9]. This prevents to write a huge amount of imperative code such as Java, C or Python by the use of a coordination language to define how the resources are manipulated in the system. A production rule is decomposed in a *precondition* and a *performance* part. The precondition part uses rd() operations combined with an inference engine in order to evaluate distributed conditions in the system. Then, the performance part uses:

- rd() to verify that conditions are still valid at performance time;
- get() to consume resources (e.g. manage critical resources, consume events);
- put() to generate resources (e.g update the system, command actuator).

A rule typically uses several bags, physically distributed or not, to access the necessary information and update the system accordingly. The particularity of LINC is that the performance part is embedded in Distributed Transactions.

Distributed Transactions: They are used in the performance part to ensure the all-or-nothing [6] property. They group in the same set of operations the verification of some conditions, the consumption of critical resources and the update of the global state of the system. Thus, the performance part is a list of transactions that are executed in sequential order.

The combination of these three paradigms enables to build transactional reactions to complex events. Complex events in a building automation context could be the combination of several events such as *people in the room* and *temperature lower than sixteen degrees* and *HVAC system is OFF*. Transactional reactions consist in *put the heating ON*, and *update the state of the system*.

2.2 Bags Abstraction

The main interest of splitting the global tuple-space into several bags is that each bag may define its own semantic associated to the rd, get and put and the tuples themselves. As a result, bags can encapsulate software or hardware components.

a database: each table of the database can be associated to a bag; rd() and put() corresponds to the reads and writes on the database.

a service: This concerns remote services as well as local services directly embedded in the bag. The partially instantiated tuple composed of the input parameters is passed to the rd(). The concerned service is invoked from the bag, using the legacy protocol imposed by the remote service (e.g. SOAP for a Webservice based approach or a native Remote Procedure Call). The output parameters obtained as the result of the service is added to the input parameters defining the fully instantiated tuple returned by the rd().

an event system: Tuples contain the topic, the ID, the timestamp and a payload; the rd() and put() operations correspond to subscribe and publish of the event system.

a sensor: Data are collected from the gateway and inserted into different bags storing the various relevant information. For instance, for a very simple approach, we can consider the three bags associating the id of the sensor to the sensed value, the type of sensor and its location. Successive values can be obtained through the rd(), changing the location of the sensor is as simple as modifying the resource by consuming it with a get() and inserting the updated information with a put(). The sampling frequency, the type of bag (e.g. set, multiset, FIFO, ...) or the precision can be adapted at this stage. The behaviour of the rd() may also be adapted to replace a simple tuple matching by a more complex matching: e.g. interval, fuzzy logic or ontologies.

an actuator: When interacting with the real world, the put operation is typically used to send actuation commands (e.g to set the speed of a motor, the direction of the wheels or to power on or off a subsystem). We can act on the physical actuator through a put() operation with a resource with the id, the command to be applied and the possible parameters p1, p2 into the associated bag. This is enough to trigger action to the actual actuator.

Finally, it is possible to associate bags. For instance, one bag can contain the number of resources contained in the bag it is associated to. More complex associations can be considered such as arithmetic functions (e.g. sum, average, max or min or even a Bayesian filter). The main advantage is to have a direct access to refined information computed from a set of resources. It has been used for instance in the application described in 4.2 to filter outliers values coming from a matrix of Rfid readers.

2.3   Coordination Language

Bags are grouped into *objects* for identification purposes, thus objects are a logical decomposition of an application. For instance an object may manage all the sensors communicating with the same protocol or located in the same space. An object may execute rules to coordinate the system by acting on its own bags and the other objects' ones. When an object executes rules, it plays the role of coordinator. Rules can be executed by any object. This means that the programmer is free to distribute them among the different objects of an application.

To illustrate how LINC rules are working Listing 1.1 gives a very simple rule involving two sensors (presence and temperature) and an actuator (heating controller) using three different technologies (e.g. different protocols). This rule adjusts the heating of a room when someone is inside and the temperature is lower than 16 °C. The rule is composed of the *precondition* (when to trigger the rule) and the *performance* (what to do) separated by the symbol : :.

```
{*,!}["Techno1", "sensors"].rd("pres_1", "True") &        1
{*,!}["Techno2", "sensors"].rd("temperature_a", temp) &
ASSERT: temp < 16 &                                       3
{1,!}["Techno1", "location"].rd("pres_1", location) &
{*,!}["Techno3", "actuators_list"].rd(id_act, "heating", location)   5
::
{                                                         7
  ["Techno1", "sensors"].rd("pres_1", "True");
  ["Techno2", "sensors"].rd("temperature_a", temp);      9
  ["Techno3", "actuators"].put(id_act, "heating","2");
}                                                         11
{ ... #other group of actions }.
```

Listing 1.1. LINC rule example

Precondition. The precondition is composed of *tokens* processed by an inference engine with a right propagation. Listing 1.1 contains 8 tokens (1 per line). The first token invokes a `rd()` operation into the bag *"sensors"* of the object *"Techno1"*. This object encapsulates the gateway of the first technology. The token looks for the resource *("pres_1", "True")* where the first field is the sensor id (generally imposed by the technology) and the second the value *"True"* meaning that a presence is detected. In a similar way, the second token asks for the temperature currently sensed by the sensor whose id is *"temperature_a"*. When the `rd` is done, all the matching tuples are returned one by one. For every returned tuple, a new branch is created with the value of the instantiated variables `temp`. The instantiated variables are right propagated. For instance in the third token this variable is compared to the threshold (16 degrees) thanks to the `ASSERT:` extension[1]. If the condition is false, the rule will not progress. If it is true, the next token asks the bag `location`, of the object `"Techno1"` (responsible for the presence sensor), for the location of sensor `"pres_1"`. With this information, the last token can ask the *id* of the co-located heating system.

The tokens in the precondition phase are preceded with modifiers embraced in curly brackets. The first field defines the number of maximum expected replies awaited by the `rd()` operation. Normally a `rd()` is blocked waiting for new matching resources that could become available. In this example, we use * for the first 2 tokens since we want to have all the replies. On the contrary, for the 4th we used 1 since a sensor has a single location and it is useless to wait for another resource. The second field is used to define the amount of time a pending `rd()` is waiting for a reply. Both are used to reduce the size of the inference tree as detailed in Section 3.2.

---

[1] The extensions `ASSERT:`, `COMPUTE:` and `SLEEP:` allows to respectively verify a condition, execute simple computation or wait for a given time.

Performance. The performance part may contain several transactions enclosed in curly brackets. The first transaction embeds the verification of the conditions presence and temperature and the operation on the heating system. Indeed, if the presence detector becomes false, this means the person is out of the room and nothing is required from the system. If the temperature has changed, it is not required to react. Indeed another inference will start with the new temperature, and a more accurate heating command will be computed. Finally, the last action of the transaction does the required operation on the heating system. Contrary to the Event-Condition-Action [32] model, events and conditions are managed in the same way. Moreover, they may be enclosed with actions in a transaction.

The transactions are executed sequentially. If several transactions perform a get() on a same unique resource, they become exclusive. It is explained in context with the guards controlled alternatives (Section 3.3) and the graceful degradation (Section 3.4) mechanisms. The distributed transactions are enforced through a classical 2 Phase-Commit [6] to provide atomicity property (all-or-nothing). However, no hypothesis is made on how the bags implement these 2 phases. Thus, it is possible on the one hand to take advantage of the context and to implement a bag fully compliant with the 2PC on small microcontroller if required. On the other hand, it allows for a given bag to relax the 2PC.

2.4   Improvement with Respect to CLF/Stitch

The explicit usage of the operations rd(), get() and put() in LINC allows to verify in the performance phase only the useful resources while in CLF/Stitch all the resources used in the precondition where systematically verified in the performance phase. The major drawback is that some rd() were verified even if it was not required. Indeed, among the rd() operations done in the precondition a significant part are just informative and not subject to change. Verifying them again in the performance was a waste of time and resources.

Another difference concerns the rd() and get() done in the performance. The presence of the resources returned in the precondition is verified in CLF / Stitch via a unique resource identifier. In LINC, it is not based on this identifier but on the value. This decreases the size of the inference tree and the amount of useless work when we have to deal with multiple resources with the same value (e.g. a sensor returning the same value).

Moreover, CLF considers in the performance a transaction for the rd() and the get() operations and the guaranty that the put() operations are eventually done by re-trying them until completion. This was motivated by the fact a put() was not supposed to fail. Indeed, for a tuple space, it is reasonable to consider that inserting a resource is always possible. However, in LINC we want also to target physical world, such as actuators that may fail when a put() is tried.

Thus, LINC enforces a transaction for (rd(), get() and put()) operations allowing a richer transactional model in the performance part.

In addition to a stronger model, we do not restrict the performance to a single transaction but we can have a sequence of transactions. This brings the possibility of alternative treatments sharing the same precondition part. This not only decreases the work to be done by the coordination engine but also offers a better view to the programmer by replacing a set of CLF/Stitch rules by a single LINC rule. Powerful mechanisms using this capability, such as guards controlled alternatives and graceful degradation are described in Section 3.

Finally, the usage of modifiers in the precondition offers the programmer to specify information that helps the inference engine to better optimise the size of its data structures. This reduces both memory footprint and CPU usage.

All these improvements brought the required scale down in the rule management that allows LINC to target smaller computing units such as Raspberry PI, Pandaboard or even ARM9 custom board.

3   LINC Features

This section presents several features offered by the LINC coordination language.

3.1   Control the Frequency of a Rule

In some circumstances it can be useful to control the pace of a rule. For instance, in Listing 1.1 the rule is triggered each time the temperature changes and a presence is detected. This is obviously too much for controlling the heating system. We can modify the rule by adding a new token at the first place of the precondition and at the first place of the performance part (cf. Listing 1.2).

We use a bag of type **set** called **tick** in which a new instance of the same resource is regularly inserted. The set property guaranties that a resource with the same value is present only once at a given time even if inserted several times (e.g. every 10 minutes). The precondition waits for the presence of this resource to start the evaluation of subsequent **rd** operations. If, in addition a token doing a **get** is added in the performance, it enforces that only one performance of the rule is performed per tick. Indeed, even if several instances of the rule reach the performance point, only one transaction will succeed. For the others, the **get** action (e.g. in line 5) will fail because the resource is not in the bag anymore.

```
{∗,!}["Control", "tick"].rd(tick) &
...  # tokens of Listing 1.1                                      2
::
{                                                                4
  ["Control", "tick"].get(tick);
  ...  # tokens of Listing 1.1                                    6
}
```

Listing 1.2. LINC rule with tick

3.2   Reduction of the Inference Tree

When a rule is executed, an inference tree is built. Its size, and the number of branches waiting for new resources to appear may become a problem, especially on embedded devices. Hence, it is important to limit the size of this inference tree to limit the memory used and to decrease the CPU load. For this, LINC relies on directives exploiting the knowledge of the developer and on an automatic process (garbage collector pruning useless branches).

Information from the Developer: Via the modifiers introduced in Section 2, the developer can:

Limit the number of matching tuples to consider is typically used when the developer knows that only a given number of resources is really useful. For instance in the rule of Listing 1.1, the 4th token asks for the presence sensor location. As a sensor has a single location, we know that we can close the flow of reply to the rd() operation right after the first reply. This can be done by replacing the * in {*,!} with 1, i.e. the number of expected replies.

Limit the time to wait for matching tuples is used to model the expiration of some tuples. For instance, in the modified rule of Listing 1.2 a tick is generated every 10 minutes. A new branch is then started at each generation of a new tick resource. Thus, if no presence is detected during 2 hours, 12 branches will be waiting for the presence detection. When a presence is detected, the 12 branches will be activated, creating useless work. If we replace the ! in {*,!} with 600, the number of seconds to wait, the rd("pres_1","True") operation will be closed after 10 minutes and thus only one branch is active at a time.

Garbage Collector. When waiting on rd for matching tuples, it might become a point where branches of the inference tree built so far do not make sense any more. For instance here, when the presence sensor becomes "False", the resource *("pres_1","True")* disappears from the bag (i.e. it is replaced by *("pres_1","False")*). Then, it is not necessary to continue to maintain the branches depending on *("pres_1","True")*. Indeed when the performance will be executed it will fail because this resource is not available.

A garbage collector periodically browses the inference tree asking the bags if the tuples are still present. By tuple we do not mean the exact same tuple but one with the same value. If the tuple is not there, the branch of inference tree starting from this node can safely be garbaged. Indeed, continuing the precondition will only lead to failures in the performance phase. If a branch is garbaged and the same value is added again in the bag, this will trigger a new inference.

3.3   Guards Controlled Alternatives

```
...                                                                          1
: :
{                                                                            3
    ["Techno1", "sensors"].rd("pres_1", "True") ; #First guard
    ["Techno2", "sensors"].rd("temperature_a", temp);                        5
    ["Techno3", "actuators"].put(id_act, "heating","2");
}.                                                                           7
{
    ["Techno1", "sensors"].rd("pres_1", "False") ; # Second guard            9
    ["Techno2", "sensors"].rd("temperature_a", temp);
    ["Techno3", "actuators"].put(id_act, "heating","1");                     11
}.
```

Listing 1.3. Extension of rule in Listing 1.1 with guards

In the rule of Listing 1.3 we show how to implement a simple guards mechanism in the performance. Here we define how to manage the heating depending on the occupant's presence (i.e. putting the set point to *"1"* or *"2"*). Here, we do not test the presence in the precondition since we want to act in both case. We use 2 transactions, one for each case and we place in each of them a `rd()` respectively on *("pres_1","True")* and *("pres_1","False")*. Depending on the actual value of the resource, one of them commits and the other aborts.

3.4 Graceful Degradation

Graceful Degradation is achieved by adding in the transactions a `get()` on a unique resource (created by the first transaction at line 3 in Listing 1.4). As transactions are tried in sequence, if transaction A succeeds, i.e. the heating command is successfully done, transaction B fails at line 9. If the heating system is not reachable, transaction A fails, transaction B succeeds (the temperature and presence have not changed). The `unique` is consumed and a SMS is sent to alert the maintenance. If the temperature has changed (or nobody is in the room anymore) at performance time, transactions A and B fail. However, as a new temperature resource is now available it is taken into account by another instance of the rule. Thus, a single rule can define what to do in the normal case and what to do in case of partial failures.

```
...
::
{["Control", "unique"].put(unique);}  #create unique              2
{ #transaction A                                                  4
  ["Control", "unique"].get(unique);
  ...                                                             6
}
{ #transaction B                                                  8
  ["Control", "unique"].get(unique);
  ["Techno1", "sensors"].rd("pres_1", "True");                   10
  ["Techno2", "sensors"].rd("temperature_a", temp);
  ["Alert", "SMS"].put("512123123", "Heating system is broken"); 12
}
{["Control", "unique"].get(unique);}. #garbage unique            14
```

Listing 1.4. Extension of rule in Listing 1.1 with graceful Degradation

3.5 Mutual Exclusion

Mutual exclusion is not easy to solve with classic programming schemes such as semaphores or monitors. In LINC, the transactions greatly simplify the problem. To illustrate this, we propose our implementation of the classical philosophers dinner. The problem is solved by the two rules of Listing 1.5.

The bag `philosopher` contains resources associating the philosopher name and the id of his left and right forks. The bag `fork` manages the critical resources: the forks. When the first rule succeeds, it means a philosopher has gotten its two forks and moved from thinking to eating. If another rule instance wants to get a fork already attributed, it will fail because the resource is not in the bag anymore. The second rule makes the philosophers go from eating to thinking and put back the fork resources in the bag. This will wake up instances of the first rule waiting for available forks.

```
# thinking -> eating
{*,!}["Dinner","philosopher"].rd(name, fork_l, fork_r) &          2
{*,!}["Dinner","fork"].rd(fork_l)&
{*,!}["Dinner","fork"].rd(fork_r)&                                 4
{*,!}["Dinner","state"].rd(name, "thinking") &
::                                                                 6
{
  ["Dinner","fork"].get(fork_l);                                  8
  ["Dinner","fork"].get(fork_r);
  ["Dinner","state"].get(name, "thinking");                       10
  ["Dinner","state"].put(name, "eating");
}.                                                                 12
# eating -> thinking
{*,!}["Dinner","state"].rd(name, "eating")&                       14
{*,!}["Dinner","philosopher"].rd(name, fork_l, fork_r) &
SLEEP: 10                                                          16
::
{                                                                 18
  ["Dinner","state"].get(name, "eating");
  ["Dinner","state"].put(name, "thinking");                       20
  ["Dinner","fork"].put(fork_l);
  ["Dinner","fork"].put(fork_r);                                  22
}.
```

Listing 1.5. Philosophers dinner problem in LINC

3.6   Rules Activation / Deactivation

One major issue when dealing with rules is how to control them and to ensure some guaranties when we decide to enable or disable some of them. To control the rules execution, we rely on the reflexivity of LINC. Indeed, in LINC everything is a resource in a bag. Naturally, rules are also controlled by resources in a dedicated bag of coordinator objects. This bag is called RulesId and contains tuples shaped as *"(rule_id, status)"*. When the rule is compiled, a rd is added at the beginning of the precondition and in each transaction as shown in Listing 1.6. The variable ego, used for object name, refers to the object executing the rule.

```
[ego, "RulesId"].rd("RU0001", "ENABLED");                         1
```

Listing 1.6. Control of rules execution

Adding these rd allows to stop a rule by simply changing the resource *("RU0001", "ENABLED")* to *("RU0001", "DISABLED")*. Indeed the rd on the rule status will make the transactions fail. To reactivate the rule, the resource status is put back to *"ENABLED"*. Note that the rd on the rule status is the first rd of the precondition. This has three main interests:

– when disabled, no new inference is started;
– when disabled, the inference tree is completely garbaged because the resource *(rule_id, "ENABLED")* is no longer in the bag;
– if *(rule_id, "ENABLED")* is put back, a new inference tree is built.

Note that this generic principle used at system level can be easily used at application level to activate and deactivate groups of rules according to application context. For instance, we can use the same principle with a resource controlling a set of rules. This can be used, for instance, to put in place a very sophisticated scenario manager in the building automation domain [10].

3.7   Dynamic Rules Generation

For some applications, it can be required to dynamically generate rules corresponding to contextual information. To do so, a resource is added in a dedicated bag, called **AddRules**. This bag receives resources of the form *(package,source)* where **package** is the logical name of a group of rules and *source* the actual code of the rules (as shown in Listing 1.1 for instance).

When a resource is added in this bag, the rule is dynamically compiled. This compilation includes syntax verifications, and various checks to prevent potential issues at execution time. For instance the coordinator object checks that the bags used by the rule are accessible, and that each variable will be instantiated at some point by a **rd()** operation in the precondition phase. If the rule contains no detectable error, the coordinator starts to execute it right away.

3.8   Registry-Based Programming

When interfacing with the hardware (very small embedded systems such as complex actuators) it is required to prepare the data in some dedicated registries and then to trigger the global action by acting on the control register. To reproduce this behaviour in a rule is straightforward because actions inside a transaction are executed sequentially. As shown in Listing 1.7, where two bags are used, one to map the data registers and one to map the control one. It is just mandatory to place the action of the control register at the last position in the transaction.

```
...                                                                    1
::
{                                                                      3
  ["object", "data"].put("r1", value1);
  ["object", "data"].put("r2", value2);                                5
  ["object", "cmd"].put("send");
}.                                                                     7
```

Listing 1.7. Registry like programming

4   Case Studies

This section presents case studies where the features of LINC have been used.

4.1   Building Automation

Building automation is a typical case where coordination is essential and may become very complex. We need to coordinate a high number of sensors (e.g. temperature, light, co2, presence) and actuators (e.g. Heating, Ventilation and Air-Conditioning (HVAC), dimmable spotlights). These devices belong to independent subsystems distributed in the building and using different protocols: BACnet [3], LONWorks [19], KNX [16] or Zigbee, 433Mhz/868Mhz for wireless. These subsystems work autonomously but most of the time cannot cooperate.

In the context of the SCUBA (Self-organising, Co-operative and robUst Building Automation) FP7 project [28], LINC has successfully been used to offer the abstraction layer required to make all these devices able to coexist. In addition

LINC has provided the coordination in order to allow the binding of devices of different constructors across a set of buildings [10]. Several scenarios have been defined to coordinate the HVAC and the lighting systems in order to improve the energy efficiency. The graceful degradation feature of LINC has proven very efficient to handle partial failure of autonomous systems. The application is currently distributed across 6 partners' sites controlling 5 buildings.

Another important role played by LINC was the administration of autonomous subsystems according to context. It has been used to reconfigure the LONWorks bindings in a room that can be either two individual offices or a single larger room, depending on the presence of a removable wall. The binding of the buttons, temperature sensors, motion detectors to the lights, shutter, HVAC have to be reconfigured accordingly. In LONWorks, this would involve the manual intervention of a skilled technician. With LINC we have coordinated the reconfiguration process with rules dynamically generated according to the current context [29].

4.2   RFID Table

To illustrate the capability of LINC to manage complex events detection, [20] describes our experiment with an original hardware. This hardware is a table stacking a 42" LCD screen with a HD 1080p resolution on top of a set of rfid readers organised as a matrix of 6 x 4 tiles, with each tile containing itself a matrix of 4 x 4 rfid readers. As a result there are 24 x 16 (384) rfid readers distributed in the table. The table works with classical rfid tags that can be attached to any physical object. The raw information received is, for each rfid reader, the set of detected tags. In addition, we have encapsulated as LINC bags two software components: a 2D engine able to display arbitrary content on the screen table allowing user interaction and a 3D engine able to render in a virtual world the tagged physical objects placed on the table.

The coordination language of LINC allowed to manage complex events resulting from the manipulation of the tags frequently added and removed from the table. The full application is managed by a dozen of rules distributed on the laptop responsible for displaying the 3D scene on the external display and the Raspberry PI managing the screen embedded in the table.

4.3   Smart Actuators

In [14] we have designed smart actuators able to directly understand the LINC coordination protocol and thus to be participant to transactions. The actuator is thus able to locally detect that it will not be able to do the requested action. For instance, this may be due to currently insufficient energy or unfeasible physical actuation (e.g. due to an obstacle or an out of range request). This simplifies the error management and allows synchronised physical actions. For instance, we used these smart devices for the obstacle avoidance of an autonomous robot where actions on the motors failed when associated sensors detect obstacles in the considered direction. The bags encapsulating the control of the motor have been implemented on small microcontrollers of type ATmega328 or PIC24.

5 Related Works

Since the introduction of tuple-spaces by Linda [13] in 1985, many contributions have been proposed to improve, extend and adapt the model.

MARS [8] extends the Linda tuple-spaces to add reactions. A reaction is implemented by an agent which triggers an operation on a matching tuple. Reactions are implemented with "meta" tuples containing a reference to the agent. In LINC, the reactions are defined by high-level coordination rules which embed actions in distributed transactions.

LIME [23] (Linda In a Mobile Environment) replaces the globally accessible persistent tuple-space of Linda by transiently shared tuple-spaces. In LIME each agent has its own tuple-space. When agents meets, they form a shared tuple-space and can exchange tuples. Strong reactions (ensuring a transaction) are restricted to a host or an agent. For distributed reactions, Weak reactions are used to ensure that eventually the reactions will be done if connectivity is preserved. LINC always uses distributed transactions in order to maintain the system in a consistent state. A similar approach to LIME is proposed in [12], with a lighter implementation of tuple-spaces.

The Holoparadigm [5] is a programming model to build context aware applications which introduces the concept of *Being* containing an interface, a behaviour and a history. History is a blackboard (similar to tuple-spaces) with Linda-like primitives. Holoparadigm offers the architecture for building agents however it mixes the coordination with the agents' code.

EgoSpaces [15] is a middleware targeting development of context aware mobile applications. It defines an agent as a unit of modularity and mobility with its own local tuple-space. EgoSpaces adds the *View* concept to limit the data seen by an agent (e.g. cost of the communication, physical location, thresholds on data). The view concept is interesting because it allows the developer to define when an agent should react.

The MobiGATE Coordination Language (MCL) [33] insists on the separation between computation and coordination which is a shared approach with LINC. Their approach seems well suited for distributing a stream or a known service in a mobile environment. However, in MCL it seems difficult to focus on the coordination when a very complex and dynamic system is considered. UbiCoMo [7] proposes a coordination model that mainly focuses on accessing data in ubiquitous environments. However, this limits too much UbiCoMo expressiveness to fit into this specific paradigm. MCL and UbiCoMo share with LINC the importance of separation between coordination and computation.

In [11] the authors propose a process-based methodology to design event-based mobile applications. They aim to translate UML activity diagram to event based models offering more flexibility. As outlined in their conclusion, event-based approaches does not make synchronisation easy. We believe this issue could be overcome by the transactional guaranties of LINC. We also believe that LINC rules could be generated from the activity diagram. This could be an interesting track to consider.

In [17] the authors present a programming model for concurrent coordination patterns targeting highly parallel and distributed applications. Similarly to LINC, they provide a language to focus on the coordination in complex environment. They aim to provide a high level language, relying on a formal language from which LINC could also take advantage of. Finally, their model relies on a tuple-space middleware. LINC seems a good candidate to implement their model. Generating LINC rules from a higher level model is in our future work.

In TOTA (Tuples On The Air) [21], tuples are not associated to a specific host, they are injected in the network and can autonomously propagate in the network according to a specified pattern. A tuple is defined by a content and a propagation rule. The TOTA approach might be interesting in some context where the data moves around the network while hosts come and go. However, in other cases this might include an overhead in the traffic because tuples are propagated even if no host is interested in them. On the contrary, in LINC, tuples are exchanged only when a rule is needing them. We believe that the autonomous and self evolution idea of TOTA could be implemented in LINC thanks to its reflexivity. Indeed objects and rules can evolve to reach an emergent behaviour.

Inspired by Gamma [4], another approach to reach self evolving system is to use chemical inspired tuple-spaces [30]. The idea is to rely on the semantic of chemical reactions to build coordination laws. High level information are then given on tuples and they autonomously evolve and move. The goal is to have an emergent behaviour with this approach. For instance, services scarcely used will automatically disappear from the tuple-space. This work only focus on the long run emerging behaviour, they do not allow to directly build coordination for the physical world. Moreover, focus has been on simulation [26] even if a middleware is under development in the scope of the SAPERE project [27]. Finally, in [31] the author define a spatial computing coordination language to extend Linda with space and time information in the tuples. As far as we understand, no implementation exists so far. LINC, with its reflexivity, could implement these proposal on large scale distributed systems.

6   Conclusion

This paper has presented the LINC coordination environment. It provides a compact yet powerful coordination language based on the three paradigms: associative memory, production rules and distributed transactions. This combination provides a language with a high expressiveness. High level coordination rules can be written while relying on the tuple-space to abstract low level implementation and communication details.

In addition, LINC is highly reflexive. Because everything is a resource it is easy to control the execution of rules or group of rules. Coordination rules can be dynamically added, removed or moved to another object. Objects themselves can migrate and independently designed applications can be merged at run-time.

With all these properties and its reflexivity, LINC is a powerful environment to tackle the challenges of the future systems of systems.

We illustrated this with several real world case studies implemented on top of LINC. This demonstrated the ability of LINC to be used in contexts such as building automation, power efficiency or monitoring network systems.

Future work will focus on providing a high-level language such as automata in order to prove the correctness of the coordination and then to automatically generate the corresponding coordination rules. We envisage to use this mechanism for self-evolving system where we can prove that the evolution will not break the running application.

Acknowledgement. This work has been partially funded by the FP7 SCUBA project under grant nb 288079.

References

1. Andreoli, J.-M., Arregui, D., Pacull, F., Willamowski, J.: Resource-based scripting to stitch distributed components. In: Han, Y., Tai, S., Wikarski, D. (eds.) EDCIS 2002. LNCS, vol. 2480, pp. 429–443. Springer, Heidelberg (2002)
2. Andreoli, J.-M., Pacull, F., Pagani, D., Pareschi, R.: Multiparty negotiation of dynamic distributed object services. Science of Computer Programming 31(2), 179–203 (1998)
3. BACNet (2014), http://www.bacnet.org/
4. Banâtre, J.-P., Fradet, P., Le Métayer, D.: Gamma and the chemical reaction model: Fifteen years after. In: Calude, C.S., Pun, G., Rozenberg, G., Salomaa, A. (eds.) Multiset Processing. LNCS, vol. 2235, pp. 17–44. Springer, Heidelberg (2001)
5. Barbosa, J., Dillenburg, F., Lermen, G., Garzão, A., Costa, C., Rosa, J.: Towards a programming model for context-aware applications. Computer Languages, Systems & Structures 38(3), 199–213 (2012)
6. Bernstein, P.A., Hadzilacos, V., Goodman, N.: Concurrency control and recovery in database systems, vol. 370. Addison-Wesley, New York (1987)
7. Bortenschlager, M., Castelli, G., Rosi, A., Zambonelli, F.: A context-sensitive infrastructure for coordinating agents in ubiquitous environments. Multiagent and Grid Systems 5(1), 1–18 (2009)
8. Cabri, G., Leonardi, L., Zambonelli, F.: Mars: A programmable coordination architecture for mobile agents. IEEE Internet Computing 4(4), 26–35 (2000)
9. Cooper, T., Wogrin, N.: Rule-based Programming with OPS5, vol. 988. Morgan Kaufmann (1988)
10. Ducreux, L.-F., Guyon-Gardeux, C., Lesecq, S., Pacull, F., Thior, S.R.: Resource-based middleware in the context of heterogeneous building automation systems. In: IECON 2012-38th Annual Conference on IEEE Industrial Electronics Society, pp. 4847–4852. IEEE (2012)
11. Fjellheim, T., Milliner, S., Dumas, M., Vayssière, J.: A process-based methodology for designing event-based mobile composite applications. Data & Knowledge Engineering 61(1), 6–22 (2007)
12. Fok, C.-L., Roman, G.-C., Hackmann, G.: A lightweight coordination middleware for mobile computing. In: De Nicola, R., Ferrari, G.-L., Meredith, G. (eds.) COORDINATION 2004. LNCS, vol. 2949, pp. 135–151. Springer, Heidelberg (2004)

13. Gelernter, D.: Generative communication in linda. ACM Transactions on Programming Languages and Systems (TOPLAS) 7(1), 80–112 (1985)
14. Iris, H., Pacull, F.: Smart sensors and actuators: A question of discipline. Sensors & Transducers Journal 18(special issue), 14–23 (2013)
15. Julien, C., Roman, G.-C.: Egospaces: Facilitating rapid development of context-aware mobile applications. IEEE Transactions on Software Engineering 32(5), 281–298 (2006)
16. KNX (2014), http://www.knx.org/
17. Kühn, E., Craß, S., Joskowicz, G., Marek, A., Scheller, T.: Peer-based programming model for coordination patterns. In: De Nicola, R., Julien, C. (eds.) COORDINATION 2013. LNCS, vol. 7890, pp. 121–135. Springer, Heidelberg (2013)
18. Lee, E.A.: Cyber physical systems: Design challenges. In: 2008 11th IEEE International Symposium on Object Oriented Real-Time Distributed Computing (ISORC), pp. 363–369. IEEE (2008)
19. LONWorks (2013), http://www.lonmark.org/
20. Louvel, M., Pacull, F.: A coordinated matrix of rfid readers as interactions input. In: SENSORDEVICES 2013, The Fourth International Conference on Sensor Device Technologies and Applications, pp. 91–96 (2013)
21. Mamei, M., Zambonelli, F.: Programming pervasive and mobile computing applications: The tota approach. ACM Transactions on Software Engineering and Methodology 18(4), 15 (2009)
22. Murphy, A.L., Picco, G.P., Roman, G.-C.: Lime: A middleware for physical and logical mobility. In: 21st International Conference on Distributed Computing Systems 2001, pp. 524–533. IEEE (2001)
23. Murphy, A.L., Picco, G.P., Roman, G.-C.: Lime: A coordination model and middleware supporting mobility of hosts and agents. ACM Transactions on Software Engineering and Methodology 15(3), 279–328 (2006)
24. Omicini, A., Viroli, M.: Coordination models and languages: From parallel computing to self-organisation. The Knowledge Engineering Review 26(01), 53–59 (2011)
25. Papadopoulos, G.A., Arbab, F.: Coordination models and languages. Advances in Computers 46, 329–400 (1998)
26. Pianini, D., Montagna, S., Viroli, M.: Chemical-oriented simulation of computational systems with alchemist. Journal of Simulation 7(3), 202–215 (2013)
27. SAPERE (2013), http://www.sapere-project.eu
28. SCUBA (2011), http://www.aws.cit.ie/scuba/
29. Scuba. Deliverable 5.3 (2013), http://linc.middlewares.info/wiki1/images/8/81/Scuba_d_5_3.pdf
30. Viroli, M., Casadei, M., Montagna, S., Zambonelli, F.: Spatial coordination of pervasive services through chemical-inspired tuple spaces. ACM Trans. Auton. Adapt. Syst. 6(2), 14:1–14:24 (2011)
31. Viroli, M., Pianini, D., Beal, J.: Linda in space-time: an adaptive coordination model for mobile ad-hoc environments. In: Sirjani, M. (ed.) COORDINATION 2012. LNCS, vol. 7274, pp. 212–229. Springer, Heidelberg (2012)
32. von Bültzingsloewen, G., Koschel, A., Lockemann, P.C., Walter, H.-D.: Eca functionality in a distributed environment. In: Active Rules in Database Systems, pp. 147–175. Springer (1999)
33. Zheng, Y., Chan, A.T.S., Ngai, G.: Mcl: a mobigate coordination language for highly adaptive and reconfigurable mobile middleware. Software: Practice and Experience 36(11-12), 1355–1380 (2006)

Safe and Efficient Data Sharing
for Message-Passing Concurrency

Benjamin Morandi, Sebastian Nanz, and Bertrand Meyer

Department of Computer Science, ETH Zurich, Switzerland
firstname.lastname@inf.ethz.ch
http://se.inf.ethz.ch/

Abstract. Message passing provides a powerful communication abstraction in both distributed and shared memory environments. It is particularly successful at preventing problems arising from shared state, such as data races, as it avoids sharing in general. Message passing is less effective when concurrent access to large amounts of data is needed, as the overhead of messaging may be prohibitive. In shared memory environments, this issue could be alleviated by supporting direct access to shared data; but then ensuring proper synchronization becomes again the dominant problem. This paper proposes a safe and efficient approach to data sharing in message-passing concurrency models based on the idea of distinguishing active and passive computational units. Passive units do not have execution capabilities but offer to active units exclusive and direct access to the data they encapsulate. The access is transparent due to a single primitive for both data access and message passing. By distinguishing active and passive units, no additional infrastructure for shared data is necessary. The concept is applied to SCOOP, an object-oriented concurrency model, where it reduces execution time by several orders of magnitude on data-intensive parallel programs.

1 Introduction

In concurrency models with message passing, such as the Actor model [14], CSP [15], and others [6], a *computational unit* encapsulates its own private data. The units interact by sending synchronous or asynchronous messages. These concurrency models are implementable in environments with and without shared memory. Based on these models, several languages and libraries support message passing, e.g., Erlang [8], Ada [16], MPI [19], and SCOOP [22].

To operate on shared data, a *client* must send a message to the *supplier* encapsulating that data. In environments with shared memory, however, the client could access this data directly and avoid the messaging overhead. The difficulty is to prevent data races and to combine the data access primitives with the messaging primitives in a developer-friendly way.

Some languages and libraries [8, 16, 19, 25] have already combined mutually exclusive shared data with message passing and observed performance gains on shared memory systems. However, as discussed in Section 6, these approaches

E. Kühn and R. Pugliese (Eds.): COORDINATION 2014, LNCS 8459, pp. 99–114, 2014.
© IFIP International Federation for Information Processing 2014

either impose restrictions on the shared data or do not provide unified primitives for data access and message passing. As a consequence of the latter limitation, programmers are required to change their code substantially when switching from messaging to shared data or vice versa.

To close this gap, this paper proposes *passive* computational units for safe and efficient data sharing in message-passing models implemented on shared memory. A passive unit is a supplier stripped from its execution capabilities. Its only purpose is to provide a container for shared data and exclusive access to it. The passive unit can contain any data that is containable by a regular supplier. A client with exclusive access uses existing communication primitives to operate on the data; instead of sending a message, these primitives access the data directly. By overloading the primitives' semantics, programmers only need to change few lines of code to set a unit passive. Furthermore, passive units are implementable with little effort as existing supplier infrastructure can be reused.

This paper develops this concept in the context of SCOOP [20,22], an object-oriented concurrency model based on message passing, where *processors* encapsulate objects and interact by sending requests. The implementation of the concept is shown to reduce execution time by several orders of magnitude on data-intensive parallel programs.

The remainder of this paper is structured as follows. Section 2 introduces a running example. Section 3 develops the concept of *passive processors* informally, and Section 4 develops it formally. Section 5 evaluates the efficiency, and Section 6 reviews related work. Finally, Section 7 discusses the applicability to other concurrency models and concludes with an outlook on future work.

2   Pipeline System

A pipeline system serves as the running example for this paper. The pipeline parallel design pattern [18] applies whenever a computation involves sending *packages* of data through a sequence of *stages* that operate on the packages. The pattern assigns each stage to a different computational unit; the stages then synchronize with each other to process the packages in the correct order. Using this pattern, each stage can be mapped for instance to a CPU core, a GPU core, an FPGA, or a cryptographic accelerator, depending on the stage's computational needs.

The pipeline pattern can be implemented in SCOOP (Simple Concurrent Object-Oriented Programming) [20,22]. The starting idea of SCOOP is that every object is associated with a processor, called its *handler*. A *processor* is an autonomous thread of control capable of executing actions on objects. An object's class describes its actions as *features*. An *entity* x belonging to a processor can point to an object with the same handler (*non-separate object*), or to an object on another processor (*separate object*). In the first case, a *feature call* x.f on the *target* x is *non-separate*: the handler of x executes the feature synchronously. In the second case, the feature call is *separate*: the handler of x, i.e., the *supplier*, executes the call asynchronously on behalf of the requester, i.e., the *client*. The possibility of asynchronous calls is the main source of concurrent execution. The asynchronous nature of separate feature calls implies a distinction between a feature call and a *feature application*: the client logs the call with the supplier (feature call) and moves on; only at some later time will the supplier actually execute the body (feature application).

In the SCOOP pipeline implementation, each stage and each package is handled by its own processor, ensuring that stages can access the packages in parallel. Each stage is numbered to indicate its position in the pipeline; it receives this position upon creation:

```
class STAGE create make feature
    position: INTEGER -- The stage's position in the pipeline.

    make (new_position: INTEGER)
            -- Create a stage at the given position.
        do position := new_position end

    process (package: separate PACKAGE)
            -- Process the package after the previous stage is done with it.
        require package.is_processed (position − 1) do
            do_work (package) -- Read from and write to the package.
            package.set_processed (position) -- Set the package processed.
        end
end
```

The *process* feature takes a package as an argument. The keyword **separate** specifies that the package may be handled by a different processor than the stage; without this keyword, the package must be handled by the same processor. To ensure exclusive access, a stage must first lock a package before accessing it. In SCOOP, such locking requirements are expressed in the formal argument list: any target of separate type within the feature must occur as a formal argument; the arguments' handlers are locked for the duration of the feature execution, thus preventing data races. In *process*, *package* is a formal argument; hence the stage has exclusive access to the package while executing *process*.

To process each package in the right order, the stages must synchronize with each other. For this purpose, each package has two features *is_processed* and *set_processed* to keep track of the stages that already processed the package. The synchronization requirement can then be expressed elegantly using a precondition (keyword **require**), which makes the execution of a feature wait until the condition is true. The precondition in *process* delays the execution until the package has been processed by the previous stage.

The SCOOP concepts require execution-time support, known as the SCOOP runtime. Each processor is protected through a lock and maintains a *request queue* of requests resulting from feature calls of other processors. When a client executes a separate feature call, it enqueues a *separate feature request* to the supplier's request queue. The supplier processes the feature requests in the order of queuing. A non-separate feature call can be processed without the request queue: the processor creates a *non-separate feature request* and processes it right away using its call stack.

A client makes sure that it holds the locks on all suppliers before executing a feature. At the end of the feature execution, the client issues an unlock request to each locked processor. Each locked processor unlocks itself as soon as it processed all previous feature requests.

3   Passive Processors

The pipeline system from Section 2 showcases an important class of concurrent programs, namely those that involve multiple processors sharing data. In SCOOP, it is necessary to assign the data to a new processor. For frequent and short read or write operations this becomes problematic:

1. Each feature call to the data leads to a feature request in the request queue of the data processor, which then picks up the request and processes it on its call stack. This chain of actions creates overhead. For an asynchronous write operation, the overhead outweighs the benefit of asynchrony. For a synchronous read operation, the client not only waits for the data processor to process the request, it also gets delayed further by the overhead.
2. The data consumes operating system resources (threads, processes, locks, semaphores) that could otherwise be freed up.

On systems with shared memory, the clients can directly operate on the data, thus avoiding the overhead. This frees most of the operating system resources attached to the data processor. Before accessing shared data, a client must ensure its access is mutually exclusive; otherwise, data races can occur. For this purpose, shared data must be grouped, and each group must be protected through a lock. Since SCOOP processors offer this functionality already along with execution capabilities, one can use processors, stripped from their execution capabilities, to group and protect shared data. This insight gives rise to passive processors:

Definition 1 (Passive processor). *A passive processor q does not have any execution capabilities. Its lock protects the access to its associated objects. A client p holding this lock uses feature calls to operate directly on q's associated objects. While operating on these objects, p assumes the identity of q. Processor q becomes passive when another processor sets it as passive. When q is not passive, it is active. Processor q becomes active again when another processor sets it as active. It can only become passive or active when unlocked, i.e., when not being used by any other processor.*

When a processor p operates on the objects of a passive processor q, it assumes q's identity. For example, if p creates a literal object or another non-separate object, it creates this object on q and not on itself; otherwise, a non-separate entity on q would reference an object on p.

Besides safe and fast data sharing, passive processors have further benefits:

- *Minimal user code changes.* The feature call primitive unifies sending messages to active processors and accessing shared data on passive processors, ensuring minimal code changes to set a processor passive or active. With respect to SCOOP's type system [22], the same types can be used to type objects on passive and active processors. The existing type system rules ensure that no object on a passive processor can be seen as non-separate on a different processor, thus providing type soundness.
- *Minimal compiler and runtime changes.* To implement passive processors, much of the existing infrastructure can be reused. In particular, no new code for grouping objects and for locking request queues is required.

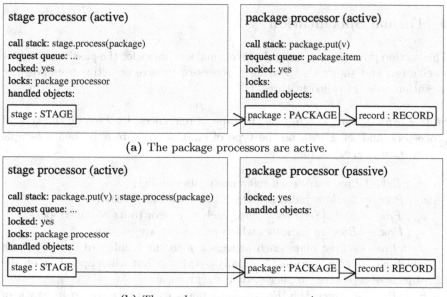

(a) The package processors are active.

(b) The package processors are passive.

Fig. 1. A stage processor processes a package. The stage object, handled by the left-hand side processor, has a separate reference (depicted by an arrow) to the package object, handled by the right-hand side processor. The package object references a non-separate record object to remember the processing history.

In the pipeline system, each package can be handled by a passive processor rather than an active one. To achieve this, it suffices to set a package's processor passive after its construction. The following code creates a package on a new passive processor and asks the stages to process the package.

```
create package.make (data, number_of_stages) ; set_passive (package)
stage_1.process (package) ; ... ; stage_n.process (package)
```

No other code changes are necessary. The existing feature calls to the packages automatically assume the data access semantics. Furthermore, a stage can still use separate $PACKAGE$ as the type of a package because the stage is still handled by a different processor than the package. Similarly, a package can still use the type $RECORD$ for its record because the package still has the same handler as the record.

Figure 1 illustrates the effect of the call to *set_passive*. In Figure 1a, active package processors have a call stack, a request queue, and a stack of locks. The stage processors send asynchronous (see *put*) and synchronous (see *item*) feature requests. In Figure 1b, passive package processors do not have any execution capabilities. Therefore, the stage processors operate directly and synchronously on the packages, thus making a better use of their own processing capabilities rather than relaying all operations to the package processors.

4   Formal Specification

This section provides a structural operational semantics for the passive processor mechanism and shows that setting a processor passive or active preserves the execution order of called features.

State Formalization. Let *Ref* be the type of references, let *Proc* be the type of processors, and let *Entity* be the type of entities. A state σ is then a 6-tuple $(\sigma_h, \sigma_l, \sigma_o, \sigma_i, \sigma_f, \sigma_e)$ of functions:

- $\sigma_h : Ref \rightarrow Proc$ maps each reference to its handler.
- $\sigma_l : Proc \rightarrow Boolean$ indicates which processors are locked.
- $\sigma_o : Proc \rightarrow Stack[Set[Proc]]$ maps each processor to its obtained locks.
- $\sigma_i : Proc \rightarrow Boolean$ indicates which processors are passive.
- $\sigma_f : Proc \rightarrow Proc$ maps each processor p to the handler of the object on which p currently operates. Normally $\sigma_f(p) = p$, but when operating on the objects of a passive supplier q, then $\sigma_f(p) = q$.
- $\sigma_e : Proc \rightarrow Stack[Map[Entity, Ref]]$ maps each processor to its stack of entity environments.

Execution Formalization. An *execution* is a sequence of configurations. Each *configuration* of the form $\langle p_1 :: s_{p1} \mid \ldots \mid p_n :: s_{pn}, \sigma \rangle$ is an execution snapshot consisting of the *schedule*, i.e., the call stacks and the request queues of processors $p_1, \ldots, p_n$, and the state σ. The call stack and the request queue of a processor are also known as the *action queue* of the processor. The commutative and associative parallel operator $\mid$ keeps the processors' action queues apart. Within an action queue, a semicolon separates statements. *Statements* are either *instructions*, i.e., program elements, or *operations*, i.e., runtime elements. The following overview shows the structure of statements, instructions, and operations. The elements e_t, e, and all items in $\overline{e_a}$ are entities of type *Entity*. The element r_t and all items in $\overline{r_a}$ are references of type *Ref*. The element f of type *Feature* denotes a feature where *f.body* returns the feature's body. Lastly, $q_1, \ldots, q_n$ and w are processors of type *Proc*, and x is a flag of type *Boolean*.

$$s \triangleq in \mid op$$
$$in \triangleq$$

$e_t.f(\overline{e_a}) \mid$	Call a feature.
create $e_t.f(\overline{e_a}) \mid$	Create an object.
set_passive(e) $\mid$	Set the handler of the referenced object passive.
set_active(e)	Set the handler of the referenced object active.

$$op \triangleq$$

apply$(r_t, f, \overline{r_a}) \mid$	Apply a feature.
revert$(\{q_1, \ldots, q_n\}, w, x) \mid$	Finish a feature application or an object creation.
unlock	Unlock a processor.

Figure 2 shows the transition rules. A processor q becomes passive when a processor p executes the *set_passive* instruction (see SET PASSIVE) with an entity e that evaluates to a reference r on q. Processor q becomes active again when a processor p executes the *set_active* instruction (see SET ACTIVE). Processor q can only become passive or active when q is unlocked, guaranteeing that q is not being used by any other processor.

To perform a feature call $e_t.f(\overline{e_a})$ (see call rules) a client p evaluates the target (see r_t) and the arguments (see $\overline{r_a}$). It then looks at the handler q of the target. If q is different from p and not passive, p creates a feature request (see apply) and appends it to the end of q's request queue. If q is p or if q is passive, then p itself immediately processes the feature request.

To process a feature request (see APPLY), a processor p first determines the missing locks $\overline{q}$ as the difference between required locks and already obtained locks. It only proceeds when all missing locks are available, in which case it obtains these locks. It also adds a new entity environment and updates σ_f with the target handler, i.e., p for non-passive calls or the handler of the target for passive calls. Processor p then executes the feature body and cleans up (see REVERT). It releases the obtained locks, restores σ_f, and removes the top entity environment. The locked suppliers unlock themselves asynchronously once they are done with the issued workload (see UNLOCK).

To execute a creation instruction create $e_t.f(\overline{e_a})$ (see creation rules), a processor p looks at the type of the target e_t. If the type is separate, i.e., its declaration has the separate keyword, p creates an active and idle processor q with a new object referenced by r_t. It then locks that processor, performs the creation call (see call rules), and cleans up. If the type of e_t is non-separate, i.e., no separate keyword, p creates a new object on the handler on whose objects p currently operates on, i.e., $\sigma_f(p)$. In case $\sigma_f(p) = q \neq p$, it is important to create the new object on q rather than on p; otherwise the non-separate entity e_t on q would point to an object not on q, thus compromising the soundness of the type system.

We embedded the transition rules from Figure 2 into the comprehensive formal specification for SCOOP [10], implemented in Maude [5]. This specification uses $\sigma_f(p)$ also in other situations where p performs an action on behalf of a passive

SET PASSIVE

$$\frac{r \overset{def}{=} \sigma_e(p).top.val(e) \quad q \overset{def}{=} \sigma_h(r) \quad \neg\sigma_l(q)}{\langle p :: set\_passive(e); s_p, \sigma \rangle \rightarrow \langle p :: s_p, (\sigma_h, \sigma_l, \sigma_o, \sigma_i[q \mapsto true], \sigma_f, \sigma_e) \rangle}$$

SET ACTIVE

$$\frac{r \overset{def}{=} \sigma_e(p).top.val(e) \quad q \overset{def}{=} \sigma_h(r) \quad \neg\sigma_l(q)}{\langle p :: set\_active(e); s_p, \sigma \rangle \rightarrow \langle p :: s_p, (\sigma_h, \sigma_l, \sigma_o, \sigma_i[q \mapsto false], \sigma_f, \sigma_e) \rangle}$$

SEPARATE CALL

$$\frac{r_t \overset{def}{=} \sigma_e(p).top.val(e_t) \quad \overline{r_a} \overset{def}{=} \sigma_e(p).top.val(\overline{e_a}) \quad q = \sigma_h(r_t) \quad p \neq q \wedge \neg\sigma_i(q)}{\langle p :: e_t.f(\overline{e_a}); s_p \mid q :: s_q, \sigma \rangle \rightarrow \langle p :: s_p \mid q :: s_q; apply(r_t, f, \overline{r_a}), \sigma \rangle}$$

NON-SEPARATE/PASSIVE CALL

$$\frac{r_t \overset{def}{=} \sigma_e(p).top.val(e_t) \quad \overline{r_a} \overset{def}{=} \sigma_e(p).top.val(\overline{e_a}) \quad q = \sigma_h(r_t) \quad p = q \vee \sigma_i(q)}{\langle p :: e_t.f(\overline{e_a}); s_p, \sigma \rangle \rightarrow \langle p :: apply(r_t, f, \overline{r_a}); s_p, \sigma \rangle}$$

APPLY

$$\frac{\overline{q} \overset{def}{=} \sigma_h(\overline{r_a}) \setminus (\sigma_o(p).flat \cup \{p\}) \quad \bigwedge_{q \in \overline{q}} \neg\sigma_l(q)}{\begin{array}{l} \langle p :: apply(r_t, f, \overline{r_a}); s_p, \sigma \rangle \rightarrow \\ \langle p :: f.body; revert(\overline{q}, \sigma_f(p), true); s_p, (\sigma_h, \sigma_l[\overline{q} \mapsto true], \sigma_o[p \mapsto \sigma_o(p).push(\overline{q})], \sigma_i, \\ \quad \sigma_f[p \mapsto \sigma_h(r_t)], \sigma_e[p \mapsto \sigma_e(p).push((current \mapsto r_t, f.formals \mapsto \overline{r_a}))]) \rangle \end{array}}$$

REVERT

$$\frac{e' \overset{def}{=} \begin{cases} \sigma_e[p \mapsto \sigma_e(p).pop] & if x \\ \sigma_e & otherwise \end{cases}}{\begin{array}{l} \langle p :: revert(\{q_1, \ldots, q_n\}, w, x); s_p \mid q_1 :: s_{q1} \mid \ldots \mid q_n :: s_{qn}, \sigma \rangle \rightarrow \\ \langle p :: s_p \mid q_1 :: s_{q1}; unlock \mid \ldots \mid q_n :: \ldots, (\sigma_h, \sigma_l, \sigma_o[p \mapsto \sigma_o(p).pop], \sigma_i, \sigma_f[p \mapsto w], e') \rangle \end{array}}$$

UNLOCK

$$\frac{}{\begin{array}{l} \langle p :: unlock; s_p, \sigma \rangle \rightarrow \\ \langle p :: s_p, (\sigma_h, \sigma_l[p \mapsto false], \sigma_o, \sigma_i, \sigma_f, \sigma_e) \rangle \end{array}}$$

PARALLELISM

$$\frac{\langle P, \sigma \rangle \rightarrow \langle P', \sigma' \rangle}{\langle P \mid Q, \sigma \rangle \rightarrow \langle P' \mid Q, \sigma' \rangle}$$

SEPARATE CREATION

$$\frac{e_t.type = separate \quad q \overset{def}{=} fresh\_proc(\sigma_h) \quad r_t \overset{def}{=} fresh\_obj(\sigma_h)}{\begin{array}{l} \langle p :: create \; e_t.f(\overline{e_a}); s_p, \sigma \rangle \rightarrow \langle p :: e_t.f(\overline{e_a}); revert(\{q\}, \sigma_f(p), false); s_p \mid q ::, \\ (\sigma_h[r_t \mapsto q], \sigma_l[q \mapsto true], \sigma_o[p \mapsto \sigma_o(p).push(\{q\})][q \mapsto ()], \sigma_i[q \mapsto false], \\ \quad \sigma_f[q \mapsto q], \sigma_e[p \mapsto \sigma_e(p).update(e_t \mapsto r_t)][q \mapsto ()]) \rangle \end{array}}$$

NON-SEPARATE CREATION

$$\frac{e_t.type = non\text{-}separate \quad r_t \overset{def}{=} fresh\_obj(\sigma_h)}{\begin{array}{l} \langle p :: create \; e_t.f(\overline{e_a}); s_p, \sigma \rangle \rightarrow \\ \langle p :: e_t.f(\overline{e_a}); s_p, (\sigma_h[r_t \mapsto \sigma_f(p)], \sigma_l, \sigma_o, \sigma_i, \sigma_f, \sigma_e[p \mapsto \sigma_e(p).update(e_t \mapsto r_t)]) \rangle \end{array}}$$

Fig. 2. Transition rules

processor, namely to create literals, to set the status of a once routine (a routine only executed once), and to import and copy object structures. We used the specification to test [21] the passive processor mechanism against other SCOOP aspects and used the results to refine the specification.

4.1 Order Preservation

The formal semantics can be used to prove Theorem 1, stating that a supplier can always be set passive or active without altering the sequence in which called features get applied. This property enables developers to use the same reasoning in determining a feature's functional correctness, irrespective of whether the suppliers are passive or active. Lemma 1 is necessary to prove Theorem 1.

Lemma 1 (Action queue order preservation). *Let p be a processor with statements $s_1, \ldots, s_l$ in its action queue. In a terminating program, p will execute $s_1, \ldots, s_l$ in the sequence order.*

Proof. The transition rules in Figure 2 only allow p to execute the leftmost statement and then continue with the next one. Since none of the rules delete or shuffle any statements, and since p's program is terminating, p must execute $s_1, \ldots, s_l$ in the sequence order.

Theorem 1 (Feature call order preservation). *Let p be a processor that is about to apply a feature f in a terminating program. Let $\overline{q}$ be the processors that p locks to apply f. For each $q \in \overline{q}$, regardless whether it is passive or active, the feature requests for q, resulting from feature calls in f's body, will be processed in the order given by f's body.*

Proof. Processor p first inserts f's instructions $s_1, \ldots, s_l$ into its action queue (see APPLY). Lemma 1 states that processor p executes all of these instructions in code order. Hence, the proof can use mathematical induction over the length l of f's body. In the base case, i.e., $l = 0$, p did not execute any instructions; hence, the property holds trivially. For the inductive step, the property holds for $l = i - 1$; the proof needs to show that the property holds for $l = i$. Consider the instruction s_i at position i:

- s_i is *set_passive* or *set_active*. Processor p does not change any action queues (see SET PASSIVE and SET ACTIVE); the property is preserved.
- s_i is a separate feature call to a passive processor q. Processor p processes the resulting feature request (see NON-SEPARATE/PASSIVE CALL). Processor q must already have been passive during earlier calls because a processor cannot be set passive when it is locked (see APPLY and SET PASSIVE). Hence, processor p must have processed all requests from earlier calls. Because of the induction hypothesis, it must have done so in the order given by the code. Consequently, processing the request for s_i now preserves the property for q. Because of the induction hypothesis, the configuration after s_{i-1} satisfied the property for all other suppliers in $\overline{q}$; Lemma 1 guarantees that these processors will execute their statements in the same order even after s_i, thus the property is preserved.

- s_i is a separate feature call to an active processor q. Processor q must already have been active during earlier calls because a processor cannot be set active when it is locked (see APPLY and SET ACTIVE). Processor p executes a separate call (see SEPARATE CALL) to add a feature request to the end of q's action queue. Because of the induction hypothesis, q must either have processed all requests from earlier calls in the code order, or some of these requests must be scheduled in q's action queue, to be executed in code order. In either case, adding a feature request for s_i to the end of the action queue preserves the property for q (see Lemma 1). As in the passive case, Lemma 1 guarantees that the property is preserved for all other suppliers in $\bar{q}$ as well.
- s_i is a non-separate feature call. Regardless of the suppliers' passiveness, p executes a non-separate feature call (see NON-SEPARATE/PASSIVE CALL). Lemma 1 guarantees that the property is preserved for all q in $\bar{q}$.
- s_i is a separate creation instruction. Regardless of the suppliers' passiveness, p executes a separate feature call (see SEPARATE CREATION), adding a new feature request to a new processor. Lemma 1 guarantees that the property is preserved for all q in $\bar{q}$.
- s_i is a non-separate creation instruction. Regardless of the supplier's passiveness, p executes a non-separate feature call (see NON-SEPARATE CREATION). Lemma 1 guarantees that the property is preserved for all q in $\bar{q}$.

5   Evaluation

The pipeline system from Section 2 is a good representative for the class of programs targeted by the proposed mechanism: multiple stages share packages of data. This section experimentally compares the performance of the pipeline system when implemented using passive processors, active processors, and low-level synchronization primitives; the latter two are the closest competing approaches. To this end, we extended the SCOOP implementation [9] with passive processors.

5.1   Comparison to Active Processors

A low-pass filter pipeline is especially suited because it exhibits frequent and short read and write operations on the packages, each of which represents a signal to be filtered. The pipeline has three stages: the first performs a decimation-in-time radix-2 fast Fourier transformation [17]; the second applies a low-pass filter in Fourier space; and the third inverses the transformation. The system supports any number of pipelines operating in parallel and splits the signals evenly.

Table 1 shows the average execution times of various low-pass filter systems processing signals of various lengths. The experiments have been conducted on a $4 \times$ Intel Xeon E7-4830 2.13 GHz server (32 cores) with 256 GB of RAM running Windows Server 2012 Datacenter (64 Bit) in a Kernel-based Virtual Machine on Red Hat 4.4.7-3 (64 Bit). A modified version of EVE 13.11 [9] compiled the programs in finalized mode with an inline depth of 100. Every data point reflects the average execution time over ten runs processing 100 signals each. Using ten

Table 1. Average execution times (in seconds) of various low-pass filter systems with various signal lengths

configuration	2048	4096	8192	16384	32768	65536	131072	262144	524288
sequential, SCOOP	1.00	1.66	3.22	6.35	12.71	26.19	55.05	120.37	272.38
sequential, thread	0.62	1.09	2.19	4.66	9.57	20.23	41.45	93.40	213.59
1 pipeline, active	337.55	682.29	1456.67	2875.23	-	-	-	-	-
1 pipeline, passive	1.64	2.72	5.02	10.99	24.68	55.29	118.30	247.29	533.83
1 pipeline, thread	0.31	0.58	1.16	2.44	5.26	11.11	23.59	53.24	122.00
2 pipelines, passive	1.19	1.77	3.05	6.35	14.19	29.82	60.24	124.99	263.96
3 pipelines, passive	1.07	1.47	2.34	4.71	9.87	20.65	41.78	85.72	185.19
5 pipelines, active	231.25	496.68	1048.95	2192.53	-	-	-	-	-
5 pipelines, passive	0.87	1.23	1.86	3.27	6.35	13.50	27.17	55.95	117.12
5 pipelines, thread	0.16	0.23	0.40	0.74	1.53	3.05	6.30	13.76	31.82
10 pipelines, active	334.93	726.83	1549.01	3322.70	-	-	-	-	-
10 pipelines, passive	0.84	1.08	1.38	2.36	4.13	8.28	16.89	35.13	76.64
10 pipelines, thread	0.16	0.22	0.33	0.59	1.08	2.09	4.26	9.21	20.93

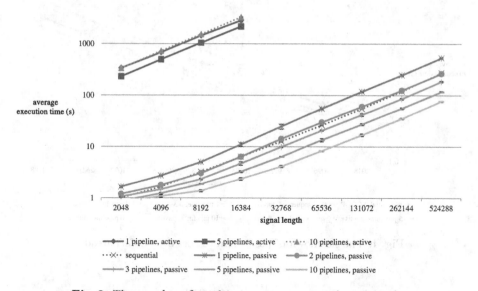

Fig. 3. The speedup of passive processors over active processors

pipelines, it took nearly ten hours to compute the average for active signals of length 16384; thus we refrained from computing data points for bigger lengths.

Figure 3 visualizes the data. The upper three curves belong to the active signal processors. The lower curves result from the passive processors and a sequential execution. As the graph indicates, the passive processors are more than two orders of magnitude faster than the active ones. In addition, with increasing number of pipelines, the passive processors become faster than the sequential program. In fact, two pipelines are enough to have an equivalent performance. The overhead is thus small enough to benefit from an increase in parallelism. In contrast, active processors deliver their peak performance with around five pipelines but never get faster than the sequential programs.

5.2 Comparison to Low-Level Synchronization Primitives

Figure 4 and Table 1 compare pipelines with passive processors to pipelines based on low-level synchronization primitives. In the measured range, the passive processors are between 3.7 to 5.4 times slower. As the signal length increases, the slowdown tends to becomes smaller. With more pipelines, the slowdown also tends to decrease at signal lengths above 8192. The two curves for sequential executions show that a slowdown can also be observed for non-concurrent programs.

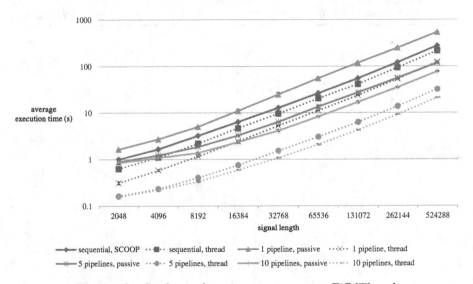

Fig. 4. The slowdown of passive processors over EiffelThread

The slowdown is the consequence of SCOOP's programming abstractions. Compare the following thread-based stage implementation to the SCOOP one from Section 2. Besides the addition of boilerplate (inherit clause, redefinition of *execute*), this code exhibits some more momentous differences. First, the thread-based stage class implements a work queue: it has an attribute to hold the packages and a loop in *execute* to go over them. In SCOOP, request queues provide this functionality. Second, each thread-based package has a mutex and a condition variable for synchronization. To process a package, stage i first locks the mutex and then uses the condition variable to wait until stage $i - 1$ has processed the package. Once stage $i - 1$ is done, it uses the condition variable to signal all waiting stages. Only stage i leaves the loop. In SCOOP, wait conditions provide this kind of synchronization off-the-shelf. We expect the cost of wait conditions and other concepts to drop further as the implementation matures.

```
class STAGE inherit THREAD create make feature
    position: INTEGER -- The stage's position in the pipeline.
    packages: ARRAY[PACKAGE] -- The packages to be processed.

    make (new_position: INTEGER; new_packages: ARRAY[PACKAGE])
        -- Create a stage at the given position to operate on the packages.
        do position := new_position ; packages := new_packages end

    execute -- Process each package after the previous stage is done with it.
        do
            across packages as package loop
                package.mutex.lock -- Lock the package.
                -- Sleep until previous stage is done; release the lock
                    meanwhile.
                from until package.is_processed (position - 1) loop
                    package.condition_variable.wait (package.mutex)
                end
                process (package) -- Process the package.
                package.condition_variable.broadcast -- Wake up next stage.
                package.mutex.unlock -- Unlock the package.
            end
        end

    process (package: PACKAGE) -- Process the package.
        do
            do_work (package) -- Read from and write to the package
            package.set_processed (position) -- Set the package processed.
        end
end
```

5.3 Other Applications

A variety of other applications could also profit from passive processors. Object structures can be distributed over passive processors. Multiple clients can thus operate on dynamically changing but distinct parts of these structures while exchanging coordination messages. For example, in parallel graph algorithms, the vertices can be distributed over passive processors. In producer-consumer programs, intermediate buffers can be passive. Normally, about half of the operations in producer-consumer programs are synchronous read accesses. Without the messaging overhead, the consumer can execute these operations much faster than the buffer. Passive processors can also be useful to handle objects whose only purpose it is to be lockable, e.g., forks of dining philosophers, or to encapsulate a shared state, e.g., a robot's state in a controller.

6 Related Work

Several languages and libraries combine shared data with message passing. In Ada [16], *tasks* execute concurrently and communicate during a *rendezvous*: upon joining a rendezvous, the client waits for a message from the supplier, and the supplier synchronously sends a message to the client. The client joins a rendezvous by calling a supplier's *entry*. The supplier joins by calling *accept* on that entry. To share data, tasks access *protected objects* that encapsulate data and provide exclusive access thereon through guarded functions, procedures, and entries. Since functions may only read data, multiple function calls may be active simultaneously. In contrast, passive processors do not support multiple readers. However, unlike protected objects, passive processors do not require new data access primitives. Furthermore, passive processors can become active at runtime.

Erlang [8] is a functional programming language whose concurrency support is based on the actor model [14]. Processes exchange messages and share data using an *ets table*, providing atomic and isolated access to table entries. A process can also use the *Mnesia* database management system to group a series of table operations into an atomic transaction. While passive processors do not provide support for transactions, they are not restricted to tables.

Schill et al. [25] developed a library offering indexed arrays that can be accessed concurrently by multiple SCOOP processors. To prevent data races on an array, each processor must reserve a *slice* of the array. Slices support fine-grained sharing as well as multiple readers using *views*, but they are restricted to indexed containers. For instance, distributed graphs cannot be easily expressed.

A group of MPI [19] processes can share data using the *remote memory access* mechanism and its *passive target* communication. The processes collectively create a *window* of shared memory. Processes access a window during an *epoch*, which begins with a collective synchronization call, continues with communication calls, and ends with another synchronization call. Synchronization includes fencing and locking. Locks can be partial or full, and they can be shared or exclusive. Passive processors neither offer fences nor shared locks; they do, however, offer automatic conditional synchronization based on preconditions. MPI can also be combined with OpenMP [23]. Just like MPI alone, this combination does not provide unified concepts. Instead, it provides distinct primitives to access shared data and to send messages. Uniformity also distinguishes passive processors from further approaches such as [13].

Several studies agree that performance gains can be realized if the setup of a program with both message passing and shared data fits the underlying architecture. For instance, Bull et al. [3] and Rabenseifner et al. [24] focus on benchmarks for MPI+OpenMP. Dunn and Meyer [7] use a QR factorization algorithm that can be adjusted to apply only message passing, only shared data, or both.

A number of approaches focus on optimizing messaging on shared memory systems instead of combining message passing with shared data. Gruber and Boyer [12] use an ownership management system to avoid copying messages between actors while retaining memory isolation. Villard et al. [26] and Bono et al. [1] employ static analysis techniques to determine when a message can be passed by reference rather than by value. Buntinas et al. [4], Graham and Shipman [11], as well as Brightwell [2] present techniques to allocate and use shared memory for messages.

7   Conclusion

Passive processors extend SCOOP's message-passing foundation with support for safe data sharing, reducing execution time by several orders of magnitude on data-intensive parallel programs. They are useful whenever multiple processors access shared data using frequent and short read or write operations, where the overhead outweighs the benefit of asynchrony. Passive processors can be implemented with minimal effort because much of the existing infrastructure can be reused. The feature call primitive unifies sending messages to active processors and accessing shared data on passive processors. Therefore, no significant code change is necessary to set a processor passive or active. This smooth integration differentiates passive processors from other approaches. The concept of passive computational units can also be applied to other message-passing concurrency models. For instance, messages to passive actors [14] can be translated into direct, synchronous, and mutually exclusive accesses to the actor's data.

Passive processors currently do not offer shared read locks, which allow multiple clients to simultaneously operate on a passive processor. Shared read locks require features that are guaranteed to be read-only. Functions could serve as a first approximation since they are read-only by convention. Further, passive processors are not distributed yet. Because frequent remote calls are expensive, implementing distributed passive processors requires an implicit copy mechanism to move the supplier's data into the client's memory.

Acknowledgments. We thank Eiffel Software for valuable discussions on the implementation. The research leading to these results has received funding from the European Research Council under the European Union's Seventh Framework Programme (FP7/2007-2013) / ERC Grant agreement no. 291389.

References

1. Bono, V., Messa, C., Padovani, L.: Typing copyless message passing. In: Barthe, G. (ed.) ESOP 2011. LNCS, vol. 6602, pp. 57–76. Springer, Heidelberg (2011)
2. Brightwell, R.: Exploiting direct access shared memory for MPI on multi-core processors. International Journal of High Performance Computing Applications 24(1), 69–77 (2010)
3. Bull, J.M., Enright, J.P., Guo, X., Maynard, C., Reid, F.: Performance evaluation of mixed-mode OpenMP/MPI implementations. International Journal of Parallel Programming 38(5-6), 396–417 (2010)
4. Buntinas, D., Mercier, G., Gropp, W.: Implementation and evaluation of shared-memory communication and synchronization operations in MPICH2 using the Nemesis communication subsystem. Parallel Computing 33(9), 634–644 (2007)

5. Clavel, M., Durán, F., Eker, S., Lincoln, P., Martí-Oliet, N., Meseguer, J., Talcott, C.: All About Maude - A High-Performance Logical Framework. LNCS, vol. 4350. Springer, Heidelberg (2007)
6. Coulouris, G., Dollimore, J., Kindberg, T., Blair, G.: Distributed Systems: Concepts and Design, 5th edn. Addison-Wesley (2011)
7. Dunn, I.N., Meyer, G.G.: Parallel QR factorization for hybrid message passing/shared memory operation. Journal of the Franklin Institute 338(5), 601–613 (2001)
8. Ericsson: Erlang/OTP system documentation. Tech. rep., Ericsson (2012)
9. ETH Zurich: EVE (2014), https://trac.inf.ethz.ch/trac/meyer/eve/
10. ETH Zurich: SCOOP executable formal specification repository (2014), http://bitbucket.org/bmorandi/
11. Graham, R.L., Shipman, G.M.: MPI support for multi-core architectures: Optimized shared memory collectives. In: Lastovetsky, A., Kechadi, T., Dongarra, J. (eds.) EuroPVM/MPI 2008. LNCS, vol. 5205, pp. 130–140. Springer, Heidelberg (2008)
12. Gruber, O., Boyer, F.: Ownership-based isolation for concurrent actors on multi-core machines. In: Castagna, G. (ed.) ECOOP 2013. LNCS, vol. 7920, pp. 281–301. Springer, Heidelberg (2013)
13. Gustedt, J.: Data handover: Reconciling message passing and shared memory. In: Foundations of Global Computing (2005)
14. Hewitt, C., Bishop, P., Steiger, R.: A universal modular ACTOR formalism for artificial intelligence. In: International Joint Conference on Artificial Intelligence, pp. 235–245 (1973)
15. Hoare, C.A.R.: Communicating Sequential Processes. Prentice Hall (1985)
16. International Organization for Standardization: Ada. Tech. Rep. ISO/IEC 8652:2012, International Organization for Standardization (2012)
17. Jones, D.L.: Decimation-in-time (DIT) radix-2 FFT (2014), http://cnx.org/content/m12016/1.7/
18. Mattson, T.G., Sanders, B.A., Massingill, B.L.: Patterns for Parallel Programming. Addison-Wesley (2004)
19. Message Passing Interface Forum: MPI: A message-passing interface standard. Tech. rep., Message Passing Interface Forum (2012)
20. Meyer, B.: Object-Oriented Software Construction, 2nd edn. Prentice-Hall (1997)
21. Morandi, B., Schill, M., Nanz, S., Meyer, B.: Prototyping a concurrency model. In: International Conference on Application of Concurrency to System Design, pp. 177–186 (2013)
22. Nienaltowski, P.: Practical framework for contract-based concurrent object-oriented programming. Ph.D. thesis, ETH Zurich (2007)
23. OpenMP Architecture Review Board: OpenMP application program interface. Tech. rep., OpenMP Architecture Review Board (2013)
24. Rabenseifner, R., Hager, G., Jost, G.: Hybrid MPI/OpenMP parallel programming on clusters of multi-core SMP nodes. In: Euromicro International Conference on Parallel, Distributed and Network-Based Processing, pp. 427–436 (2009)
25. Schill, M., Nanz, S., Meyer, B.: Handling parallelism in a concurrency model. In: Lourenço, J.M., Farchi, E. (eds.) MUSEPAT 2013 2013. LNCS, vol. 8063, pp. 37–48. Springer, Heidelberg (2013)
26. Villard, J., Lozes, É., Calcagno, C.: Proving copyless message passing. In: Hu, Z. (ed.) APLAS 2009. LNCS, vol. 5904, pp. 194–209. Springer, Heidelberg (2009)

Affine Sessions

Dimitris Mostrous and Vasco Thudichum Vasconcelos

University of Lisbon, Faculty of Sciences and LaSIGE
Lisbon, Portugal

Abstract. Session types describe the structure of protocols from the
point of view of each participating channel. In particular, the types describe the type of communicated values, and also the dynamic alternation
of input and output actions on the same channel, by which a protocol can
be statically verified. Crucial to any term language with session types is
the notion of linearity, which guarantees that channels exhibit exactly
the behaviour prescribed by their type. We relax the condition of linearity to that of affinity, by which channels exhibit at most the behaviour
prescribed by their types. This more liberal setting allows us to incorporate an elegant error handling mechanism which simplifies and improves
related works on exceptions. Moreover, our treatment does not affect the
progress properties of the language: sessions never get stuck.

1 Introduction

A session is "*a semantically atomic chain of communication actions which can
interleave with other such chains freely, for high-level abstraction of interaction-
based computing*" [21]. *Session types* capture this intuition as a description of the
structure of a protocol, in the simplest case between two programs (binary sessions). This description consists of types that indicate whether a communication
channel will next perform an output or input action, the type of the value to send
or receive, and what to do next, inductively. For example, !nat.!string.?bool.end
is the type of a channel that will first send a value of type nat, then one of type
string, then wait for a value of type bool, and nothing more. This type can be
materialised by the π-calculus [19] process $\bar{a}5.\bar{a}$"hello".$a(x).\mathbf{0}$. To compose two
processes that communicate over a channel, we require that each has a comple-
mentary (or *dual*) type, so that an input will match an output, and vice versa.
The dual of the previous type is ?nat.?string.!bool.end, and can be implemented
by $a(x).a(y).\bar{a}(x + 1 < 2).\mathbf{0}$. To ensure that the actions take place in the prescribed order, session typing relies crucially on the notion of *linearity* [12], which
means that a causal chain can be assumed. To see why, imagine that we write the
first process as $\bar{a}5.\mathbf{0} \mid \bar{a}$"hello".$a(x).\mathbf{0}$. Now we cannot determine which output
can react first, and the second process can receive a "hello" first, which would
clearly be unsound and would most likely raise an error.

Beyond the basic input/output types, sessions typically provide constructors
for alternative sub-protocols, which are very useful for structured interaction.
For example, & {go: T_1, cancel: T_2} can be assigned to an (external) choice $a \triangleright$

E. Kühn and R. Pugliese (Eds.): COORDINATION 2014, LNCS 8459, pp. 115–130, 2014.
© IFIP International Federation for Information Processing 2014

$\{go.P_1 \,[\![\, cancel.P_2\}$. The dual type, where $\overline{T}$ denotes T with an alternation of all constructors, is $\oplus\{go: \overline{T_1}, cancel: \overline{T_2}\}$, and corresponds to a process that will make a (internal) choice, either $\overline{a} \triangleleft go.Q_1$ or $\overline{a} \triangleleft cancel.Q_2$. In the first case the two processes will continue as P_1 and Q_1, respectively.

As can be seen, sessions are very suitable as a static verification mechanism for interacting programs. However, they are also quite rigid, since everything in the description of a session type *must* be implemented by a program with that type. Indeed, in many real world situations, interactions are structured but can be aborted at any time, for example an online store should be prepared for clients that get disconnected, that close their web browsers, or for general *errors* that abruptly severe the expected pattern of interaction.

In this work, we address the above issues. In technical terms, we relax the condition of linearity to that of *affinity*, inspired by Affine Logic (which is the variation of Linear Logic with unrestricted weakening; see [2] for an introduction), and this allows processes to terminate their sessions prematurely. However, a naive introduction of affinity can leave programs in a stuck state: let us re-write the first process into $\overline{a}5.\overline{a}$"hello".**0**, i.e., without the final input; then, after two communications the dual process will be stuck trying to perform $\overline{a}(5+1<2).\mathbf{0}$. One of the basic tenets of sessions, *progress*, is now lost. Actually, the study of Proof Nets for Affine Logic [2] reveals that weakening is not, and should not be, invisible. In particular, there exists a device that will perform the weakening step by step, progressing through the dependencies of a proof, and removing all that must be removed. This is exactly what we need in order to handle an abrupt termination of an interaction in an explicit way, and we denote it by $a\xi$, which reads *cancel a*. Now we can write $\overline{a}5.\overline{a}$"hello".$a\xi$, and after two steps against the dual process we obtain $\overline{a}(5 + 1 < 2).\mathbf{0} \mid a\xi$, which results in the cancellation of the output (and in general, of any subsequent actions on a). We take this idea a step further: if cancellation of a session is explicit, we can treat it as an *exception*, and for this we introduce a *do-catch* construct that can provide an alternative behaviour activated when a cancellation is encountered. For example, we can write do $\overline{a}(5 + 1 < 2).\mathbf{0}$ catch P, and a composition with $a\xi$ will *replace* $\overline{a}(5 + 1 < 2).\mathbf{0}$ with the exception handler P. A do-catch is not the same as the try-catch commonly found in sequential languages: it does not define a persistent scope that captures exceptions from the inside, but rather it applies to the first communication and is activated by exceptions from the outside (as in the previous example). Thus, do $\overline{a}(5 + 1 < 2).\mathbf{0}$ catch P in parallel to $a(x).\mathbf{0}$ becomes **0**, because the communication was successful.

2   Affine Sessions by Example

We describe a simple interaction that implements a book purchase taking place between three processes, Buyer, Seller, and Bank. The buyer sends the title of a book, receives the price, and makes a choice to either buy it or cancel. If the buyer chooses to buy the book, the credit card is sent over the session, and the buyer is informed whether or not the transaction was successful. The diagram in Figure 1 shows the interactions of a specific purchase.

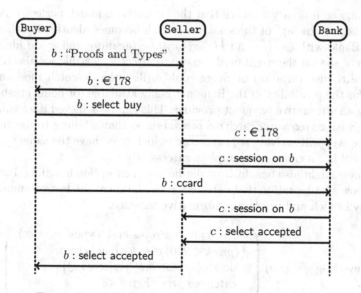

Fig. 1. Sequence Diagram for Succesful Book Purchase

We now show how this scenario can be implemented using sessions, and how our treatment of affinity can be used to enable a more concise and natural handling of exceptional outcomes. Our language is an almost standard π-calculus where replication is written acc $a(x).P$ and plays the role of "accept" in sessions terminology [15]. Dually, an output that activates a replication is written req $\overline{a}b.P$, and is called a "request". We will use some standard contructs that are encodable in π-calculus, like $\overline{a}e$ for an expression e. Also, we use if t then P else Q that can be implemented by a new session, specifically $a \triangleright \{true.P \;[]\; false.Q\}$ against some process representing the test t that communicates the result by a selection of one of the labels, $\overline{a} \triangleleft true$ or $\overline{a} \triangleleft false$.

An implementation of the protocol we described in Figure 1 is shown below:

$$\text{Buyer} \doteq (\boldsymbol{\nu}b) \left(\begin{array}{l} \text{req } \overline{seller}\,b \mid \overline{b}\,\text{``Proofs and Types''}.b(price).\text{if } (price < 200) \\ \text{then } \overline{b} \triangleleft \text{buy}.\overline{b}\,\text{ccard}.b \triangleright \{\text{accepted}.P \;[]\; \text{rejected}.Q\} \text{ else } \overline{b} \triangleleft \text{cancel} \end{array} \right)$$

$$\text{Seller} \doteq \text{acc } seller(s). \left(\begin{array}{l} s(prod).\overline{s}\,price(prod). \\ s \triangleright \{\text{buy}.(\boldsymbol{\nu}c)(\text{req } \overline{bank}\,c \mid \overline{c}\,price(prod).\overline{c}s.c(r). \\ \quad c \triangleright \{\text{accepted}.\overline{r} \triangleleft \text{accepted} \;[]\; \text{rejected}.\overline{r} \triangleleft \text{rejected}\}) \\ \;[]\; \text{cancel}.0\} \end{array} \right)$$

$$\text{Bank} \doteq \text{acc } bank(k). \left(\begin{array}{l} k(amount).k(r).r(card).\overline{k}r. \\ \text{if charge}(amount, card) \text{ then } \overline{k} \triangleleft \text{accepted else } \overline{k} \triangleleft \text{rejected} \end{array} \right)$$

First we note how sessions are established. For example, in Buyer the fresh name b is sent to Seller via the request req $\overline{seller}\,b$, where it will substitute s in a copy of the replication, and it appears also locally. These are the two endpoints of the session, and it is easy to check that the interactions match perfectly. Another point is the "borrowing" of the session b (which becomes identified with s) from Seller to Bank, with $\bar{c}s.c(r)$ and $k(r).r(card).\bar{k}r$ (again, c and k are identified), respectively, so that the credit card is received directly by Bank; see also Figure 1.

A more robust variation of Seller could utilise the do-catch mechanism to account for the possibility of the Bank not being available (or being crashed), by providing an alternative payment provider. This can be achieved if we substitute req $\overline{bank}c$ with do req $\overline{bank}c$ catch req $\overline{paymate}c$, so that a failure to use the bank service ($bank\!\!\!/$) will activate req $\overline{paymate}c$ (which must have the same type) and the protocol has a chance to complete successfully.

The Buyer might also benefit from our notion of exception handling. For example, we show an adaptation that catches a cancellation at the last communication of the buy branch and prints an informative message:

$$
\text{BuyerMsg} \doteq (\nu b)
\left(
\begin{array}{l}
\text{req } \overline{seller}\,b \mid \bar{b}\text{"Proofs and Types"}.b(price). \\
\text{if } (price < 200) \text{ then } \bar{b} \lhd \text{buy}.\bar{b}\,\text{ccard.} \\
\quad \text{do } b \rhd \{\text{accepted}.P \;[]\; \text{rejected}.Q\} \\
\quad \text{catch req } \overline{print}\text{"Error 42"} \\
\text{else } \bar{b} \lhd \text{cancel}
\end{array}
\right)
$$

As mentioned in the Introduction, a do-catch on some communication does not catch subsequent cancellations. For instance, if in the above example the do-catch was placed on $\bar{b}$"Proofs and Types", then any $b\!\!\!/$ generated *after* this output was performed would be uncaught, since req $\overline{print}$"Error 42" would have been already discarded. However, a do-catch does catch cancellations emitted *before* the point of definition, so placing it near the end of a protocol is very useful if we just want a single exception handler that catches everything.

Indeed, exception handlers that persist for the lifetime of the whole session are definable. Specifically, we can write try P catch $(b\colon Q)$ to mean that one endpoint of b is implemented in P and that Q should be activated if b is canceled at *any* point from the *outside* of P. This try-catch notation translates to a do-catch on the last prefix on b in P, in multiple branches as required, assuming that b is not delegated (i.e., sent over another channel), as is the case in BuyerMsg.[1] Then we have, for example, that try $\bar{b}5.P'$ catch $(b\colon Q) \mid b(x).\mathbf{0}$ becomes try P' catch $(b\colon Q)$ and try $\bar{b}5.P'$ catch $(b\colon Q) \mid b\!\!\!/$ becomes $P'' \mid Q$ where P'' is P' with b and all its dependencies canceled. In general, however, our mechanism is very fine-grained, and a single session can have multiple, nested do-catch on crucial points of communication.

Note also that $a\!\!\!/$ can be very useful in itself, even without the do-catch mechanism. Here are two ways to implement a process that starts a protocol with Seller only to check the price of a book:

---

[1] We assume that in BuyerMsg P and Q do not use b. The restriction to non-delegated sessions is for simplicity: if the last action on b was to send it over some channel k, e.g., using $\bar{k}b$, the encoding would be more complicated, because we would not have access to the end of the session and anything after that output would not be caught.

CheckPriceA $\doteq$ $(\nu b)\,(\,\mathsf{req}\ \overline{seller}\,b\mid \overline{b}\,\text{``The Prince''}.b(price).(\overline{b}\triangleleft\mathsf{cancel}\mid R)\,)$

CheckPriceB $\doteq$ $(\nu b)\,(\,\mathsf{req}\ \overline{seller}\,b\mid \overline{b}\,\text{``Beyond Good and Evil''}.b(price).(b\lightning\mid R)\,)$

Both the above processes can be typed. However, the first requires a knowledge of the protocol, which in that case includes an exit point (branch cancel), while the second is completely transparent. For example, imagine a buyer that selects buy by accident and then wishes to cancel the purchase: without cancellation it is impossible because it is not *predicted* by the session type; with cancellation it is extremely simple, as shown below.

BuyerCancel $\doteq$ $(\nu b)\,(\,\mathsf{req}\ \overline{seller}\,b\mid \overline{b}\,\text{``Gödel, Escher, Bach''}.b(price).\overline{b}\triangleleft\mathsf{buy}.b\lightning\,)$

We now make a small digression to discuss how our affine sessions can be encoded in standard sessions. The purpose is to shed light on the complexity that is required, which motivates even more our development. First of all, it is possible that both endpoints of a session emit a cancellation, possibly at different moments. Therefore, if we are to encode this behaviour in a standard session system, we must allow a protocol to end at any point and by the request of either of the participants. This can be achieved by an exchange of a decision, to go or to cancel, by both endpoints, before all communications. We show the translation for output and input; the rest is similar.

$$[\![!T_1.T_2]\!]\ \doteq\ \oplus\left\{\begin{array}{l}\mathsf{go}:\&\,\{\mathsf{go}:!T_1.[\![T_2]\!],\mathsf{cancel}:\mathsf{end}\},\\ \mathsf{cancel}:\&\,\{\mathsf{go}:\mathsf{end},\mathsf{cancel}:\mathsf{end}\}\end{array}\right\} \qquad \begin{array}{l}[\![?T_1.T_2]\!]\doteq\overline{[\![!T_1.\overline{T_2}]\!]}\\[6pt][\![\mathsf{end}]\!]\doteq\mathsf{end}\end{array}$$

The notable point is that by an alternation of constructors we obtain a translation that preserves duality, and it is easy to check that it preserves soundness. Moreover, the only way to proceed is if both ends agree to go. The term-level translation follows the structure of the types, and $a\lightning$ becomes $\overline{a}\triangleleft\mathsf{cancel}$. All free sessions in the term must be canceled in the branches that do not result in normal execution so as to obtain the same typing environment, but this is always possible.

The above translation only handles cancellation. Our do-catch mechanism can also be encoded within the branches of the previous translation, but it becomes quite complicated due to the typing contraints that must be respected. In any case, we think it is obvious that the burden is heavy if one wishes to obtain a functionality as general as the one available in the affine system, and types would become completely illegible from the multiplication of constructors.

3   The Process Calculus of Affine Sessions

Syntax. Our language is a small extension of standard π-calculus [19]. With respect to standard sessions systems [11,22], we avoid the need for *polarities* and *double binders* by carefully introducing a logically-founded typing principle, detailed later. For technical convenience we shall consider all indexing sets I

to be totally ordered, so that we can speak, e.g., of the maximum element. Also for technical convenience, we separate the prefixes denoted by ρ, i.e., all communication actions except for accept (replication). We only added two non-standard constructs: the *cancellation* $a\notz$ and the *do-catch* construct that captures a cancellation, denoted by $\mathsf{do}\,\rho\,\mathsf{catch}\,P$. Notice that we restricted the action to a prefix in ρ, but this is not so limiting. In the case of replication, it does not make sense to catch an event that never occurs, since as we shall see we never explicitly cancel a persistent service. For parallel composition, it would be ambiguous to allow $\mathsf{do}\,(P \mid Q)\,\mathsf{catch}\,R$ since more than one action can be active in $(P \mid Q)$, and moreover we do not think it would really add any benefit since we can add a separate do-catch for each session. Similarly, $\mathsf{do}\,a\notz\,\mathsf{catch}\,P$ would be strange: it would allow to trigger some behaviour when the other end is canceled, but while at the same time the protected session is canceled too. It can be added if a good use is discovered, but we preferred to keep the semantics simpler.

$$
\begin{array}{lll}
\rho ::= & a(x\colon T).P & \text{(input)} \\
\mid & \bar{a}b.P & \text{(output)} \\
\mid & a \vartriangleright \{l_i.P_i\}_{i\in I} & \text{(branching)} \\
\mid & \bar{a} \vartriangleleft l_k.P & \text{(selection)} \\
\mid & \mathsf{req}\,\bar{a}b.P & \text{(request)}
\end{array}
$$

$$
\begin{array}{lll}
P ::= & \rho & \text{(prefix)} \\
\mid & \mathsf{acc}\,a(x\colon T).P & \text{(replicated accept)} \\
\mid & \mathbf{0} & \text{(nil)} \\
\mid & P \mid Q & \text{(parallel)} \\
\mid & (\nu a\colon T)P & \text{(restriction)} \\
\mid & a\notz & \text{(cancel)} \\
\mid & \mathsf{do}\,\rho\,\mathsf{catch}\,P & \text{(catch)}
\end{array}
$$

Structural Congruence. With $\equiv$ we denote the least congruence on processes that is an equivalence relation, equates processes up to α-conversion, satisfies the abelian monoid laws for parallel composition, the usual laws for scope extrusion, and satisfies the axiom:

$$(\nu a\colon T)(a\notz \mid \cdots \mid a\notz) \equiv \mathbf{0}$$

We added this axiom mainly for the left-to-right direction which allows "leftover" cancellations to disappear; this is convenient for technical reasons.

Reduction. We use two kinds of contexts, $C[\,]$ which are standard, and $H[\,]$ for (possible) exception handling, defined below.

$$
\begin{array}{ll}
\textit{Standard Contexts}: & C[\cdot] ::= \cdot \mid (C[\cdot] \mid P) \mid (\nu a\colon T)\,C[\cdot] \\
\textit{Do-Catch Contexts}: & H[\cdot] ::= \cdot \mid \mathsf{do}\,\cdot\,\mathsf{catch}\,P
\end{array}
$$

Reduction is defined in two parts, first the standard rules, and then the cancellation rules. The standard reductions are defined below:

$$H_1[\overline{a}b.P] \mid H_2[a(x\colon T).Q] \longrightarrow P \mid Q\{^b/x\} \qquad\qquad\qquad \text{(R-Com)}$$

$$H_1[\overline{a} \triangleleft l_k.P] \mid H_2[a \triangleright \{l_i.Q_i\}_{i \in I}] \longrightarrow P \mid Q_k \qquad (k \in I) \qquad\qquad \text{(R-Bra)}$$

$$H[\,\mathsf{req}\ \overline{a}b.P\,] \mid \mathsf{acc}\ a(x\colon T).Q \longrightarrow P \mid Q\{^b/x\} \mid \mathsf{acc}\ a(x\colon T).Q \qquad \text{(R-Ses)}$$

$$P \equiv P' \longrightarrow Q' \equiv Q \ \Rightarrow\ P \longrightarrow Q \qquad\qquad\qquad\quad \text{(R-Str)}$$

$$P \longrightarrow Q \ \Rightarrow\ C[P] \longrightarrow C[Q] \qquad\qquad\qquad\qquad\quad \text{(R-Ctx)}$$

The only notable point is that we discard any do-catch handlers, since there is no cancellation, which explains why the H-contexts disappear.

The cancellation reductions follow:

$$\mathsf{req}\ \overline{a}b.P \mid a \lightning \longrightarrow a \lightning \mid b \lightning \mid P \qquad\qquad\qquad\qquad \text{(C-Req)}$$

$$\overline{a}b.P \mid a \lightning \longrightarrow a \lightning \mid b \lightning \mid P \qquad\qquad\qquad\qquad\quad \text{(C-Out)}$$

$$a(x\colon T).P \mid a \lightning \longrightarrow (\boldsymbol{\nu} x\colon T)(a \lightning \mid x \lightning \mid P) \qquad\qquad \text{(C-Inp)}$$

$$\overline{a} \triangleleft l_k.P \mid a \lightning \longrightarrow P \mid a \lightning \qquad\qquad\qquad\qquad\quad\ \text{(C-Sel)}$$

$$a \triangleright \{l_i.P_i\}_{i \in I} \mid a \lightning \longrightarrow P_k \mid a \lightning \qquad \max(I) = k \qquad \text{(C-Bra)}$$

$$\mathsf{do}\ \rho\ \mathsf{catch}\ P \mid a \lightning \longrightarrow P \mid a \lightning \qquad \mathsf{subject}(\rho) = a \qquad \text{(C-Cat)}$$

We discuss some notable points.

Only what is strictly needed will be deleted, in particular one might have expected $a(x\colon T).P \mid a \lightning$ to result in the annihilation of P, which can be done by generating $b \lightning$ for each b in the free names of P. However, this has several drawbacks: first, it is too absolute, since some interactions in P may not depend on a or x, and we prefer to preserve them; second, it is technically simpler, since in this setting we can use typing restrictions to avoid the creation of any $b \lightning$ for a replication $\mathsf{acc}\ b(x).Q$ inside P, which follows our decision to never delete services; finally, it is what happens in Proof Nets for Affine Logic (see [2]).

In the cancellation of branching, (C-Bra), we choose the maximum index k which exists by our assumption that index sets are totally ordered. This is a simple way to avoid non-determinism solely by cancellation.[2] Notice that it follows the pattern of activating a continuation, motivated above.

In the rule (C-Cat), we use a function $\mathsf{subject}(\rho)$ which returns the subject in the prefix of ρ. This is defined in the obvious way, e.g., $\mathsf{subject}(\overline{a}b.P) = \mathsf{subject}(\mathsf{req}\ \overline{a}b.P) = a$, and similarly for the other cases. The typing system will ensure that a does not appear in P, so it is ok to leave $a \lightning$ in the result; this is needed for canceled requests, where the $a \lightning$ should remain until it reacts with all of them.

---

[2] The language remains confluent, as expected in a logically founded system.

We clarify some of the main points:

i) Consider $a(x).(Q \mid \mathsf{acc}\, b(z).R) \mid a\lightning$. The replication provided on b may or may not depend on x. A cancellation of a does not necessarily mean that b will be affected, but if x appears in R it is possible that subsequent sessions will be canceled.

ii) Consider $a(x).(\mathsf{acc}\, x(z).Q \mid \bar{b}x.R) \mid a\lightning$. As can be seen, the replicated channel x is delegated on b, and it should not be deleted just because a is canceled. Indeed, this situation is not allowed by the restrictions in our type system. In other words, some sessions *cannot* be canceled.

iii) Consider $a(x).(Q \mid \bar{b}e.R) \mid a\lightning$. The session output $\bar{b}e.R$ will not be canceled, but since it is possible that $e = x$ and in general e could appear in R, other cancellations may eventually be generated.

iv) A communication discards any handlers: do $\bar{a}b.P$ catch $Q \mid a(x:T).R \longrightarrow P \mid R\{^b/x\}$. The type system ensures that it is sound to discard Q, since it contains the same sessions as $\bar{a}b.P$, except for a.

v) A cancellation activates a handler, which may provide some default values to a session, completing it or eventually re-throwing a cancellation, as in: do $\bar{a}b.P$ catch $(\bar{b}5.b\lightning) \mid a\lightning \longrightarrow \bar{b}5.b\lightning \mid a\lightning$.

4   Typing Affine Sessions

Types. The session types we use are standard [15] with two exceptions. First, following [22] we allow a session type to evolve into a shared type. Second, we decompose shared types into accept types $\mathsf{acc}\, T$ and request types $\mathsf{req}\, T$, following the logical principles of Affine Logic. Technically, $\mathsf{acc}\, T$ corresponds to $!T$ ("of course T") and $\mathsf{req}\, T$ to $?\overline{T}$ ("why not $\overline{T}$") [12]. This has several technical advantages that simplify our development, for example $\mathsf{acc}\, T$ retains information on the persistence of a term with that type, since it must be replicated, which is useful for typing. Moreover, $\mathsf{req}\, T$ is the only type allowed in the context of a resource that can be used zero or more times.

$$
\begin{array}{llll}
T ::= & \mathsf{end} & & \text{(nothing)} \\
& \mid\ !T.T & & \text{(output)} \\
& \mid\ ?T.T & & \text{(input)} \\
& \mid\ \oplus\{l_i : T_i\}_{i \in I} & & \text{(selection)} \\
& \mid\ \&\{l_i : T_i\}_{i \in I} & & \text{(branching)} \\
& \mid\ \mathsf{req}\, T & & \text{(request)} \\
& \mid\ \mathsf{acc}\, T & & \text{(accept)}
\end{array}
$$

Duality. The two ends of a session are composed when their types are *dual*, which is defined as an involution over the type constructors, similarly to Linear Logic's negation except that end is self-dual.[3]

$$\overline{!T_1.T_2} \doteq ?T_1.\overline{T_2} \qquad \overline{?T_1.T_2} \doteq !T_1.\overline{T_2}$$

$$\overline{\oplus \{l_i : T_i\}_{i \in I}} \doteq \& \{l_i : \overline{T_i}\}_{i \in I} \qquad \overline{\& \{l_i : T_i\}_{i \in I}} \doteq \oplus \{l_i : \overline{T_i}\}_{i \in I}$$

$$\overline{\text{req } T} \doteq \text{acc } T \qquad \overline{\text{acc } T} \doteq \text{req } T \qquad \overline{\text{end}} \doteq \text{end}$$

Typing Rules. Typing judgements take the form:

$$P \triangleright \Gamma \qquad \text{where} \qquad \Gamma ::= \emptyset \mid \Gamma, a : T$$

meaning that term P has interface Γ. We shall also use Γ, Δ, Θ for interfaces.

We restrict replications to be unique, but allow multiple requests to take place against them. This means that processes can have multiple uses of $a : \text{req } T$, which corresponds to the logical principle of contraction. For this, we make use of the splitting relation from [22]:

$$\overline{\emptyset = \emptyset \circ \emptyset} \qquad \frac{\Gamma = \Gamma_1 \circ \Gamma_2}{\Gamma, a : \text{req } T = (\Gamma_1, a : \text{req } T) \circ (\Gamma_2, a : \text{req } T)}$$

$$\frac{\Gamma = \Gamma_1 \circ \Gamma_2}{\Gamma, a : T = (\Gamma_1, a : T) \circ \Gamma_2} \qquad \frac{\Gamma = \Gamma_1 \circ \Gamma_2}{\Gamma, a : T = \Gamma_1 \circ (\Gamma_2, a : T)}$$

In the typing rules, req Γ stands for an interface of the shape $a_1 : \text{req } T_1, \ldots, a_n : \text{req } T_n$. Similarly, end Γ stands for an interface $a_1 : \text{end}, \ldots, a_n : \text{end}$.

We also define a predicate no-requests(T), used to forbid any request type from appearing in the type of $a \xi$, since this maps by duality to the deletion of a persistent accept on the other side, which we do not allow.[4]

$$\text{no-requests}(\text{req } T) = \text{false}$$

$$\text{no-requests}(\text{acc } T) = \text{no-requests}(T) \qquad \text{no-requests}(\text{end}) = \text{true}$$

$$\text{no-requests}(!T_1.T_2) = \text{no-requests}(\overline{T_1}) \wedge \text{no-requests}(T_2)$$

$$\text{no-requests}(?T_1.T_2) = \text{no-requests}(T_1) \wedge \text{no-requests}(T_2)$$

$$\text{no-requests}(\oplus \{l_i : S_i\}_{i \in I}) = \text{no-requests}(\& \{l_i : S_i\}_{i \in I}) = \wedge_{i \in I} \text{no-requests}(S_i)$$

The typing rules are presented in Figure 2. We focus on some key points. First, we type modulo structural equivalence, a possibility suggested by [18] and used in [4]. This is because associativity of " | " does not preserve typability, i.e.,

---

[3] The expert might notice that logical negation suggests a dualisation of all components, e.g., $\overline{!T.T'} \doteq ?\overline{T}.\overline{T}'$ In fact the output type $!T.T'$ and the request req T hide a duality on T, effected by the type system, so everything is compatible.

[4] This method works fine until one adds a second-order fragment: then type substitutions must be carefully controlled, or some results will become slightly weaker.

(Out)
$$\frac{P \,\triangleright\, \Gamma, a : T_2}{\overline{a}b.P \,\triangleright\, (\Gamma, a : !T_1.T_2) \circ b : T_1}$$

(In)
$$\frac{P \,\triangleright\, \Gamma, x : T_1, a : T_2}{a(x : T_1).P \,\triangleright\, \Gamma, a : ?T_1.T_2}$$

(Sel)
$$\frac{P \,\triangleright\, \Gamma, a : T_k \qquad k \in I}{\overline{a} \triangleleft l_k.P \,\triangleright\, \Gamma, a : \oplus \{l_i : T_i\}_{i \in I}}$$

(Bra)
$$\frac{\forall i \in I \,.\, P_i \,\triangleright\, \Gamma, a : T_i \qquad I \neq \emptyset}{a \triangleright \{l_i.P_i\}_{i \in I} \,\triangleright\, \Gamma, a : \& \{l_i : T_i\}_{i \in I}}$$

(Req)
$$\frac{P \,\triangleright\, \Gamma}{\mathsf{req}\ \overline{a}b.P \,\triangleright\, \Gamma \circ a : \mathsf{req}\ T \circ b : T}$$

(Acc)
$$\frac{P \,\triangleright\, \mathsf{req}\ \Gamma, x : T}{\mathsf{acc}\ a(x : T).P \,\triangleright\, \mathsf{req}\ \Gamma, a : \mathsf{acc}\ T}$$

(Par)
$$\frac{P \,\triangleright\, \Gamma_1 \qquad Q \,\triangleright\, \Gamma_2}{P \mid Q \,\triangleright\, \Gamma_1 \circ \Gamma_2}$$

(ParSes)
$$\frac{P \,\triangleright\, \Gamma_1, a : \mathsf{acc}\ T \qquad Q \,\triangleright\, \Gamma_2, a : \mathsf{req}\ T}{P \mid Q \,\triangleright\, (\Gamma_1 \circ \Gamma_2), a : \mathsf{acc}\ T}$$

(Res)
$$\frac{P \,\triangleright\, \Gamma_1, a : T \qquad Q \,\triangleright\, \Gamma_2, a : \overline{T}}{(\boldsymbol{\nu} a : T)(P \mid Q) \,\triangleright\, \Gamma_1 \circ \Gamma_2}$$

(Str)
$$\frac{Q \,\triangleright\, \Gamma \qquad Q \equiv P}{P \,\triangleright\, \Gamma}$$

(Nil)
$$\overline{0 \,\triangleright\, \mathsf{req}\ \Gamma, \mathsf{end}\ \Delta}$$

(Catch)
$$\frac{\rho \,\triangleright\, \Gamma, a : T \qquad P \,\triangleright\, \Gamma \qquad \mathsf{subject}(\rho) = a}{\mathsf{do}\ \rho\ \mathsf{catch}\ P \,\triangleright\, \Gamma, a : T}$$

(Cancel)
$$\frac{\mathsf{no\text{-}requests}(T)}{a \lightning \,\triangleright\, a : T}$$

Fig. 2. Affine Session Typing

a composition between P and $(Q \mid R)$ may be untypable as $(P \mid Q) \mid R$; see (ParSes), (Res). This applies also to $(\boldsymbol{\nu} a)$ that causes similar problems. In fact, the splitting of the terms in (Res) is inspired by the work [4] which interprets sessions as propositions in a form of Intuitionistic Linear Logic. It is because of this separation of terms, which applies also to (ParSes), that we can avoid channel polarities: the two ends of a session can never become causally dependent or intermixed. The purpose of (ParSes) is to type multiple requests against a persistent accept, which explains why $a : \mathsf{acc}\ T$ remains in the conclusion. An output $\overline{a}b.P$ records a conclusion $b : T_1$, so in fact it will compose against $b : \overline{T_1}$. Therefore $!T_1.T_2$ really means "send $\overline{T_1}$," which matches with the dual input. A cancellation $a \lightning$ can be given any type that does not contain a request, as explained previously.

A do-catch is typed as follows: if ρ is an action on a and has an interface $\Gamma, a : T$, then the handler P will implement Γ, i.e., all sessions of ρ *except* for $a : T$ which has been canceled. Of course, inside P these other sessions can be canceled anyway, which corresponds to "re-throwing" the cancellation, but they can also be implemented in whole or in part. The rule is sound, since no session is damaged, irrespectively of which term we execute, ρ or P.

Motivating the "no requests" Restriction on the Type of $a \lightning$. There are pragmatic motivations behind our decision to not allow cancellation of replicated terms, namely that we do not wish a request to cancel a service possibly shared by many processes. However, there are also technical challenges, stemming from the fact that multiple actions of type a: req T can appear in a well-typed term, which as we explain below can create ambiguity in cancellation reductions.

Let us assume that the no-requests(T) restriction was lifted. Now, as an example consider the composition req $\overline{a}b.P \mid a\frac{\prime}{} \mid \overline{c}a.Q \mid c(x).\text{acc } x(y).R$. First, let us look at the underlined term: it is impossible to know what is the type of $a\frac{\prime}{}$, as it could be either acc T or req T. If the type is acc T, which means that the (dual) accept is canceled, we should apply cancellation to req $\overline{a}b.P$; if the type is req T, i.e., if $a\frac{\prime}{}$ is in fact the cancellation of another request, then we should not touch req $\overline{a}b.P$. In our example, it is easy to check that the replication will appear after a communication on c so the type of $a\frac{\prime}{}$ must be req T, but in general it is not possible to determine this information (again, consider just the underlined term). Our restriction on the type of $a\frac{\prime}{}$ ensures that, in a case like the underlined term above, we can be sure that the type cannot be req T, so it must be acc T and we can proceed to cancel req $\overline{a}b.P$ using (C-Req). Indeed, the full composition is not typable since in that case the type of $a\frac{\prime}{}$ must be req T, and no-requests(req T) is not true. In fact, without our restriction, (C-Req) does not work any more, since it assumes $a\frac{\prime}{}$ to be of type acc T, so we would need to replace it with:

$$(\boldsymbol{\nu} a\colon T)(\textstyle\prod_{i\in I} \text{req } \overline{a}b_i.P_i \mid a\tfrac{\prime}{}) \longrightarrow (\boldsymbol{\nu} a\colon T)(\textstyle\prod_{i\in I}(b_i\tfrac{\prime}{} \mid P_i) \mid a\tfrac{\prime}{}) \qquad \text{(C-Req')}$$

This is the special case in which we know the type of $a\frac{\prime}{}$ must be acc T, since it is bound and all other elements are requests. This variation is more complex, and we would also have to forego the ability to use do-catch on req $\overline{a}b.P$, so we chose not to introduce it. Even if we did use this seemingly more liberal system, we would anyway not want replications to be deleted, so it would be of limited value. The only advantage of this alternative solution is that it does not put restrictions on the shape of types assigned to $a\frac{\prime}{}$, and therefore it works also with polymorphism (i.e., a second-order setting).

Typing the Book Purchase Example

It is easy to verify that the examples from Section 2 are well-typed. For the Buyer we obtain the following (for some req Γ_1 and end Δ_1):

$$\text{Buyer} \triangleright \text{req } \Gamma_1, \text{end } \Delta_1, seller\colon \text{req } T_1$$

with $\overline{T_1} = \text{!string.?double.}\oplus \left\{ \begin{array}{l} \text{buy}\colon \text{!string.\& } \{\text{accepted}\colon \text{end}, \text{rejected}\colon \text{end}\}, \\ \text{cancel}\colon \text{end} \end{array} \right\}.$

The type $\overline{T_1}$ is the behaviour of b inside Buyer.

For the Seller we obtain:

$$\text{Seller} \triangleright \text{req } \Gamma_2, bank\colon \text{req } T_2, seller\colon \text{acc } T_1$$

with $T_2 = \text{?double.?(?string.}T_3).!T_3.T_3)$ and $T_3 = \oplus\{\text{accepted}\colon \text{end}, \text{rejected}\colon \text{end}\}.$

For the Bank we obtain:

$$\text{Bank} \triangleright \text{req } \Gamma_3, \text{bank: acc } T_2$$

Interestingly, no type structure is needed for the affine adaptations: cancellation is completely transparent. The variation of Seller with an added do-catch, do req $\overline{bank}\,c$ catch req $\overline{paymate}\,c$, will simply need $paymate$: req T_2 in its interface, i.e., with a type matching that of $bank$, but the original Seller can also be typed in the same way by weakening. Similarly, BuyerMsg has the same interface as Buyer, except that it must include $print$: req string, and again the two processes can be assigned the same interface by weakening, if needed. The processes Check-PriceA, CheckPriceB, and BuyerCancel can be assigned the same type for $seller$, namely req T_1, exactly like Buyer.

Finally, as we shall see next affinity does not destroy any of the good properties we expect to obtain with session typing.

5 Properties

Typed terms enjoy the expected soundness properties. In particular we have:

Lemma 1 (Substitution). *If $P \triangleright \Gamma$ and $a \notin dom(\Gamma)$ then $Q\{a/b\} \triangleright \Gamma\{a/b\}$.*

Theorem 1 (Subject Reduction). *If $P \triangleright \Gamma$ and $P \longrightarrow Q$ then $Q \triangleright \Gamma$.*

Proof. The proof relies on several results including Lemma 1. The non-standard case is for cancellations and in particular for do ρ catch $P \mid Q$. However, it can be easily checked that the substitution of ρ by P is sound, because both terms offer the same interface except for the canceled session (and dually P can be thrown away in standard communication).

Theorem 2 (Diamond property). *If $P \triangleright \Gamma$ and $Q_1 \longleftarrow P \longrightarrow Q_2$ then either $Q_1 \equiv Q_2$ or $Q_1 \longrightarrow R \longleftarrow Q_2$.*

Proof. The result is actually easy to establish, since the only critical pairs arise from multiple requests to the same replication or to the same cancellation. However, even in that case the theorem holds because: a) replications are immediately available and functional (*uniform availability*); b) cancellations are persistent. The fact that $a\frac{\iota}{}$ can never be assigned req T simplifies the proof.

The above strong confluence property indicates that our sessions are completely deterministic, even considering the possible orderings of requests.

Progress

Our contribution to the theory of session types is *well-behaved affinity*, in the sense that we can guarantee that any session that ends prematurely will not affect the quality of a program. Indeed, if we simply allowed unrestricted weakening, for example by a type rule $\Gamma \vdash \mathbf{0}$ as done in [13], but without any apparatus at the language level, it would be easy to type a process such as $(\boldsymbol{\nu}a)\overline{a}b.P \mid b(x).Q$ and clearly not only a but also b would be stuck for ever. In this section we prove that this never happens to a well-typed term.

Let us write λ for a prefix ρ that is not a request, i.e., such that $\rho \neq \mathsf{req}\,\overline{a}b.P$.

Proposition 1. *If* $P \triangleright \Gamma$ *and* $P \equiv (\boldsymbol{\nu}\widetilde{a})(H[\lambda] \mid Q)$ *and* subject$(\lambda) = b$ *and* $b \in \mathsf{fn}(Q)$ *then* $b \in \widetilde{a}$.

This is proved very easily by induction on typing derivations.

We now define a notion of permanently blocked process, which intuitively is a process that cannot proceed in *any* context, either because of deadlock or because of (restricted) sessions without a dual. We will use the fact that linear communications are always under the corresponding bound name, from Proposition 1. As usual $P \not\rightarrow$ means that P cannot reduce.

Definition 1 (Blocked process). *A process* P *is* blocked *if* $P \not\rightarrow$ *and:*

$$P \equiv (\boldsymbol{\nu}\widetilde{a}: \widetilde{T})(H_1[\rho_1] \mid \cdots \mid H_n[\rho_n]) \qquad n \geq 1 \quad \forall i \in \{1, \ldots, n\}\,.\,subject(\rho_i) \in \{\widetilde{a}\}$$

We give some examples to clarify the definition:

i) $\mathsf{req}\,\overline{a}x.\mathsf{req}\,\overline{b}y.P \mid \mathsf{req}\,\overline{b}r.\mathsf{req}\,\overline{a}k.Q$ is not considered blocked since it can reduce properly if we add the appropriate replications.
ii) $(\boldsymbol{\nu}a)(\mathsf{req}\,\overline{a}x.\mathsf{req}\,\overline{b}y.P \mid \mathsf{req}\,\overline{b}r.\mathsf{req}\,\overline{a}k.Q)$ is not considered blocked because we can add a replication $\mathsf{acc}\,b(x).R$ and it will perform one step (before becoming blocked).
iii) both $(\boldsymbol{\nu}a)(\mathsf{req}\,\overline{a}x.\mathsf{req}\,\overline{b}y.P \mid \mathsf{req}\,\overline{a}k.\mathsf{req}\,\overline{b}r.Q)$ and $(\boldsymbol{\nu}a,b)(\mathsf{req}\,\overline{a}x.\mathsf{req}\,\overline{b}y.P \mid \mathsf{req}\,\overline{b}r.\mathsf{req}\,\overline{a}k.Q)$ are blocked, and indeed they have no chance of reducing.
iv) $a(x).\overline{b}y.P \mid b(z).\overline{a}r.Q$ is not considered blocked, even if it can never reduce, but from Proposition 1 we don't need to consider this case.
v) $(\boldsymbol{\nu}a,b,c)(a(x).\overline{b}y.P \mid b(z).\overline{c}r.Q \mid c(s).\overline{a}e.R)$ is blocked; there is a cycle spanning all three sub-processes.
vi) $(\boldsymbol{\nu}a)\overline{a}b.P$ and $(\boldsymbol{\nu}a,b)(\overline{a}b.P \mid b(x).Q)$ are blocked; this is "bad" affinity.
vii) The above examples can be extended with do-catch, which explains the H-contexts in the definition.

We can now present the main result:

Theorem 3 (Progress). *If* $P \triangleright \Gamma$ *then:*

a) for all $Q, C[\ ]$ *such that* $P \equiv C[Q]$, Q *is not blocked.*
b) if $P \not\rightarrow$, *then either* $P \equiv \mathbf{0}$ *or there exists* $Q, \widetilde{a}, \Delta, \Theta$ *with* $Q \triangleright \Delta$ *and* $Q \not\rightarrow$, *such that* $(\boldsymbol{\nu}\widetilde{a})(P \mid Q) \triangleright \Theta$ *and* $(\boldsymbol{\nu}\widetilde{a})(P \mid Q) \longrightarrow$.

Part *a)* is shown by Theorem 1 and with the help of a lemma: if $P \triangleright \Gamma$ then P is not blocked. Part *b)*, which is similar to the formulation in [9], is shown by induction on the type derivation.

The theorem is actually very strong, since it holds also for requests, contrary to related works such as [9] where terms enjoy progress only for the linear part of sessions, i.e., where a request (that may never be activated) can permanently disable any sessions that depend on it.

Moreover, notice that b) in itself is not enough: we could have a blocked subterm in parallel to a request req $\overline{a}_1 b.P'$, then we could iterate compositions with forwarders acc $a_i(x)$.req $\overline{a}_{i+1}x$ and there would always be a reduction. In general, the existence of a "good" Q does not exclude a "bad" one that leads to deadlock. However, from a) we know that there is no subterm that is blocked.

Also, we have not considered circular dependencies for replications; it is easy to check that they cannot lead to deadlock, and actually they cannot be typed.

Finally, we have checked that typed processes are strongly normalising, which is not so surprising since we followed closely the logical principles of Affine Logic. We leave the complete proof of this result, which uses the technique of Reducibility Candidates [12] in conjunction with Theorem 2, to a longer version. Note that Progress (Theorem 3) is in a sense more important, for two reasons: first, a system without progress can still be strongly normalising, since blocked terms are by definition irreducible; second, practical systems typically allow divergence, and in that case the progress property (which we believe can be transferred without surprises to this setting) becomes much more relevant.

6   Related Work and Future Plans

We divide our discussion on the related work in three parts: relaxing linearity in session types, dealing with exceptional behaviour, and logical foundations.

The study of language constructs for exceptional behavior (including exceptional handling and compensation handling) has received significant attention; we refer the reader to a recent overview [10], while concentrating on those works more closely related to ours. Carbone at al. are probably the first to introduce exceptional behaviour in session types [7]. They do so by extending the programming language (the π-calculus) to include a throw primitive and a try-catch process. The language of types is also extended with an abstraction for a try-catch block: essentially a pair of types describing the normal and the exceptional behaviour. The extensions allow communication peers to escape, in a *coordinated* manner, from a dialogue and reach another point from where the protocol may progress. Carbone [6] and Capecchi et al. [5] port these ideas to the multi-party setting. Hu et al. present an extension of multi-party session types that allow to specify conversations that may be interrupted [16]. Towards this end, an interruptible type constructor is added to the type language, requiring types that govern conversations to be designed with the possible interrupt points in mind. In contrast, we propose a model where programs with and without exceptional behaviour are governed by the same (conventional) types, as it is the norm in functional and object-oriented programming languages.

Caires et al. proposed the conversation calculus [23]. The model introduces the idea of conversation context, providing for a simple mechanism to locally handle exceptional conditions. The language supports error recovery via throw and try-catch primitives. No type abstraction is proposed.

Contracts take a different approach by using process-algebra languages [8] or labeled transition systems [3] for describing the communication behaviour of processes. In contrast to session types, where client-service compliance is given by a symmetric duality relation, contracts come equipped with an asymmetric notion of compliance usually requiring that a client and a service reach a successful state. In these works it is possible to end a session (usually on the client side only) prematurely, but there is no mechanism equivalent to our cancellation, no relationship with exception handling, and no clear logical foundations.

Caires and Pfenning gave a Curry-Howard correspondence relating Intuitionistic Linear Logic and session types in a synchronous π-calculus [4]. Although we do not use their types, there is a clear correspondence between $!T_1.T_2$ and $[\![\overline{T_1}]\!] \otimes [\![T_2]\!]$, and similarly for input. The splitting of the term when composing session endpoints, in our case with (Res), which is standard from [1], was never used in sessions before the work [4]. For output (and request) we followed a different but equivalent approach in which b in $\overline{a}b.P$ is free, when in [4] it would be restricted to appear strictly under P. In fact, we did not change anything compared to the usual output rule [15], which shows that a logical system can be obtained from a standard session system simply by an adaptation of (Res) so that it plays the role of a logical "cut."

Indeed, the system we presented can be mildly adapted to obtain an embedding of typed processes to proofs of Affine Logic. In any case, our formulation allows to type more processes than Linear Logic interpretations, and to our knowledge it is the first logical account of exceptions in sessions, based on an original interpretation of weakening. Moreover, Propositional Affine Logic is decidable, a result by Kopylov [17], so there are better prospects for type inference.

As part of future work, we would like to develop an algorithmic typing system, along the lines of [22]. We also believe it would be interesting to apply our technique to multiparty sessions [14] based on Proof Nets [20].

Acknowledgments. This work was supported by FCT through funding of MULTICORE project, ref. PTDC/EIA-CCO/122547/2010, and LaSIGE Strategic Project, ref. PEst-OE/EEI/UI0408/2014. We would like to thank the anonymous reviewers and also Nobuko Yoshida, Hugo Torres Vieira, Francisco Martins, and the members of the GLOSS group in the University of Lisbon, for their detailed and insightful comments.

References

1. Abramsky, S.: Computational interpretations of linear logic. Theoretical Computer Science 111, 3–57 (1993)
2. Asperti, A., Roversi, L.: Intuitionistic light affine logic. ACM Transactions on Compututational Logic 3(1) (2002)
3. Bravetti, M., Zavattaro, G.: Contract-based discovery and composition of web services. In: Bernardo, M., Padovani, L., Zavattaro, G. (eds.) SFM 2009. LNCS, vol. 5569, pp. 261–295. Springer, Heidelberg (2009)

4. Caires, L., Pfenning, F.: Session types as intuitionistic linear propositions. In: Gastin, P., Laroussinie, F. (eds.) CONCUR 2010. LNCS, vol. 6269, pp. 222–236. Springer, Heidelberg (2010)
5. Capecchi, S., Giachino, E., Yoshida, N.: Global escape in multiparty sessions. In: FSTTCS. LIPIcs, pp. 338–351. Schloss Dagstuhl (2010)
6. Carbone, M.: Session-based choreography with exceptions. In: PLACES. ENTCS, vol. 241, pp. 35–55. Elsevier (2009)
7. Carbone, M., Honda, K., Yoshida, N.: Structured interactional exceptions in session types. In: van Breugel, F., Chechik, M. (eds.) CONCUR 2008. LNCS, vol. 5201, pp. 402–417. Springer, Heidelberg (2008)
8. Castagna, G., Gesbert, N., Padovani, L.: A theory of contracts for web services. ACM Transactions on Programming Languages and Systems 31(5), 1–61 (2009)
9. Dezani-Ciancaglini, M., de'Liguoro, U., Yoshida, N.: On progress for structured communications. In: Barthe, G., Fournet, C. (eds.) TGC 2007. LNCS, vol. 4912, pp. 257–275. Springer, Heidelberg (2008)
10. Ferreira, C., Lanese, I., Ravara, A., Vieira, H.T., Zavattaro, G.: Advanced Mechanisms for Service Combination and Transactions. In: Wirsing, M., Hölzl, M. (eds.) SENSORIA Project. LNCS, vol. 6582, pp. 302–325. Springer, Heidelberg (2011)
11. Gay, S.J., Hole, M.J.: Subtyping for session types in the pi calculus. Acta Informatica 42(2/3), 191–225 (2005)
12. Girard, J.-Y.: Linear logic. Theoretical Computer Science 50, 1–102 (1987)
13. Giunti, M.: Algorithmic type checking for a pi-calculus with name matching and session types. The Journal of Logic and Algebraic Programming 82(8), 263–281 (2013)
14. Honda, K., Yoshida, N., Carbone, M.: Multiparty asynchronous session types. In: POPL, pp. 273–284. ACM (2008)
15. Honda, K., Vasconcelos, V.T., Kubo, M.: Language primitives and type disciplines for structured communication-based programming. In: Hankin, C. (ed.) ESOP 1998. LNCS, vol. 1381, pp. 122–138. Springer, Heidelberg (1998)
16. Hu, R., Neykova, R., Yoshida, N., Demangeon, R., Honda, K.: Practical interruptible conversations: Distributed dynamic verification with session types and Python. In: Legay, A., Bensalem, S. (eds.) RV 2013. LNCS, vol. 8174, pp. 130–148. Springer, Heidelberg (2013)
17. Kopylov, A.P.: Decidability of linear affine logic. Information and Computation 164(1), 173–198 (2001)
18. Milner, R.: Functions as processes. Mathematical Structures in Computer Science 2(2), 119–141 (1992)
19. Milner, R., Parrow, J., Walker, D.: A calculus of mobile processes, parts I and II. Information and Computation 100(1) (1992)
20. Mostrous, D.: Multiparty sessions based on proof nets. In: Programming Language Approaches to Concurrency and Communication-cEntric Software, PLACES (2014)
21. Takeuchi, K., Honda, K., Kubo, M.: An interaction-based language and its typing system. In: Halatsis, C., Philokyprou, G., Maritsas, D., Theodoridis, S. (eds.) PARLE 1994. LNCS, vol. 817, pp. 398–413. Springer, Heidelberg (1994)
22. Vasconcelos, V.T.: Fundamentals of session types. Information and Computation 217, 52–70 (2012)
23. Vieira, H.T., Caires, L., Seco, J.C.: The conversation calculus: A model of service-oriented computation. In: Drossopoulou, S. (ed.) ESOP 2008. LNCS, vol. 4960, pp. 269–283. Springer, Heidelberg (2008)

Multiparty Session Actors

Rumyana Neykova and Nobuko Yoshida

Imperial College London

Abstract. Actor coordination armoured with a suitable protocol description language has been a pressing problem in the actors community. We study the applicability of multiparty session type (MPST) protocols for verification of actor programs. We incorporate sessions to actors by introducing minimum additions to the model such as the notion of actor roles and protocol mailboxes. The framework uses Scribble, which is a protocol description language based on multiparty session types. Our programming model supports actor-like syntax and runtime verification mechanism guaranteeing communication safety of the participating entities. An actor can implement multiple roles in a similar way as an object can implement multiple interfaces. Multiple roles allow for cooperative inter-concurrency in a single actor. We demonstrate our framework by designing and implementing a session actor library in Python and its runtime verification mechanism. Benchmark results demonstrate that the runtime checks induce negligible overhead.

1 Introduction

The actor model [2,3] is (re)gaining attention in the research community and in the mainstream programming languages as a promising concurrency paradigm. Unfortunately, the programming model itself does not ensure correct sequencing of interactions between different computational processes. A study in [26] points out that "the property of no shared space and asynchronous communication can make implementing coordination protocols harder and providing a language for coordinating protocols is needed". This reveals that the coordination of actors is a challenging problem when implementing, and especially when scaling up an actor system.

To overcome this problem, we need to solve several shortcomings existing in the actor programming models. First, although actors often have multiple states and complex policies for changing states, no general-purpose specification language is currently in use for describing actor protocols. Second, a clear guidance on actor discovery and coordination of distributed actors is missing. This leads to adhoc implementations and mixing the model with other paradigms which weaken its benefits [26]. Third, no verification mechanism (neither static nor dynamic) is proposed to ensure correct sequencing of actor interactions. Most actor implementations provide static typing within a single actor, but the communication between actors – the complex communication patterns that are most likely to deadlock – are not checked.

We tackle the aforementioned challenges by studying applicability of multyparty session types (MPST) [14], a type theory for communicating processes, to actor systems. The tenet of MPST safety assurance methodology is the use of a high-level, global specification (also called protocol) for describing the interactions of communication entities.

E. Kühn and R. Pugliese (Eds.): COORDINATION 2014, LNCS 8459, pp. 131–146, 2014.

From the global protocol each entity is given a local session type defining the order and the payload type of the interactions. Programs are then written as a collection of possibly interleaved conversations, verified against prescribed protocols and constraints at runtime. The practical incarnation of the theoretical MPST is the protocol specification language Scribble [24]. Scribble is equipped with a verification mechanism, which makes protocol creation easier and protocol verification sound. Declarative protocol specifications in Scribble can readily avoid typical errors in communications programming, including type errors, disrespect of call orders, circular service dependencies and deadlocks. We call these safety properties ensured by MPST *communication safety*.

Recent works from [18,15] prove the suitability of Scribble and its tools for the dynamic verification of real world complex protocols [20] and present a runtime verification framework that guarantees safety and session fidelity of the underlying communications. The verification mechanism is applied to a large cyberinfrastructure. The MPST dynamic verification framework is built on a runtime layer for protocol management and developers use MPST primitives for communication, which limits the verification methodology to a specific infrastructure. In this paper, we take the MPST one step further. We adapt and distil the model to present a MPST verification of actors systems. A main departure from our previous work is that [18,15] required special conversation runtime, built into the application, which restrict the programming style and the model applicability. In this paper, we prove the generality of MPST framework by showing Scribble protocols offer a wider usage, in particular, for actor programming.

Our programming model is grounded on three new design ideas: (1) use Scribble protocols and their relation to finite state machines for specification and runtime verification of actor interactions; (2) augment actor messages and their mailboxes dynamically with protocol (role) information; and (3) propose an algorithm based on virtual routers (protocol mailboxes) for the dynamic discovery of actor mailboxes within a protocol. We implement a session actor library in Python to demonstrate the applicability of the approach. To the best of our knowledge, this is the first design and implementation of session types and their dynamic verification toolchain in an actor library.

The paper is organised as follows: § 2 gives a brief overview of the the key features of our model and presents the running example. § 3 describes the constructs of Session Actors and highlights the main design decisions. § 4 presents the implementation of the model on concrete middleware. § 5 evaluates the framework overheads, compares it with a popular Scala actor library [4] and shows applications. Finally, § 6 discusses related work and concludes. The code for the runtime and the monitor tool, example applications and omitted details are available at [25].

2   Session Actors Programming Model

2.1   Actor Models and Design Choices

Actor Model Overview. We assume the following actor features to determine our design choices. Actors are concurrent autonomous entities that exchange messages asynchronously. An actor is an entity (a class in our framework) that has a mailbox and a behaviour. Actors communicate between each other only by exchanging messages. Upon receiving a message, the behaviour of the actor is executed, upon which the actor can send a number of messages to other actors, create a number of actors or change its internal state. Each actor is equipped with a mailbox where messages are buffered. Actors have states and behaviours. Behaviours of an actor can only be changed by that actor itself, while processing a message. Active threads within actors continuously process messages whenever their mailboxes are not empty. There are only three primitive operations each actor can perform: (1) create new actors; (2) send messages to other actors whose address the sender knows; and (3) become an actor with a new state and behaviour. All these operations are atomic. The only order inherent is a causal order, and the only guarantee provided is that messages sent by actors will eventually be processed by their receivers. Other synchronisation and coordination constraints need to be externally enforced, by the unit called *roles*. The notion of roles is crucial in our framework and is explained below.

Session Actors. To verify actor interactions, we introduce *multiparty roles* that enable multiple local control flows inside an actor. Each actor is annotated with supported protocols and roles it implements. As a result, session actors are containers for roles. Each actor also holds a reference to the other participating roles in the protocols. These references are bound to their physical actor containers through the actor discovery mechanism (during the protocol creation, explained in § 4.3), Without session annotations a session actor behaves identically to a plain actor. In a nutshell, an actor can be transformed to a session actor by applying the following design methodology:

1. the global protocol the actor is part of is written in Scribble and projected to local specifications;
2. the actor class is annotated with a `@protocol` decorator, which links to the local protocol specification;
3. each method is annotated with `@role` decorator that exposes a role instance (acting as a container for all protocol roles); and
4. interactions with other actors are performed via the exposed role instance.

The changes and additions that the MPST annotations bring to the original actor model are as follows (we link to the subsections where they are explained):

(a) different passive objects (called roles) that run inside an actor are given a session type (§ 4.2);
(b) an actor engages in structured protocol communications via a protocol mailbox (§ 4.3) and dynamically learns the roles it is communicating with; and
(c) an actor message execution is bound to a protocol structure (§ 4.4). This structure is checked via the internal FSM-based monitor.

This design choice (incorporating roles inside actors) enables to apply the MPST verification framework to actors, as explained in this and the next two sections.

Scribble Overview. Scribble [24,13] is a practical and human-readable language for protocol specification that is designed from the multiparty session types theory [14,6]. It is a language to describe application-level protocols among communicating systems and aims to prevent communication mismatches and type errors during communications. A Scribble protocol represents an agreement on how participating systems interact with each other by describing an abstract structure of message exchanges between roles. Roles abstract from the actual identity of the endpoints that may participate in a

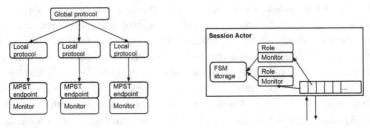

Fig. 1. MPST-development methodology (left) and session actors (right)

run-time conversation instantiating the protocol. The core structures supported in Scribble are asynchronous message passing, choice, parallel and recursion constructs. The Scribble toolkit comes with libraries for parsing, well-formedness checking algorithms and several language bindings. An implementation of Python-based Scribble tools for projection and validation [24], as well as static verification for various languages, e.g.[19] are explained in the literature [12].

MPST Verification Framework. The top-down development methodology for MPST verification is shown in the left part of Fig. 1 and the additions for session actors is illustrated on the right.

A distributed protocol is specified as a global Scribble protocol, which collectively defines the admissible communication behaviours between the participating entities, called *roles* inside the protocol. Then, the Scribble toolchain is used to algorithmically project the global protocol to local specifications.

For each role a finite state machine (FSM), which prescribes the allowed actions and communicating parties, is generated from the local specification and stored in a distributed storage to be retrieved whenever a role is instantiated. When a party requests to start or join a session, the initial message specifies which role it intends to play as. Its monitor retrieves the local specification based on the protocol name and the role. A runtime monitor ensures that each endpoint program conforms to the core protocol structure.

To guarantee session fidelity we perform two main checks. First, we verify that the type (operation and payload) of each message matches its specification (operations can be mapped directly to message headers, or to method calls, class names or other relevant artefacts in the program). Second, we verify that the overall order of interactions is correct, i.e. interaction sequences, branches and recursions proceed as expected, respecting the explicit dependencies (for example, m1() from A to B; m2() from B to C; where A, B and C denote roles and m1() and m2() denote methods imposes an input-output causality). These measures rule out errors, e.g. communication mismatches, that violate the permitted protocol.

Verification of Session Actors. We explain how we apply the above methodology. As observed in [23] in many actor systems an actor encapsulates a number of passive objects, accessed from the other actors through asynchronous method calls. Similarly session actors are a collection of interleaving control flows of actor roles. An actor role is associated with a FSM, generated from a global protocol. This verification structure is depicted in the right hand side of Fig. 1.

The association is done through annotating the actor type (class) and receive messages (methods) with protocol information. Annotating the actor type with protocol information results in registering the type for a particular role. When a session is started, a join message is sent (in a round-robin style) to all registered actors. When this join message is received, the generated FSM is loaded into the actor role and all subsequent messages on that protocol (role) are tracked and checked via the verification mechanism explained above. Message receive is delegated to the appropriate FSM via pattern matching on the protocol id, contained in the message. If all actors messages comply to their assigned FSMs, the whole communication is guaranteed to be safe. If participants do not comply, violations (such as deadlocks, communication mismatch or breakage of a protocol) are detected and delegated to a Policy actor. Further implementation details are explained in § 4.

2.2   Warehouse Management Use Case

To illustrate and motivate central design decisions of our model, we present the buyer-seller protocol from [14] and extend it to a full warehouse management scenario. A warehouse consists of multiple customers communicating to a warehouse provider. It can be involved in a Purchase protocol (with customers), but can also be involved in a StoreLoad protocol with dealers to update its storage.

Scribble Protocol. The interactions between the entities in the system are presented as two Scribble protocols, shown in Fig. 2(a) and 2(b). The protocols are called Purchase and StoreLoad and involve three (a Buyer (B), a Seller (S) and an Authenticator (A)) and two (a Store (S), a Dealer (D)) parties, respectively. At the start of a purchase session, B sends login details to S, which delegates the request to an Authentication server. After the authentication is completed, B sends a request quote for a product to S and S replies with the product price. Then B has a choice to ask for another product, to proceed with buying the product, or to quit. By buying a product the warehouse decreases the product amount it has in the store. Products in stock are increased as prescribed by the StoreLoad protocol, Fig. 2(b). The protocol starts with a recursion where the warehouse (in the role of S) has a choice to send a product request to a dealer (D) to load the store with n numbers of a product. After receiving the request, D delivers the product (operation put on Line 8). These interactions are repeated in a loop until S decides to quit the protocol (Line 11). The reader can refer to [24] for the full specification of the Scribble syntax.

Challenges. There are several challenging points to implement the above scenario. First, a warehouse implementation should be involved in both protocols, therefore it can play more than one role. Second, initially the user does not know the exact warehouse it is buying from, therefore the customer learns dynamically the address of the warehouse. Third, there can be a specific restriction on the protocol that cannot be expressed as system constants (such as specific timeout depending on the customer). The next section explains the implementation of this example in Session Actors.

```
1   global protocol Purchase(role B,          1   global protocol StoreLoad
2       role S, role A)                       2       (role D, role S)
3   {                                         3   {
4       login(string:user) from B to S;      4       rec Rec{
5       login(string:user) from S to A;      5       choice at S
6       authenticate(string:token) from A to B, S   6       {request(string:product, int:n)
                                              ;                 7                 from S to D;)
7       choice at B                           8           put(string:product, int:n) from
8           {request(string:product) from B to S;              D to S;
9           (int:quote) from S to B;}         9           continue Rec;}
10      or                                    10      or
11          {buy(string:product) from B to S  11          {quit() from S to D;
12          delivery(string) from S to B; }   12          acc() from D to S;}}}
13      or
14          {quit() from B to S; }}
```

Fig. 2. Global protocols in Scribble for (a) Purchase protocol and (b) StoreLoad protocol

3   Session Actor Language

This section explains the main operations in the session actor language and its usecase implementation in Python.

Session Actor Language Operations. Fig. 3 presents the main session actor operations and annotations. The central concept of the session actor is the *role*. A role can be considered as a passive object inside an actor and it contains meta information used for MPST-verification. A session actor is registered for a role via the @protocol annotation. The annotation specifies the name of the protocol and role the session actor is registered for and the rest of the participants in the protocol. The aforementioned meta information is stored in a role instance created in the actor. To be used for communication, the method should be annotated with the role using the @role decorator and passing the role instance name. The instance serves as a container for references to all protocol roles, which allows sending a message to a role in the session actor without knowing the actor location. A message is sent via c.role.method, where c is the self role instance and role is the role the message is intended for.

Sending to a role without explicitly knowing the actor location is possible by the actor discovery mechanism (the details will be explained in § 4). When a session is started via the create method, actors receive an invitation for joining the protocol. The

Conversation API operation	Purpose
@protocol(variable_name, protocol_name, self_role, other_roles) actor_class	Annotating actor class
@role(self_role, sender_role) msg_handler	Annotating message handler
c.create(protocol_name, invitation_config.yml)	Initiating a conversation, sending invitations
c.role.method(payload)	Sending a message to an actor in a role
join(self, role, principal_name)	Actor handler for joining a protocol
actor.send.method(payload)	Sending a message to a known actor

Fig. 3. Session Actor operations

```
1    @protocol(c, Purchase, seller, buyer, auth)    13
2    @protocol(c1, StoreLoad, store, dealer)        14    @role(c, buyer)
3    class Warehouse(SessionActor):                 15    def quit(self, c):
4        @role(c, buyer)                            16        c.send.buyer.acc()
5        def login(self, c, user):                  17
6            c.auth.send.login(user)                18    @role(c1, self)
7                                                    19    def update(self, c1, product):
8        @role(c, buyer)                            20        c1.dealer.send.request(product, n)
9        def buy(self, c, product):                 21
10           self.purchaseDB[product]-=1;           22    @role(c1, dealer)
11           c.seller.send.delivery(product.        23    def put(self, c1, product):
                 details)                            24        self.purchaseDB[product]+=1:
12           self.become(update, product)
```

Fig. 4. Session Actor implementation for the Warehouse role

operation join is a default handler for invitation messages. If a session actor changes the join behaviour and applies additional security policies to the joiners, the method should be overloaded. Introducing actor roles via protocol executions is a novelty of our work: without roles and the actor discovery mechanism, actors need additional configurations to introduce their addresses, and this would grow the complexity of configurations.

Warehouse Service Implementation. We explain the main constructs by an implementation of a session actor accountable for the Warehouse service. Fig. 4 presents the implementation of a warehouse service as a single session actor that keeps the inventory as a state (self.purchaseDB). Lines 1–2 annotate the session actor class with two protocol decorators – c and c1 (for seller and store roles respectively). c and c1 are accessible within the warehouse actor and are holders for mailboxes of the other actors, involved in the two protocols.

All message handlers are annotated with a role and for convenience are implemented as methods. For example, the login method (Line 5) is invoked when a login message (Line 4, Fig. 2 (a)) is sent. The role annotation for c (Line 4) specifies the sender to be buyer.

The handler body continues following Line 5, Fig. 2 (a) – sending a login message via the send primitive to the session actor, registered as a role auth in the protocol of c. Value c.auth is initialised with the auth actor mailbox as a result of the actor discovery mechanism (explained in the next section). The handling of authenticate (Line 6, Fig. 2 (a)) and request (Line 6, Fig. 2 (b)) messages is similar, so we omit it and focus on the buy handler (Line 9–12), where after sending the delivery details (Line 11), the warehouse actor sends a message to itself (Line 12) using the primitive become with value update. Value update is annotated with another role c1, but has as a sender self. This is the mechanism used for switching between roles within an actor. Update method (Line 19–20) implements the request branch (Line 6–9, Fig. 2 (b)) of the StoreLoad protocol – sending a request to the dealer and handling the reply via method put.

The correct order of messages is verified by the FSM attached to c and c1. As a result, errors such as calling put before update or executing two consecutive updates, will be detected as invalid.

4   Implementations of Session Actors

This section explains our implementation of Session Actors. The key design choices follow the actor framework explained in § 2.1. We have implemented the multiparty session actors on top of Celery [8] (a Python framework for distributed task processing) with support for distributed actors [1]. Celery uses advanced message queue protocol (AMQP 0-9-1 [5]) as a transport. The reason for choosing AMQP network as base for our framework is that AMQP middleware shares a similar abstraction with the actor programming model, which makes the implementation of distributed actors more natural.

4.1   AMQP Background

We first summarise the key features of the AMQP model. In AMQP, messages are published by producers to entities, called exchanges (or mailboxes). Exchanges then distribute message copies to queues using binding rules. Then AMQP brokers (virtual routers) deliver messages to consumers subscribed to queues. Exchanges can be of different types, depending on the binding rules and the routing strategies they implement. We explain the three exchange types used in our implementation: *round-robin* exchange (deliver messages, alternating to all subscribers), *direct* exchange (subscribers subscribe with a binding key and messages are delivered when a key stored in the message meta information matches the binding key of the subscription) and *broadcast* exchange (deliver a message to all subscribers).

Distributed actors are naturally represented in this AMQP context using the abstractions of exchanges. Each actor type is represented in the network as an exchange and is realised as a consumer subscribed to a queue based on a pattern matching on the actor id. Message handlers are implemented as methods on the actor class.

Our distributed actor discovery mechanism draws on the AMPQ abstractions of exchanges, queues and binding, and our extensions to the actor programming model are built using Python advanced abstraction capabilities: two main capabilities are *greenlets* (for realising the actors inter-concurrency) and *decorators* (for annotating actor types and methods).

A greenlet (or micro/green thread) is a light-weight cooperatively-scheduled execution unit in Python. A Python decorator is any callable Python object that is used to modify the function, method or class definition it annotates using the @ symbol. A decorator is passed the original object being defined and returns a modified object, which is then bound to the name in the definition. These decorators in Python are partly inspired by Java annotations.

4.2   Actor Roles

A key idea of actor roles is each role to run as a micro-thread in an actor (using Python greenlet library). Actors are assigned to session roles by adding the @protocol decorator to the actor class declaration. Methods that implement a part of a protocol are annotated with the @role decorator. A role is activated when a message is received and ready to be processed. Switching between roles is done via the become primitive (as demonstrated in Fig. 4), which is realised as sending a message to the internal queue of the actor. Roles are scheduled cooperatively. This means that at most one role can be active in a session actor at a time.

4.3 Actors Discovery

Fig. 5 presents the network setting (in terms of AMQP objects) for realising the actor discovery for buyer and seller of the protocol Purchase. We use the three types from AMQP explained in § 4.1. For simplicity, we create some of the objects on starting of the actor system – round-robin exchange per actor type (warehouse and customer in Fig. 5) and broadcast exchange per protocol type (purchase in Fig. 5). All spawned actors alternate to receive messages addressed to their type exchange. Session actors are registered for roles via the protocol decorator and as a result their type exchange is bound to the protocol exchange (Line 1 in Fig. 4 binds warehouse to purchase in Fig. 5).

We now explain the workflow for actor discovery. When a protocol is started, a fresh protocol id and an exchange with that id are created. The type of the exchange uses AMPQ type, direct explained in § 4.1. A direct type is used so that messages with a routing key are delivered to actors linked to the exchange with binding to that key (it corresponds to protocol id in Fig. 5). Then join message is sent to the protocol exchange and delivered to one actor per registered role (join is broadcasted to warehouse and customer in Fig. 5). On join, an actor binds itself to the protocol id exchange with subscription key equal to its role (bindings seller and buyer in Fig. 5). When an actor sends a message to another actor within the same session (for example c.buyer.send in Fig. 4), the message is sent to the protocol id exchange (stored in c) and from there delivered to the buyer actor.

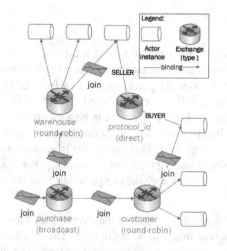

Fig. 5. Organising Session Actors into protocols   **Fig. 6.** Session Actors Monitoring

4.4 Preservation through FSM checking

Before a message is dispatched to its message handler, the message goes through a monitor. Fig. 6 illustrates the monitoring process. Each message contains meta information (a routing key) with the role name the message is intended for and the id of the protocol the message is in the part of. When an actor joins a protocol, the FSM, generated from the Scribble compiler (as shown in Fig. 1) is loaded from a distributed storage to the actor memory.

Then the checking goes through the following steps. First, depending on the role and the protocol id the matching FSM is retrieved from the actor memory. Next the FSM checks the message labels/operators (already in the part of the actor payload) and sender and receiver roles (in the part of the message binding key implemented as our extension) are valid.

The *check assertions* step verifies that if any constraints on the size/value of the payload are specified in Scribble, they are also fulfilled. If a message is detected as wrong the session actor throws a distributed exception and sends an error message back to the sending role and does not pass the message to its handler for processing. This behaviour can change by implementing the `wrong_message` method of the session actor.

5 Evaluations of Session Actors

This section reports on the performance of our framework. The goal of our evaluation is two fold. First, we compare our host distributed actor framework [8] with a mainstream actor library (AKKA [4]) to show our host framework is a suitable choice. Second, we show that our main contribution, verification of MPST protocols, can be realised with reasonable cost. The full source code of the benchmark protocols and applications and the raw data are available from the project page [25].

5.1 Session Actors Performance

We test the overhead in message delivery implementation using the pingpong benchmark [16] in which two processes send each other messages back and forth. The original version of the code was obtained from Scala `pingpong.scala` from `http://scala-lang.org/old/node/54` and adapted to use distributed AKKA actors (instead of local). We distinguish two protocols. Each pingpong can be a separate session (protocol `FlatPingPong`) or the whole iteration can be part of one recursive protocol (`RecPingPong`). The protocols are given in Fig. 7(b). This distinction is important only to session actors, because the protocol shape has implications on checking. For AKKA actors the notion of session does not exist and therefore the two protocols have the same implementation.

Set Up. We prepared each scenario 50 times and measured the overall execution time (the difference between successive runs was found to be negligible). The creation and population of the network was not measured as part of the execution time. The client and server actor nodes and the AMQP broker were each run on separate machines (Intel Core2 Duo 2.80 GHz, 4 GB memory, 64-bit Ubuntu 11.04, kernel 2.6.38). All hosts are

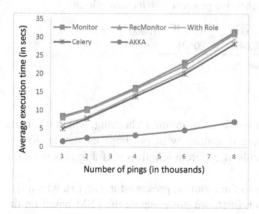

```
global protocol FlatPingPong(
    role C, role S)
{
    ping(string) from C to S;
    pong(string) from S to C;
}


global protocol RecPingPong(
    role C, role S)
{
    rec Loop{
        ping(string) from C to S;
        pong(string) from S to C;
        continue Loop
    }
}
```

Fig. 7. (a) The PingPong benchmark (the overhead of message delivery) and (b) The PingPong protocol

interconnected through Gigabit Ethernet and Latency between each node was measured to be 0.24 ms on average (ping 64 bytes). The version of Python used was 2.7, of Scala – 2.10.2 and of the AKKA-actors – 2.2.1.

Results. Fig. 7(a) compares three separate benchmark measurements for session actors. The base case for comparison. "Celery" is a pure actor implementation without the addition of roles. "With Role" measures the overhead of roles annotations without having the monitor capabilities enabled. The two main cases, "Rec Monitor" and "Monitor", measure the full overhead of session actors. This separation aims to clearly illustrate the overhead introduced by each of the additions, presented in the paper: roles annotations, MPST verification and actor discovery. Note that the FSMs for the recursive and for the flat protocol have the same number of states. Therefore, the observed difference in the performance is a result of the cost of the actor discovery.

The goal of the benchmarks is two fold. First, to compare the actor framework that we use with one of the most widely used frameworks for distributed actors. Second, to evaluate the performance implications of our extensions. A difference between the performance of AKKA and Celery is not surprising and can be explained with a distinct nature of the frameworks. AKKA runs on top of JVM and the remote actors in these benchmarks use direct TCP connections. On the other hand, Celery is Python-based framework which uses a message middleware as a transport, which adds additional layer of indirection. Given these differences, Celery actors have reasonable performance and are a viable alternative.

Regarding our additions we can draw several positive conclusions from the benchmarks: (1) the cost of the FSM checking is negligible and largely overshadowed by the cost of the communication (such as latency and routing); and (2) the cost of the actor discovery is reasonable, given the protocol load.

Table 1. Execution Time for checking protocol with increasing length

States	100	1000	10000
Time (ms)	0.0479	0.0501	0.0569

5.2   MPST Verification Overhead

In this subsection, we discuss the row overhead of monitor checking, which is a main factor that can affect the performance and scalability of our implementation. Knowing the complexity of checking protocols of different length is useful to reason on the applicability of the model.

We have applied two optimisations to the monitor, presented in [18,15], which significantly reduce the runtime overhead. First, we pre-generate the FSM based on the global protocol. Second, we cache the FSM protocols the first time when a role is loaded. Therefore, the slight runtime overhead, observed in the previous section is a result of the time required to choose the correct FSM among all in-memory FSMs inside the actor and the time required to check the FSM transition table that the message is expected. Both have the linear complexity on the number of roles running inside the actor and the number of states inside the FSM respectively. Table 1 shows the approximate execution time for checking a protocols of increasing length. The small numbers are omitted since the time taken is negligible.

5.3   Applications of Session Actors

As a practical evaluation of our framework, we have implemented two popular actor applications and adapted them to session actors.

The first application is a distributed chat with multiple chat rooms, where a number of clients connect to a reactive server and execute operations based on their privileges. Depending on privileges some clients might have extended number of allowed messages. We impose this restriction dynamically by annotating the restricted operations with different roles. An operation is allowed only if its actor has already joined a session in the annotated role.

The second usecase is a general `MapReduce` for counting words in a document. It is an adaptation from an example presented in the official website for celery actors: `http://cell.readthedocs.org/en/latest/getting-started/index.html`. The session actor usage removes the requirement for the manual actor spawning of `Reducers` actors inside the `Mapper` actor, which reduces the code size and the complexity of the implementation.

We give in Fig. 8 the implementation of the latter example. For sake of space and clarity, the implementation reported here abstracts from technical details that are not important for the scope of this paper–interested readers can find the full sources in [25]. The protocol is started on Line 26 specifying the type of the actors for each role and passing the arguments for the initial execution – n (the number of reducers) and `file` (the name of the source file to be counted). The `Mapper` implements the `join` method, which is invoked when the actor joins a protocol. Since the `Mapper` is the starting role,

```
1    #======SCRIBBLE CODE======          25   #start the protocol
2    global protocol WordCount(           26   Protocol.create(WordCount,
3        A, R[n], M):                     27       M=Mapper, R=Reducer, A=Aggregator,
4        rec Loop{                        28       n=10, file="file1.txt")
5            count_lines(string) from M to R[1..n];  29
6            aggregate(string) from R[1..n] to A;    30   @protocol(c, WordCount, A, M, R)
7            continue Loop;}              31   class Aggregator(Actor):
8    #======PYTHON CODE======             32       @role(c, master)
9    @protocol(c, WordCount, R, A, M)     33       def aggregate(self, c, words):
10   class Mapper(Actor):                 34           for word, n in words.iteritems():
11       # invoked on protocol start      35               self.result.setdefault(word, 0)
12       @role(c)                         36               self.result[word] += n
13       def join(self, c, file, n):      37           # when a treshhold is reached
14           self.count_document(self, file, n)  38           # print the results
15                                        39           c.close()
16       @role(c, self)                   40
17       def count_document(self, c, file, n):  41   @protocol(c, WordCount, R, A, M)
18           with open(file) as f:        42   class Reducer(Actor):
19               lines = f.readlines()     43       @role(c, M)
20               count = 0                 44       def count_lines(self, c, line):
21               for line in lines:        45           words = {}
22                   reducer = c.R[count % n]  46           for word in line.split(" "):
23                   count+=1              47               words.setdefault(word, 0)
24                   reducer.count_lines(line)  48               words[word] += 1
                                          49           c.A.aggregate(words)
```

Fig. 8. WordCount in Session Actors

when it joins, it sends a message to itself, scheduling the execution of count_document. Note that spawning and linking of the actors are not specified in the code because the actor discovery mechanism accounts for it. The protocol proceeds by Mapper sending one message for each line of the document. The receiver of each message is one of the Reducers. Each Reducer counts the words in its line and sends the result to the Aggregator (c.A, Line 48), which stores all words in a dictionary and aggregates them. When a threshold for the result is reached, the Aggregator prints the result and stops the session explicitly.

Our experiences with session actors are promising. Although they introduce new notions, i.e. a protocol and a role, we found that their addition to a class-based actor framework is natural to integrate without requiring a radical new way of thinking. The protocol and role annotations are matched well with typical actor applications, and even they result in simplifying the code by removing the boilerplate for actor discovery and coordination. The protocol-oriented approach to actor programming accounts for the early error detection in the application design and the coordination of actors. The runtime verification guarantees and enforces the correct order of interactions, which is normally ensured only by hours of testing.

6   Related Work

Behavioural and Session Types for Actors and Objects. There are several theoretical works that have studied the behavioural types for verifying actors [17,9]. The work [9] proposes a behavioural typing system for an actor calculus where a type describes a sequence of inputs and outputs performed by the actor body. In [17], a concurrent fragment of Erlang is enriched with sessions and session types. Messages are linked to a session via correlation sets (explicit identifiers, contained in the message), and clients create the required references and send them in the service invocation message. The developed typing system guarantees that all within-session messages have a chance of being received. The formalism is based on only binary sessions.

Several recent papers have combined session types, as specification of protocols on communicating channels, with object-oriented paradigm. A work close to ours is [10], where a session channel is stored as a field of an object, therefore channels can be accessed from different methods. They explicitly specify the (partial) type for each method bound to a channel. Our implementation also allows modularised sessions based on channel-based communication. Their work [10] is mainly theoretical and gives a static typing system based on binary session types. Our work aims to provide a design and implementation of runtime verification based on multiparty session types, and is integrated with existing development frameworks based on Celery [8] and AMQP [5].

The work in [7] formalises behaviours of non-uniform active objects where the set of available methods may change dynamically. It uses the approach based on spatial logic for a fine grained access control of resources. Method availability in [7] depends on the state of the object in a similar way as ours.

See [27] for more general comparisons between session types and other frameworks in object-oriented paradigms.

Other Actor Frameworks. The most popular actor's library (the AKKA framework [4] in Scala studied in [26]) supports FSM verification mechanism (through inheritance) and typed channels. Their channel typing is simple so that it cannot capture structures of communications such as sequencing, branching or recursions. These structures ensured by session types are the key element for guaranteeing deadlock freedom between multiple actors. In addition, in [4], channels and FSMs are unrelated and cannot be intermixed; on the other hand, in our approach, we rely on external specifications based on the choreography (MPST) and the FSMs usage is internalised (i.e. FSMs are automatically generated from a global type), therefore it does not affect program structures.

Several works study an extension of actors in multicore control flows. Multithreaded active objects [11] allow several threads to co-exist inside an active object and provide an annotation system to control their concurrent executions. Parallel Actor Monitors (PAM) [23] is another framework for intra actor parallelism. PAMs are monitors attached to each actor that schedule the execution of the messages based on synchronisation constraints. Our framework also enables multiple control flows inside an actor as [11,23]. In addition, we embed monitors inside actors in a similar way as [23,11] embed schedulers. The main focus of the monitors in [11,23] is scheduling the order of the method executions in order to optimise the actor performance on multi-core machines, while our approach aims to provide explicit protocol specifications and verification among interactions between distributed actors in multi-node environments.

The work [22] proposes a solution to have multiple cooperatively scheduled tasks within a single active object similar to our notion of cooperative roles within an actor. The approach is implemented as a Java extension with an actor-like concurrency where communication is based on asynchronous method calls with objects as targets. They resort to RMI for writing distributed implementations and do not allow specifying sequencing of messages (protocols) like ours.

The work [21] proposes a framework of three layers for actor roles and coordinators, which resembles roles and protocol mailboxes in our setting. Their specifications focus on QoS requirements, while our aim is to describe and ensure correct patterns of interactions (message passing).

Comparing with the above works, our aim is to provide effective framework for multi-node environments where actors can be distributed transparently to different machines and/or cores.

7 Conclusion

We propose an actor specification and verification framework based on multiparty session types, providing a Python library with actor communication primitives. Cooperative multitasking within sessions allows for combining active and reactive behaviours in a simple and type-safe way. The framework is naturally integrated with Celery [8] which uses advanced message queue protocol (AMQP [5]), and uses effectively its types for realising the key mechanisms such as the actor discovery. We demonstrate the overhead of our implementation is very small. We then show that programming in session actors is straightforward by implementing and rewriting usecases from [4]. To our best knowledge, no other work is linking FSMs, actors and choreographies in a single framework. As a future work, we plan to extend to other main stream actor-based languages such as Scala and Erlang to test the generality of our framework. As actor languages and frameworks are getting more and more attractions, we believe that our work would offer an important step for writing correct large-scale actor-based communication programs.

Acknowledgement. We thank Ask Solem for his support and guidance. This work has been partially sponsored by VMWare, Pivotal and EPSRC EP/K011715/1 and EP/K034413/1.

References

1. Cell - actors for celery, http://cell.readthedocs.org/
2. Agha, G.: Actors: a model of concurrent computation in distributed systems. MIT Press, Cambridge (1986)
3. Agha, G., Mason, I.A., Smith, S.F., Talcott, C.L.: A foundation for actor computation. Journal of Functional Programming 7, 1–72 (1997)
4. Akka - scala actor library, http://akka.io/
5. Advanced Message Queuing Protocol homepage, http://www.amqp.org/
6. Bettini, L., Coppo, M., D'Antoni, L., De Luca, M., Dezani-Ciancaglini, M., Yoshida, N.: Global progress in dynamically interleaved multiparty sessions. In: van Breugel, F., Chechik, M. (eds.) CONCUR 2008. LNCS, vol. 5201, pp. 418–433. Springer, Heidelberg (2008)
7. Caires, L.: Spatial-behavioral types for concurrency and resource control in distributed systems. Theor. Comput. Sci. 402(2-3), 120–141 (2008)
8. Celery, http://www.celeryproject.org/
9. Crafa, S.: Behavioural types for actor systems. arXiv:1206.1687
10. Gay, S.J., Vasconcelos, V.T., Ravara, A., Gesbert, N., Caldeira, A.Z.: Modular session types for distributed object-oriented programming. In: POPL, pp. 299–312. ACM (2010)

11. Henrio, L., Huet, F., István, Z.: Multi-threaded active objects. In: De Nicola, R., Julien, C. (eds.) COORDINATION 2013. LNCS, vol. 7890, pp. 90–104. Springer, Heidelberg (2013)

12. Honda, K., Hu, R., Neykova, R., Chen, T.-C., Demangeon, R., Deniélou, P.-M., Yoshida, N.: Structuring Communication with Session Types. In: COB 2012. LNCS (2012) (to appear)

13. Honda, K., Mukhamedov, A., Brown, G., Chen, T.-C., Yoshida, N.: Scribbling interactions with a formal foundation. In: Natarajan, R., Ojo, A. (eds.) ICDCIT 2011. LNCS, vol. 6536, pp. 55–75. Springer, Heidelberg (2011)

14. Honda, K., Yoshida, N., Carbone, M.: Multiparty asynchronous session types. In: POPL 2008, pp. 273–284. ACM (2008)

15. Hu, R., Neykova, R., Yoshida, N., Demangeon, R., Honda, K.: Practical Interruptible Conversations: Distributed Dynamic Verification with Session Types and Python. In: Legay, A., Bensalem, S. (eds.) RV 2013. LNCS, vol. 8174, pp. 130–148. Springer, Heidelberg (2013)

16. Imam, S.M., Sarkar, V.: Integrating task parallelism with actors. SIGPLAN Not. 47(10), 753–772 (2012)

17. Mostrous, D., Vasconcelos, V.T.: Session Typing for a Featherweight Erlang. In: De Meuter, W., Roman, G.-C. (eds.) COORDINATION 2011. LNCS, vol. 6721, pp. 95–109. Springer, Heidelberg (2011)

18. Neykova, R., Yoshida, N., Hu, R.: SPY: Local Verification of Global Protocols. In: Legay, A., Bensalem, S. (eds.) RV 2013. LNCS, vol. 8174, pp. 358–363. Springer, Heidelberg (2013)

19. Ng, N., Yoshida, N., Honda, K.: Multiparty session C: Safe parallel programming with message optimisation. In: Furia, C.A., Nanz, S. (eds.) TOOLS 2012. LNCS, vol. 7304, pp. 202–218. Springer, Heidelberg (2012)

20. Ocean Observatories Initiative, http://www.oceanobservatories.org/

21. Ren, S., Yu, Y., Chen, N., Marth, K., Poirot, P.-E., Shen, L.: Actors, roles and coordinators - a coordination model for open distributed and embedded systems. In: Ciancarini, P., Wiklicky, H. (eds.) COORDINATION 2006. LNCS, vol. 4038, pp. 247–265. Springer, Heidelberg (2006)

22. Schäfer, J., Poetzsch-Heffter, A.: Jcobox: Generalizing active objects to concurrent components. In: D'Hondt, T. (ed.) ECOOP 2010. LNCS, vol. 6183, pp. 275–299. Springer, Heidelberg (2010)

23. Scholliers, C., Tanter, É., Meuter, W.D.: Parallel actor monitors: Disentangling task-level parallelism from data partitioning in the actor model. Sci. Comput. Program. 80, 52–64 (2014)

24. Scribble project home page, http://www.scribble.org

25. Online appendix for this paper, http://www.doc.ic.ac.uk/~rn710/sactor

26. Tasharofi, S., Dinges, P., Johnson, R.E.: Why do Scala developers mix the actor model with other concurrency models? In: Castagna, G. (ed.) ECOOP 2013. LNCS, vol. 7920, pp. 302–326. Springer, Heidelberg (2013)

27. BETTY WG3 - Languages Survey, http://www.doc.ic.ac.uk/~yoshida/WG3/BETTY_WG3_state_of_art.pdf

Typing Liveness in Multiparty Communicating Systems

Luca Padovani[1], Vasco Thudichum Vasconcelos[2], and Hugo Torres Vieira[2]

[1] Dipartimento di Informatica, Università di Torino, Italy
[2] LaSIGE, Faculdade de Ciências, Universidade de Lisboa, Portugal

Abstract. Session type systems are an effective tool to prove that communicating programs do not go wrong, ensuring that the participants of a session follow the protocols described by the types. In a previous work we introduced a typing discipline for the analysis of progress in binary sessions. In this paper we generalize the approach to multiparty sessions following the conversation type approach, while strengthening progress to liveness. We combine the usual session-like fidelity analysis with the liveness analysis and devise an original treatment of recursive types allowing us to address challenging configurations that are out of the reach of existing approaches.

1 Introduction

The importance of error detection in the early cycles of software development, and the consequent savings arising from it, can never be overemphasized. The problem becomes even more acute when concurrency comes into play, for concurrency faults are notoriously hard to track down. This work focuses on early error detection of concurrent message passing systems, and addresses, apart from the usual communication safety, the static identification of states in which liveness is compromised.

The setting in which we operate is that of (multi-party) sessions [2–4, 8, 10–12]. *Sessions* are private conversations occurring between two or more interacting participants. Each participant behaves according to a *session type* that describes the messages that the participant is supposed to send/receive and their relative order. One of the strengths of sessions is that they provide a structuring construct on top of which complex systems can be built in a modular way. The relatively simple typing discipline imposed by session types ensures strong properties such as *liveness*, that is the eventual completion of communication operations. This point in favor of sessions is also, somewhat paradoxically, a weakness: since session types describe only *intra*-session communications, but say nothing on *inter*-session dependencies, it may be the case that a well-typed participant simultaneously involved in two or more sessions finds itself in a deadlocked situation because of mutual dependencies between sessions. We address this problem by identifying potentially dangerous dependencies between sessions, so that liveness is ensured also when communications on several different sessions are interleaved.

To illustrate the basic ingredients of our approach, consider the process

$$(\nu s)(\operatorname{rec} \mathcal{X} . s?x. \mathcal{X} \mid \operatorname{rec} \mathcal{X} . s?y. \mathcal{X} \mid \operatorname{rec} \mathcal{X} . s!5.s!\operatorname{true}.\mathcal{X}) \tag{1}$$

describing three participants (say A, B, and C, composed in parallel) that interact within the scope of a multiparty session s. The aim of C is to repeatedly send two messages

E. Kühn and R. Pugliese (Eds.): COORDINATION 2014, LNCS 8459, pp. 147–162, 2014.
© IFIP International Federation for Information Processing 2014

(here exemplified as the constants 5 and true) respectively to A and B. All participants interact within the same session s. However, the order of the synchronizations cannot be predicted and it may well be the case that a 5 message is received by B and a true message is received by A or, in fact, that one of A or B does not receive any message at all! In order to recover the *linearity* of communications (i.e., at most one possible synchronization per session channel at a given moment) we tag messages with *labels*, following the approach of [4]. In this way, we refine (1) to

$$(vs)(\text{rec } \mathcal{X}.s?1x.\mathcal{X} \mid \text{rec } \mathcal{X}.s?my.\mathcal{X} \mid \text{rec } \mathcal{X}.s!15.s!m\text{true}.\mathcal{X}) \qquad (2)$$

so that 1- and m-tagged messages respectively and uniquely identify synchronizations with A and B. We are then able to characterize the overall protocol that takes place on session s with the following type.

$$T_s \triangleq \mu\alpha.\tau 1\text{int}.\tau m\text{bool}.\alpha$$

The type describes a conversation consisting of an infinite exchange of alternated 1- and m-tagged messages whose payload is described by the int and bool types, respectively. The occurrences of τ in the type denote *synchronizations* that are supposed to occur in a session typed by T_s. To specify the behavior of the participants involved in the conversation, we *split* T_s into "slices" which we distribute among the participants. First of all, we separate the behavior of C from the rest of the system, and obtain

$$T_s = T_C \circ T' \quad \text{where} \quad T_C \triangleq \mu\alpha.!1\text{int}.!m\text{bool}.\alpha \quad \text{and} \quad T' \triangleq \mu\alpha.?1\text{int}.?m\text{bool}.\alpha$$

In particular, T_C says that C repeatedly sends alternated 1 and m messages and T' says that the rest of the system should be ready to receive the very same messages, in this order. Then, we further split T' in the behaviors of A and B, thus:

$$T' = T_A \circ T_B \quad \text{where} \quad T_A \triangleq \mu\alpha.?1\text{int}.\alpha \quad \text{and} \quad T_B \triangleq \mu\alpha.?m\text{bool}.\alpha$$

Note that this splitting is valid *assuming* that the environment in which A and B execute guarantees that the synchronization on each 1 message occurs before the synchronization on each m message. This is indeed guaranteed by the sequential structure of process C. Since T_A, T_B, and T_C match the behaviors of A, B, and C with respect to s we may show that (2) is well typed and consequently that it enjoys *communication safety* (no message with wrong type is ever sent), *session fidelity* (the interactions follow the protocol described by T_s), and *liveness* (each interaction described in T_s eventually occurs).

Of all these properties, liveness is the most delicate one, in the sense that it may easily break up when two or more sessions are interleaved with each other. To illustrate the issue, consider the following refinement of (2)

$$(vs)((vr)(\text{rec } \mathcal{X}.r?ny.s?1x.\mathcal{X} \mid \text{rec } \mathcal{X}.s?my.r!ny.\mathcal{X}) \mid \text{rec } \mathcal{X}.s!15.s!m\text{true}.\mathcal{X}) \qquad (3)$$

in which A and B are engaged in another session r, different from s, while C behaves exactly as before. Now B forwards y in a n-tagged message to A, perhaps so that A and B can double-check that they are given consistent information from C. Session s is still well typed according to T_s and session r is well typed according to $T_r \triangleq \mu\alpha.\tau n\text{bool}.\alpha$. Yet, (3) is stuck because A waits for the message from B *before* having received the message from C, but C sends its message to B only *after* it has successfully delivered the message to A. So, none of the synchronizations in T_s and T_r ever happens, although the structure of the participants in (3) agrees to these types.

One possibility for detecting the problem in (3) stems from the observation that the two sessions s and r are mutually dependent on each other. So, one may devise a static analysis technique that keeps track of inter-session dependencies and flags any system that gives rise to circularities as ill typed. This approach has been pursued, for instance, in [3, 6, 7]. The limit of this approach is that, by considering sessions as atomic units, it is quite coarse grained when it comes to analyzing dependencies. For instance,

$$(vs)((vr)(\operatorname{rec} \mathscr{X}.s?1x.r?ny.\mathscr{X} \mid \operatorname{rec} \mathscr{X}.s?my.r!ny.\mathscr{X}) \mid \operatorname{rec} \mathscr{X}.s!15.s!m\operatorname{true}.\mathscr{X}) \quad (4)$$

is a simple variation of (3) where A performs the same two inputs, but in the "correct" order. Also in (4) there are actions on session s interleaving with actions on session r *and* vice versa, so the approach based on session dependencies also flags (4) as ill typed, which is unfortunate because (4), contrarily to (3), enjoys liveness.

The approach we pursue here is based on the idea of tracking the dependencies between *actions* instead of sessions. Towards this aim, we annotate each interaction in a type with an identifier—which we call *event*—and we keep track of the dependencies between events by means of a *strict partial order* $\prec$. To get the flavor of the technique at work, let us apply it to the sessions s and r discussed above. First of all, we annotate the actions in the types of s and r with three events e, f, and g:

$$s : \mu\alpha.e\tau 1\operatorname{int}.f\tau m\operatorname{bool}.\alpha \qquad r : \mu\alpha.g\tau n\operatorname{bool}.\alpha$$

Then, we analyze the dependencies between the actions in the participants of (3): it must be $e \prec f$ (read, e precedes f) because C first sends the 1-tagged message, and only then it sends the m-tagged message; it must be $g \prec e$ because A waits for the n-tagged message before waiting for the 1-tagged one; finally, it must be $f \prec g$ by looking at the structure of B. Overall, $\prec$ is not a strict partial order because of the circularity in the relation $g \prec e \prec f \prec g$ between the two sessions s and r, hence (3) is ill typed.

Our approach builds on previous works [16, 22] that use analogous annotations for reasoning on the dependencies between actions. With respect to these works, our contributions are along two major axes. First of all, we show that the techniques can be applied to sessions/conversations with an arbitrary number of participants. Second, we support complex recursive process structures. The latter aspect requires a non-trivial extension of the technique described in [22] because, in order to declare that a system like (4) is well typed, we must be able to distinguish occurrences of the same event that pertain to different iterations of a recursive process.

The next section formally describes our language. Sections 3 and 4 introduce the notion of types, the type system and the main results. Section 5 concludes the paper including a more detailed comparison with related work and hints on future developments. Additional material can be found in the associated technical report [18].

2 Process Model

We consider an infinite set of *names* ranged over by $x, y, \ldots$ representing communication channels, an infinite set of *process variables* ranged over by $\mathscr{X}, \ldots$, and a set of

$$
\begin{aligned}
P, Q ::= \quad & \mathbf{0} && \text{(Inaction)} && \mid \quad x!l\,y.P && \text{(Output)}\\
& \mid \;\; P \mid Q && \text{(Parallel)} && \mid \quad x?\{l_i y_i.P_i\}_{i \in I} && \text{(Input Summation)}\\
& \mid \;\; (vx)P && \text{(Restriction)} && \mid \quad \text{rec}\,\mathscr{X}.P && \text{(Recursion)}\\
& \mid \;\; \mathscr{X} && \text{(Recursion Variable)}
\end{aligned}
$$

Fig. 1. Syntax of processes

$$
\frac{k \in I}{x?\{l_i y_i.P_i\}_{i \in I} \mid x!l_k z.Q \to P_k\{z/y_k\} \mid Q} \qquad \frac{P \to Q}{(vx)P \to (vx)Q} \qquad \text{(R-Com,R-New)}
$$

$$
\frac{P \to P'}{P \mid Q \to P' \mid Q} \qquad \frac{P \equiv P' \quad P' \to Q' \quad Q' \equiv Q}{P \to Q} \qquad \text{(R-Par,R-Cong)}
$$

Fig. 2. Reduction relation

message labels $l, \ldots$. Processes, ranged over by $P, Q, \ldots$, are the terms defined by the grammar in Fig. 1. The language is that of TyCO [20] that extends the π-calculus [15] by considering labeled communications. The terms $\mathbf{0}$, $P \mid Q$, and $(vx)P$ respectively denote the inactive process, the parallel composition of P and Q, and the restriction of name x to P. Terms $\text{rec}\,\mathscr{X}.P$ and $\mathscr{X}$ are used to build recursive processes. The term $x!l\,y.P$ denotes a process that sends a message on channel x and then continues as P. A *message* is made of a label l and an argument y. The term $x?\{l_i y_i.P_i\}_{i \in I}$ denotes a process that waits for a message from channel x and then continues as P_i according to the label of the received message. The argument of the received message replaces the name y_i in P_i. To keep the setting as simple as possible, we have not included conditional or non-deterministic processes. These constructs can be easily added.

The binders of the language are name restriction $(vx)P$, which binds the name x in P, the input prefix $x?l\,y.P$, which binds the name y in P, and the recursion $\text{rec}\,\mathscr{X}.P$, which binds the recursion variable $\mathscr{X}$ in P. The notions of free and bound names (as well as free and bound process variables) are defined in the usual way. We identify processes modulo renaming of bound names and of bound process variables. By convention, we exclude recursive processes where unguarded recursion variables occur.

The semantics of the language is defined via a structural congruence and a reduction relation. Structural congruence is standard, except that it includes the law $\text{rec}\,\mathscr{X}.P \equiv P\{\text{rec}\,\mathscr{X}.P/\mathscr{X}\}$ for unfolding recursive processes, where $P\{Q/\mathscr{X}\}$ denotes the capture-avoiding substitution of the free occurrences of $\mathscr{X}$ by process Q in P. Reduction is defined by the rules in Fig. 2. Rule (R-Com) describes the synchronization of two processes exchanging a message: the sender emits a message with a label l_k that is among those accepted by the receiver and the argument z of the message replaces the bound input parameter in the appropriate continuation P_k of the receiver. The remaining rules close the relation under language contexts—name restriction and parallel composition—as well as under structural congruence.

3   Types and Typing Contexts

This section starts by introducing the notion of strict partial orders which allows to identify well-formed communication dependencies in processes. It then introduces types and operations on these, most notably type split which allows to separate a type in two disjoint "slices" of behavior.

$$p ::= \ ! \ | \ ? \ | \ \tau \qquad \text{(Polarity)}$$
$$T ::= a^n \, p \, l \, T \qquad \text{(Shared type, S)}$$
$$| \ B^{\prec} \qquad \text{(Linear type, L)}$$
$$\Gamma ::= \cdot \ | \ \Gamma, x : T \qquad \text{(Context)}$$
$$\Delta ::= \cdot \ | \ \Delta, X : (\Gamma; \prec) \ \text{(Recursion context)}$$

$$B ::= \text{end} \qquad \text{(Stop)}$$
$$| \ B_1 \, | \, B_2 \qquad \text{(Parallel)}$$
$$| \ \mu\alpha.B \qquad \text{(Recursion)}$$
$$| \ \alpha \qquad \text{(Variable)}$$
$$| \ a^n \, p \{ l_i.T_i.B_i \}_{i \in I} \ \text{(Prefix summation)}$$

Fig. 3. Syntax of types and typing contexts

Strict Partial Orders. We consider an infinite set of event identifiers $\mathcal{E}$ and the set of natural numbers $\mathbb{N}$, and use $a, b, \ldots$ to range over $\mathcal{E}$ and $n, m, \ldots$ to range over $\mathbb{N}$. We use a^n to denote an element in set $\mathcal{E} \times \mathbb{N}$. We further introduce a distinguished event, $\top$, use $e, f, \ldots$ to range over $(\mathcal{E} \times \mathbb{N}) \cup \{\top\}$, and call this set the *set of events*. A *strict (or irreflexive) partial order* $\prec$ over the set of events is a binary relation that is asymmetric (hence irreflexive) and transitive. We write $e \prec f$ when the pair (e, f) is in $\prec$, and $supp(\prec)$ for the *support* of $\prec$, namely the set of events that occur in $\prec$.

Next we define two *partial* operations over strict partial orders. We write $e + \prec$ for the strict partial order obtained by *adding a least event e* to $\prec$, provided that e does not occur in $supp(\prec)$. Formally, $e + \prec \triangleq \prec \cup \{(e, f) \mid f \in supp(\prec)\} \cup \{(e, \top)\}$, where we explicitly add the pair $(e, \top)$ since $\prec$ may be empty (in which case $e + \emptyset$ is defined as $\{(e, \top)\}$). We write $\prec_1 \uplus \prec_2$ for the least strict partial order that includes both $\prec_1$ and $\prec_2$, if it exists. We use $\uplus$ to gather the communication dependency structures of, e.g., two parallel processes.

Types. The syntax of types is given in Fig. 3. Our types are based on conversation types [4] extended with event annotations following the approach introduced in [22]. A polarity p describes a communication capability: ! specifies an output; ? specifies an input; and τ specifies a synchronization, i.e., a matched communication pair (cf., [4]). At the type level we distinguish two separate categories of channels: *shared* (or unrestricted) channels—ranged over by S—are used for modeling (possibly persistent) services having a publicly known name, with which sessions can be established; *linear* channels—ranged over by L—are used for modeling the private conversations within sessions. Note that such distinction between shared and linear channels appears at the type level only, while they are treated uniformly in the process model. For the sake of simplicity we omit non-channel types (e.g., Int) which could be easily added.

A type $a^n \, p \, l \, T$ describes the behavior of a shared channel via an event a^n, a polarity p, a message label l and a type T describing the message argument. We associate shared types with events to temporally relate shared communications with others, in particular with the communications specified by the message type T.

A type $B^{\prec}$ captures the linear usage of a channel: B specifies the *behavior* of a process w.r.t. the channel, whereas $\prec$ specifies the ordering of events expected from the external environment. Informally, $\prec$ is used in a type $B^{\prec}$ to represent the sequentiality information that B admits but does not impose. For example, when typing a process that concurrently sends messages hello and bye the type *may* specify that the outputs on hello and bye actually take place one after the other if such order is imposed by the corresponding inputs (present in the external process environment).

Behavioral types B include inaction end, parallel composition $B_1 \, | \, B_2$ of two independent behaviors B_1 and B_2, recursive types $\mu\alpha.B$, recursion variables α, and (prefixed) summation $a^n p\{l_i T_i.B_i\}_{i \in I}$. Sums capture communication capabilities associated with event a^n, polarity p, and a menu of synchronization options. Each entry in the menu is identified by a distinct label l_i, the type of the argument of the message T_i, and the behavior B_i that takes place after the synchronization. We say that a linear type $B^{\prec}$ is well-formed if $supp(\prec)$ does not include events associated with communication actions of polarity τ in B (since no further ordering information can be provided for such actions by the external environment). In the remainder, whenever we write $B^{\prec}$, we assume that $B^{\prec}$ is well formed. We also identify α-equivalent (recursive) types by convention.

Following the ideas presented in [22], we associate with each linear communication an event a^n so as to temporally relate the communication action described by the summation with respect to others, establishing an overall ordering of communications. In this work, we introduce the notion of *iteration*, by adding to events a natural number n, allowing to describe infinite chains of (related) events. Informally, the index allows to capture the several "stages" of a type by means of an *increment*, so, for example, $\mu\alpha.a^1 \tau 1 T.b^1 \tau m T'.\alpha$ unfolds to $a^1 \tau 1 T.b^1 \tau m T'.\mu\alpha.a^2 \tau 1 T.b^2 \tau m T'.\alpha$ so as to associate the first iteration with index 1 and the second iteration with index 2 and so on and so forth.

Operations on Types. We write $labels(B)$ for the set of labels occurring in B. We say that B_1 and B_2 are *behaviorally independent*, and denote it by $B_1 \# B_2$, if $labels(B_1) \cap labels(B_2) = \emptyset$ so that disjoint message sets ensure behavioral independence. We also need an operation to *remove* part of the partial order in a type, defined as $B^{\prec} \setminus \prec \triangleq B^{\prec \setminus \prec}$, and $S \setminus \prec \triangleq S$. Since linear types may contain sequentiality assumptions, we use this operation to clear hypotheses that are proved externally.

In order to capture the several iterations of a communication that may repeat itself in the context of recursion, we introduce an operator that *increments* the index associated with an event by a given factor, defined as $inc(a^n, m) \triangleq a^{n+m}$ and $inc(\top, m) \triangleq \top$. We then extend inc to strict partial orders, pointwise, and to behavior types so that $inc(a^n p\{l_i T_i.B_i\}_{i \in I}, m) \triangleq a^{n+m} p\{l_i inc(T_i, m).inc(B_i, m)\}_{i \in I}$. The increment of a behavior is an homomorphism for all other constructs. The increment operation on types affects only linear types, $inc(B^{\prec}, m) \triangleq inc(B, m)^{inc(\prec, m)}$, since events associated with shared communications are not considered to be repeated in different stages but rather to be repeated always at the same stage, hence $inc(a^n p l T, m) \triangleq a^n p l T$. Essentially, we model shared communication repetition using replication (via recursion), so shared replicated communication actions have the same temporal ordering, while we model linear recursive repetition using a sequential chain of events. The index is then used to capture repetition (without cycles) in the orderings.

To simplify the typing rules, we define a type equivalence relation $\equiv$ that includes commutativity, associativity and neutral end for $|$, as well as iso-recursive equivalence for recursive types $\mu\alpha.B \equiv B\{\mu\alpha.inc(B, m)/\alpha\}$ for some $m > 0$, saying that the next iteration of the behavior is captured by the increment of the events (we use any positive m so as to support misalignment between processes and types).

We now introduce operations that capture the temporal ordering prescribed by types. We write $events(B)$ for the set of elements of $\mathscr{E} \times \mathbb{N}$ occurring in a behavior B, not including the events in message types. Formally:

$$events(B) \triangleq \begin{cases} \emptyset & \text{if } B = \text{end or } B = \alpha \\ events(B_1) \cup events(B_2) & \text{if } B = B_1 | B_2 \\ \{e\} \cup \bigcup_{i \in I} events(B_i) & \text{if } B = e\, p\{l_i T_i.B_i\}_{i \in I} \\ \{inc(e,k) \mid e \in events(B') \text{ and } k \geq 0\} & \text{if } B = \mu\alpha.B' \end{cases}$$

Notice that $events(\mu\alpha.B)$ includes all the events in the body of the recursion, incremented zero or more times so as to capture the first and the following iterations. We extend the operation to types, by defining $events(B^\prec) \triangleq events(B)$, as we are only interested in linear types where $supp(\prec) \subseteq events(B)$, and by defining $events(e\,p\,|\,T) \triangleq \{e\}$.

We write $B\!\downarrow$ for the strict partial order over $\mathscr{E} \times \mathbb{N}$ induced by a type B. Notice that $B\!\downarrow$ is a partial operator since it uses $\uplus$ and $+$. Formally:

$$B\!\downarrow \triangleq \begin{cases} \emptyset & \text{if } B = \text{end or } B = \alpha \\ B_1\!\downarrow \uplus B_2\!\downarrow & \text{if } B = B_1 | B_2 \\ e + (\uplus_{i \in I} B_i\!\downarrow) & \text{if } B = e\, p\{l_i T_i.B_i\}_{i \in I} \\ \{(inc(e,k), inc(f,k)) \mid (e,f) \in B'\!\downarrow \text{ and } k \geq 0\} \cup \\ \quad \{(inc(e,m), inc(f,n)) \mid e, f \in events(B') \text{ and } 0 \leq m < n\} & \text{if } B = \mu\alpha.B' \end{cases}$$

Notice that the operation adds a least event in the case of the prefix summation, and for recursions it adds all pairs obtained from the body of the recursion (incremented zero or more times) and all pairs that pertain to different iterations. We extend the definition to types by taking $(e\,p\,|\,T)\!\downarrow \triangleq (e, \top)$ and $B^\prec\!\downarrow \triangleq B\!\downarrow \setminus \prec$, where $\setminus$ denotes set difference. The definition for linear types considers the order obtained from the behavioral type removing the ordering expected from the external environment, so $B^\prec\!\downarrow$ characterizes exclusively the ordering imposed by the type.

To identify types that characterize channels that do not depend on the external environment to evolve, and hence are "self-sustained" communication wise, we introduce a predicate that is true for types containing no unmatched communication actions. We say that a behavioral type B is *matched* if it contains no top-level (i.e., excluding message types) input or output polarities. We extend the definition to linear types by considering $matched(B^\prec) \triangleq matched(B)$ (which, by well-formedness, implies $\prec = \emptyset$), and $matched(e\,p\,|\,T) \triangleq p = ?$. A message type of polarity ? says that a shared input is available. Since we are only interested in capturing continuously available shared inputs, ? shared types "absorb" (as will be clear from the definition of type splitting) ! shared types, so as to capture the fact that (replicated) shared inputs are still available after synchronization. Hence, the definition of $matched()$ for shared types excludes solely (unmatched) shared outputs, and considers the (infinitely available) shared inputs to be matched (regardless whether they are used or not).

Typing Contexts. The syntax of typing contexts is given in Fig. 3. We assume by convention that, in a typing context $\Gamma, x : T$ and in a recursion environment $\Delta, \mathscr{X} : (\Gamma; \prec)$, the name x and the process variable $\mathscr{X}$ do not occur in Γ and in Δ, respectively, as usual. Also, we consider contexts up to permutations of their entries.

We denote by Γ_{un} contexts that contain only outputs on shared channels and linear types with end behavior, that is, if $x : T$ is in Γ_{un}, then T is either $e\,!\,l\,T'$ or end^0. We use such contexts to describe systems that only use shared resources, namely to describe (the continuation of) processes that input on shared channels. We exclude shared inputs

$$\frac{}{B = B \circ \mathsf{end}} \qquad \frac{B_1 = B_1' \circ B_1'' \quad B_2 = B_2' \circ B_2'' \quad B_1 \# B_2}{B_1 \mid B_2 = B_1' \mid B_2' \circ B_1'' \mid B_2''} \qquad \text{(B-End,B-Par)}$$

$$\frac{B = B_1 \circ B_2}{\mu\alpha.B = \mu\alpha.B_1 \circ \mu\alpha.B_2} \qquad \frac{\forall i \in I \quad B_i = B_i' \circ B \quad e\,p\{l_i T_i.\mathsf{end}\}_{i \in I} \# B}{e\,p\{l_i T_i.B_i\}_{i \in I} = e\,p\{l_i T_i.B_i'\}_{i \in I} \circ B} \qquad \text{(B-Rec,B-Break)}$$

$$\frac{}{\alpha = \alpha \circ \alpha} \qquad \frac{\forall i \in I \quad B_i = B_i' \circ B_i''}{e\,\tau\{l_i T_i.B_i\}_{i \in I} = e\,?\{l_i T_i.B_i'\}_{i \in I} \circ e\,!\{l_i T_i.B_i''\}_{i \in I}} \qquad \text{(B-Var,B-Sync)}$$

Fig. 4. Behavioural type splitting

$$\frac{B = B_1 \circ B_2 \quad \prec = \prec_1 \setminus B_2^{\prec_2}{\downarrow} \cup \prec_2 \setminus B_1^{\prec_1}{\downarrow} \cup B{\downarrow} \setminus (B_1{\downarrow} \cup B_2{\downarrow})}{B^{\prec} = B_1^{\prec_1} \circ B_2^{\prec_2}} \qquad \text{(L-Split)}$$

Fig. 5. Linear type splitting

from Γ_{un} in order to avoid "nested" shared inputs, so that inputs on shared channels are continuously active (cf. uniform receptiveness [1, 19]). Similarly, we denote by Γ_{lin} contexts that contain only linear types, that is, types of the form $B^{\prec}$.

We are interested in systems where all communications are matched, i.e., typed against *matched* contexts, defined as the pointwise extension of the *matched* predicate on types. We also lift the notions of type *increment*, *inc*, type *equivalence*, $\equiv$, and partial order difference, $\setminus$, pointwise to contexts.

Splitting and Conformance. We now introduce two notions crucial to our development, namely *splitting* (inspired by [2] and by the *merge* operation of [4]) that explains how behaviors can be decomposed and safely distributed to distinct parts of a process (e.g., to the branches of a parallel composition), and *conformance* that captures the desired relation between typing contexts and strict partial orders.

We say type T conforms to order $\prec$, noted *conforms*$(T, \prec)$, if $T{\downarrow} \subseteq \prec$. Notice that since $T{\downarrow}$ excludes the ordering expected from the external environment, conformance focuses on the order imposed by the types (which is the focus of the overall ordering). The *conforms* predicate is defined on typing contexts as the pointwise extension of the predicate on types, so *conforms*$(\Gamma, \prec)$ ensures that every communication action specified in Γ is ordered by $\prec$.

Splitting is defined both on types and on typing contexts. We write $T = T_1 \circ T_2$ to mean that type T is split in types T_1 and T_2, and likewise for $\Gamma = \Gamma_1 \circ \Gamma_2$. Behavioral type splitting, linear type splitting, shared type splitting and context splitting are given by the rules in Figs. 4–7 (where we omit symmetric rules).

We briefly describe the rules in Fig 4. A behavioral type may be split in itself and in end, so as to allow, e.g., to give away the behavior completely to one branch of a parallel composition—rule (B-End). A parallel composition $B_1 \mid B_2$ (where B_1 and B_2 are apart #) may be split in two parallel compositions, the components of which are obtained by decomposing B_1 and B_2—rule (B-Par). A recursive type is split in two recursive types, the bodies of which are obtained by splitting the body of the incoming recursive type—rule (B-Rec). Also, a recursion variable may be split in itself—rule (B-Var).

A prefix summation may be split in an independent (#) behavior, obtained by splitting (all) the continuations, and in the prefix whose continuations specify the remaining

$$\frac{p \in \{?,!\}}{e?!T = e?!T \circ epIT}\text{(S-In-L)} \qquad \frac{}{\cdot = \cdot \circ}\text{(C-Empty)} \qquad \frac{\Gamma = \Gamma_1 \circ \Gamma_2}{\Gamma,x\colon T = \Gamma_1,x\colon T \circ \Gamma_2}\text{(C-Left)}$$

$$\frac{}{e!IT = e!IT \circ e!IT}\text{(S-Out)} \qquad \frac{\Gamma = \Gamma_1 \circ \Gamma_2 \quad T = T_1 \circ T_2}{\Gamma,x\colon T = \Gamma_1,x\colon T_1 \circ \Gamma_2,x\colon T_2}\text{(C-Split)}$$

Fig. 6. Shared type splitting   **Fig. 7.** Context splitting

behavior—rule (B-Break). A synchronized (τ) prefix summation may be split in prefix with dual polarities (? and !) whose continuations are obtained by splitting the synchronized prefix continuations—rule (B-Sync).

Notice that rule (B-Break) may decompose a type in such a way that the overall ordering is not guaranteed by the splitted types. To this end we keep track of the ordering assumptions in the linear type splitting, defined in Fig. 5. A linear type split is defined by the behavioral split and also by a separation of the ordering assumptions $\prec$, such that everything $\prec$ assumes may be assumed by $\prec_1$ or $\prec_2$, but $\prec_1$ and $\prec_2$ may specify other assumptions which are actually ensured by $B_2^{\prec_2}$ and by $B_1^{\prec_1}$, respectively. Also, $\prec$ necessarily contains the ordering present in B (i.e., $B\!\downarrow$) that is not supported by either B_1 or B_2, hence any sequentiality information that B specifies introduced via (B-Break).

Shared type splitting (Fig. 6) decomposes shared communication capabilities in two distinct ways, depending on whether the polarity of the incoming type is ? or !. A shared input is split in a shared input and either in an output or another input, via rule (S-In-L). Essentially, the latter allows for typing processes that separately offer the input capability (e.g., a service that is provided by two distinct sites), and the former allows for typing processes that offer the dual communication capabilities (e.g., a service provider and a service client). A shared output is split in two shared outputs—rule (S-Out)—which allows for typing processes that offer the output capability separately (e.g., two clients of some service). Notice type splitting preserves the message types and event association so as to guarantee the dual communication actions agree on the type of what is communicated and on the ordering.

Context splitting (Fig. 7) allows to divide a context in two distinct ways: context entries either go into the left or the right outgoing contexts—(C-Left) as well as the omitted symmetric rule—or they go in both contexts—(C-Split). The latter form lifts the (type) behavior distribution to the context level, while the former allows to delegate the entire behavior to a part of the process, leaving no usage at all to the other part. To lighten notation we use $\Gamma_1 \circ \Gamma_2$ to represent any Γ such that $\Gamma = \Gamma_1 \circ \Gamma_2$ (if such Γ exists). Notice that, given Γ_1 and Γ_2, there may be more than one Γ such that $\Gamma = \Gamma_1 \circ \Gamma_2$.

4 Typing System

This section introduces our typing system and the main results of the paper, namely soundness of the type system (Theorem 1) and liveness (Theorem 2).

Typing System. The typing system characterizes processes according to typing assumptions for free process variables (Δ) and for names (Γ), as well as an overall ordering of events ($\prec$). We say process P is well-typed if $\Delta;\Gamma;\prec \vdash P$ is derivable using the

$$\frac{\Delta;\Gamma_1;\prec_1 \vdash P \quad \Delta;\Gamma_2;\prec_2 \vdash Q}{\Delta;\Gamma_1 \circ \Gamma_2;\prec_1 \uplus \prec_2 \vdash P \mid Q} \qquad \frac{\Delta;\Gamma,x:T;\prec \vdash P \quad matched(T)}{\Delta;\Gamma;\prec \vdash (vx)P} \qquad \text{(T-Par,T-New)}$$

$$\frac{}{\Delta;\Gamma_{un};\emptyset \vdash 0} \qquad \frac{\Delta,\mathscr{X}:(inc(\Gamma_{lin},n);inc(\prec,n));\Gamma_{lin};\prec \vdash P \quad n \in \mathbb{N}}{\Delta;\Gamma_{lin};\prec \vdash \mathsf{rec}\,\mathscr{X}.P} \qquad \text{(T-Inact,T-LRec)}$$

$$\frac{\Delta,\mathscr{X}:(\Gamma;\prec);\Gamma;\prec \vdash P \quad \Gamma = \Gamma_{un},x:e?lT \quad \prec = (e + \prec'') \uplus \prec' \quad e \notin supp(\prec')}{\Delta;\Gamma;\prec \vdash \mathsf{rec}\,\mathscr{X}.P} \qquad \text{(T-URec)}$$

$$\frac{\Delta(\mathscr{X}) = (\Gamma;\prec) \quad conforms(\Gamma,\prec)}{\Delta;\Gamma;\prec \vdash \mathscr{X}} \qquad \frac{\Delta,\Gamma_2;\prec \vdash P \quad \Gamma_1 \equiv \Gamma_2}{\Delta;\Gamma_1;\prec \vdash P} \qquad \text{(T-Var,T-Equiv)}$$

$$\frac{\forall_{i\in I}\; \Delta;\Gamma,x:B_i^{\prec_i},y_i:T_i;\prec_i \vdash P_i}{\Delta;\Gamma,x:e?\{l_iT_i.B_i\}_{i\in I}^{\uplus_{i\in I}\prec_i};\; e + (\uplus_{i\in I}\prec_i) \vdash x?\{l_iy_i.P_i\}_{i\in I}} \qquad \text{(T-LinIn)}$$

$$\frac{\Delta;\Gamma,x:B_k^{\prec'};\prec \vdash P \quad k \in I}{\Delta;(\Gamma,x:e!\{l_iT_i.B_i\}_{i\in I}^{\prec'}) \circ y:T_k;\; e + (\prec \uplus T_k\!\downarrow) \vdash x!l_k y.P} \qquad \text{(T-LinOut)}$$

$$\frac{\Delta;\Gamma_{un},x:e?lT,y:T;e + \prec \vdash P}{\Delta;\Gamma_{un},x:e?lT;e + \prec \vdash x?l y.P} \qquad \frac{\Gamma = (\Gamma_{un},x:e!lT) \circ y:T \quad \cdot;\cdot;\emptyset \vdash P}{\Delta;\Gamma;e+T\!\downarrow \vdash x!l y.P} \qquad \text{(T-UIn,T-UOut)}$$

Fig. 8. Typing rules

rules in Fig. 8. We briefly comment on the rule. In rule (T-Par) the parallel composition is typed if the branches are typed in splittings ($\circ$) of the context and a decomposition of the order. In rule (T-New) the name restriction is typed if the process in the scope of the restriction is typed in the same contexts together with the typing assumption for the usage of the restricted name which must be a *matched* type (all communication prefixes are matched). Notice that the overall ordering $\prec$ is preserved, hence the ordering prescribed by name x is still present in the conclusion, even if the type T of x is not.

In rule (T-Inact) the inaction process is typed with any usage of recursion variables (Δ), and with only outputs on shared labels and end linear types (Γ_{un}), and an empty overall ordering ($\emptyset$). In rule (T-LRec) a recursive process is well typed if so is the body of the recursion in the same typing context Γ_{lin} (which only includes linear usages) and overall ordering $\prec$, and in the recursion environment augmented with an assumption for the recursion variable: the variable is assumed to have exactly the same usage and overall ordering *up to* an increment (for some n) of the natural exponent of the events. Rule (T-LRec) therefore captures, in a fairly intuitive way, subsequent iterations of a (linear) recursion: the point of the next iteration is characterized by an increment of the typing and ordering.

Rule (T-URec) addresses a recursive process that uses only shared resources where no increment is involved since shared communications do not have iterations (their repetition is considered to happen at the level of a single iteration). So the recursion environment is augmented with the typing and ordering that types the body of the recursion. The typing mentions only shared exponential resources (Γ_{un}) together with a shared input (on x), as we intend to capture replicated shared inputs. In order to ensure that the shared input is an immediate action of the body of the recursion, the ordering makes e a minimal event. Given the above explanation, rule (T-Var) is straightforward:

the assumption for the variable provides the context and ordering for the process. In rule (T-Equiv) we embed the notion of context equivalence in the type system, since we need to unfold recursive types when typing the body of a recursion.

Communication prefixes are also typed in separate rules, depending on the type of the subject of the communication. In rule (T-LinIn) the input on a channel x with linear usage is typed if the continuation processes are typed with the usages for x prescribed in the prefix summation type, together with a separation of the ordering assumptions; also, by adding a typing assumption for the usage of the received name (according to the corresponding message type), and a separation of the events *greater than e* in the overall ordering. The e is the event associated with the prefix summation (notice that we pick *fresh* events since $+$ is undefined otherwise). The fact that events in the continuation are of greater order ensures that the communications in the continuation are in fact prescribed to take place after the prefix itself. Notice that the overall ordering registered in the conclusion is a tree rooted in e. Further notice that the communication dependency structure of the received name is transparently kept in the conclusion (the ordering prescribed by the channel usages is *invariantly* registered in the overall ordering). This allows us to type systems where communications on received channels are interleaved with others, configurations out of reach of related approaches.

The reasoning is similar in rule (T-LinOut). The continuation is typed by considering the continuations of the prefix summation (any prefix summation containing the only label mentioned by the process) which is uniquely associated with event e, together with the same ordering assumptions $\prec'$ (as we are only interested that the environment guarantees the order of one branch). The typing context Γ is actually the result of a split of the context registered in the conclusion, which also mentions the usage delegated in the communication for the sent name. Finally, the overall ordering in the conclusion also registers the ordering (of events greater than e) prescribed by the message type.

Rules (T-UIn) and (T-UOut) explain the typing for communications on shared channels. In rule (T-UIn) the input with shared usage is typed if the continuation process is typed adding the usage for the received name to the context. Notice that since we type the continuation with the shared input usage, the continuation must offer again the shared input behavior (so shared inputs can be typed only in the context of a recursion). Notice also that the overall ordering in the conclusion is that of the premise, as expected in a replicated process, and specifies that the event associated with the shared input is minimal (so as to ensure it is immediately available). Furthermore, we require that the remaining context mentions exclusively shared outputs (Γ_{un}) so that no other shared inputs are defined in the continuation. This would be a problem for liveness since shared inputs on *free* names defined in the continuation might leave a matching output dangling. However, we may freely type processes in the continuation that specify shared inputs in restricted names (or even in the received name).

In rule (T-UOut) we type the output on a shared channel if the continuation is typed in the empty context and empty ordering. This means that our model for shared channel communications is an asynchronous one. There are at least two approaches to guarantee that shared inputs are always active (*uniform receptiveness*): one is to exclude usage of the shared name in the continuations of *both* input and output prefixes [19] (we followed a similar approach in [22] excluding the corresponding *event* in the continuations); the other relies on an asynchronous model of communication [1]—which we adopt here for shared channels. The advantage of this approach is that it supports processes that specify in the continuation of a shared input a matching output (intuitively, think of a recursive "service" call). Also, looking at (T-UOut) and (T-Par) we argue that every process P that we have used in examples in the continuation of a shared output $x!ly.P$ can be specified (and typed) using the parallel composition $P \mid x!ly.\mathbf{0}$, essentially since the type delegated in the communication is obtained via a split of the context nonetheless. Notice that rule (T-UOut) says that the event associated with the output is minimal w.r.t. the message type in the conclusion. Notice also that the rules for communication prefixes make no distinction whatsoever on the type of the channel communicated.

One can now show that process (4) is well typed. Consider the following types.

$$T_s \triangleq \mu\alpha.e^1\,\tau\mathtt{1}\mathsf{int}.f^1\,\tau\mathsf{m}\mathsf{bool}.\alpha \qquad T_r \triangleq \mu\alpha.g^1\,\tau\mathsf{n}\mathsf{bool}.\alpha$$

Each unfolding of a type increments the indexes of the events. The splitting of these behaviors produces

$$T_{As} \triangleq \mu\alpha.e^1\,?\mathtt{1}\mathsf{int}.\alpha \qquad T_{Bs} \triangleq \mu\alpha.f^1\,?\mathsf{m}\mathsf{bool}.\alpha \qquad T_{Cs} \triangleq \mu\alpha.e^1\,!\mathtt{1}\mathsf{int}.f^1\,!\mathsf{m}\mathsf{bool}.\alpha$$

$$T_{Ar} \triangleq \mu\alpha.g^1\,?\mathsf{n}\mathsf{bool}.\alpha \qquad T_{Br} \triangleq \mu\alpha.f^1\,!\mathsf{n}\mathsf{bool}.\alpha$$

regarding sessions s and r. Now, looking at the structure of the participants in (4), we realize that the following relations must hold: the structure of A requires $e^1 \prec g^1 \prec e^2$; the structure of B requires $f^1 \prec g^1 \prec f^2$; finally, the structure of C requires $e^1 \prec f^1 \prec e^2$. Overall, it is possible to find a typing derivation for the whole process by considering the strict partial order

$$\prec \triangleq T_s{\downarrow} \cup T_r{\downarrow} \cup \{(f^i,g^i),(g^i,e^{i+1}) \mid i \in \mathbb{N}\}$$

Results. We start by mentioning some auxiliary results, in particular that conformance between the typing context and the overall ordering is ensured for all derivations. This result may be viewed as a sanity check saying that the conditions imposed by our rules are enough to keep conformance invariant in a derivation. We may also show that split is an associative relation, in particular for behavioral types. This result in particular ensures that the derivation (sub-)trees may be moved around, and used in the proof of the following (standard) results.

Lemma 1 (Subject Congruence). *If* $\Delta;\Gamma;\prec \vdash P$ *and* $P \equiv Q$ *then* $\Delta;\Gamma;\prec \vdash Q$.

Lemma 2 (Substitution). *If* $\Delta;\Gamma_1,x\colon T;\prec \vdash P$ *and* $\Gamma_2 = \Gamma_1 \circ y\colon T$ *then* $\Delta;\Gamma_2;\prec \vdash P\{x/y\}$.

The proofs follow by induction on the structure of the process and on the length of the typing derivation (respectively) along unsurprising lines. Notice that substitution uses context splitting to characterize the context that types the resulting process, since name y may already be used by P and the soundness of the substitution is guaranteed by the split. Before presenting our first main result we need to introduce two auxiliary notions that characterize reduction of contexts and of strict partial orders. As expected from a behavioral type system, as processes evolve so must the types that characterize the processes. The reduction relations for behavioral types and contexts are given in

$$\frac{k \in I}{e\,\tau\{l_i T_i.B_i\}_{i \in I} \to B_k} \qquad \frac{B_1 \to B_1'}{B_1 \,|\, B_2 \to B_1' \,|\, B_2} \qquad \frac{B_1 \equiv B_1' \to B_2' \equiv B_2}{B_1 \to B_2}$$

$$\frac{}{\cdot \to \cdot} \qquad \frac{B_1 \to B_2}{\Gamma, x: B_1^{\prec} \to \Gamma, x: B_2^{\prec}} \qquad \frac{\Gamma_1 \to \Gamma_2}{\Gamma_1, x: T \to \Gamma_2, x: T}$$

Fig. 9. Type and context reduction

$$\frac{}{\prec \to \prec} \qquad \frac{e \in supp(\prec)}{\prec \to \prec \backslash e} \qquad \frac{\Gamma_1 \to \Gamma_2 \quad \prec_1 \to \prec_2}{\Gamma_1; \prec_1 \to \Gamma_2; \prec_2}$$

Fig. 10. Order and typing reduction

Fig. 9. Note that τ-prefixed summations (in "active contexts") may reduce and a context reduces if it has an entry on a linear type prefix that reduces. Also, the empty context reduces so as to mimic synchronizations on restricted and shared channels (embedding reflexivity in context reduction); these synchronizations do not change the types.

Fig. 10 shows the reduction for orders and context/order pairs. Strict partial order reduction is also reflexive to capture both shared synchronizations and communications that *depend* on shared communications (as they take place repeatedly for each of the continuation of the shared input). Reduction is also defined by removing an event of the ordering, so as to capture *one shot* synchronizations (which includes infinite chains of synchronizations). We may now present our first main result.

Theorem 1 (Preservation). *If* $\Delta; \Gamma_1; \prec_1 \vdash P_1$ *and* $P_1 \to P_2$ *then* $\Gamma_1; \prec_1 \to \Gamma_2; \prec_2$ *and* $\Delta; \Gamma_2; \prec_2 \vdash P_2$.

The proof follows by induction on the length of the derivation of $P_1 \to P_2$. The theorem says that typing is preserved under process reduction, up to a reduction in the context and ordering. Fidelity is an immediate consequence of Theorem 1, as usual (cf. [2]), thanks to the precise correspondence between reduction in processes and in typing contexts. We now turn our attention to the liveness result, where we use $\to^n$ to denote a sequence of n reductions.

Theorem 2 (Liveness). *Let* $\Delta; \Gamma_1; \prec_1 \vdash P_1$ *with* $matched(\Gamma_1)$, *and let* $x: L_1$ *in* Γ_1 *with* $e \in events(L_1)$. *Then* $P_1 \to^n P_2$ *and* $(\Gamma_1; \prec_1) \to^n (\Gamma_2; \prec_2)$ *and* $\Delta; \Gamma_2; \prec_2 \vdash P_2$ *with* $x: L_2$ *in* Γ_2 *and* $e \notin events(L_2)$, *for some* $n > 0$.

In words, every event e occurring in the type of a linear channel used by a well-typed process can eventually disappear from the type environment. This means that either e is associated with an (inter)action that can eventually be performed by the process, or that e occurs in a branch of a choice which is not selected. This property is akin to *lock freedom* [13] or *progress* [3, 6, 12] except that e in Theorem 2 can be associated with an action that is arbitrarily deep within the process structure, whereas lock freedom and progress are usually formulated for top-level actions only. The proof invariant is that for each linear synchronization prescribed by the types there is either an immediate corresponding synchronization in the process or there are preceding actions which necessarily are of "lesser" order. The fact that behaviors described by linear types have a correspondence with the communication capabilities of processes is a standard property of linear type theories.

Notice that we are not able to characterize shared usages in the same way, as the events associated with them are persistent. However, we may immediately conclude that since any linear synchronization that depends on a shared synchronization takes place then so does the shared synchronization (in fact, our proof relies on the fact that also shared synchronizations are live, along with communications in restricted channels with matched typings). Notice also that our type-based approach addresses processes with "unmatched" typing, just as long as we consider them up to the composition with any other processes for which the resulting typing is *matched*—in particular via rule (T-Par) of Fig. 8. An immediate consequence of Theorem 1 and Theorem 2 combined is that any configuration reachable from a matched typed one (as the matched predicate is invariant under context reduction) also has the liveness property.

5 Concluding Remarks

We have presented a type system for multiparty session-based communication-centred systems that guarantees *liveness* in addition to session *fidelity* even when multiple sessions are interleaved. Compared to other models for multiparty session communication, our approach strives to achieve minimality of both language and type features. Regarding language features, we rely on message labels for preventing communication races on linear channels, whereas other approaches make use of *channel polarities* [9], of distinct *channel endpoints* [21], or *roles* [3, 6]. Moreover, we do not make use of dedicated session initialization primitives. Regarding type features, our work exploits notions introduced in [2, 4] (e.g., the τ polarity and the split operator), allowing us to use the same type language for specifying both *global* and *local* types. This is in contrast with common multiparty session type theories such as [3, 6, 12], which introduce distinct languages for global and local types connected by a projection operation from the former into the latter.

A number of type-based techniques guaranteeing deadlock freedom, progress, or liveness properties have been proposed. Kobayashi [13, 14] presents type systems for *lock-free* and *deadlock-free* processes written in the pure π-calculus. Roughly speaking, every top-level input/output prefix in a lock-free process is guaranteed to be eventually consumed, whereas a deadlock-free process is one that is always able to reduce, unless it has terminated. The type systems rely on *channel usages*, which are behavioral types resembling session types where actions are annotated with pairs of *obligation/capability* levels, roughly denoting the time at which actions begin/are supposed to end. Top-level actions with a finite capability level are guaranteed to succeed in a finite amount of time (and possibly under some fairness assumption). For session-based languages, the relevant works on binary sessions are [8, 16], while [3, 6] deal with multiparty sessions. The basic idea of [3, 6, 8] is to devise a type system that detects the *dependency graph* between different sessions, where a dependency arises if a (blocking) action in one session guards an action pertaining a different session. Liveness is guaranteed if the dependency graph is acyclic. [16] leverages Kobayashi's technique (in [13]) from channel usages to session types showing that such technique can achieve a greater accuracy when compared to [3, 6, 8]. The present work differs from these in several minor and major ways.

In particular, our process model is synchronous, while the ones in [3, 6, 16] is asynchronous. Asynchrony has a non-trivial impact in the type system for progress, mainly because output actions are *non-blocking*. The progress property considered in [3, 6] assumes that missing session participants can eventually join the system at any time. In practice, this assumption implies that any action on shared channels is considered non-blocking, because it is always possible to add some (well-typed) processes that provide for the missing messages. Also, [6] defines a syntax-directed type system and automatic inferences are known for the systems described in [13, 14]. In our case, the definition of a syntax-directed type system and of an inference algorithm remain open problems.

One major difference between our work and the aforementioned ones, which constitutes the main technical contribution, regards the treatment of recursive types. In all previous works, annotations such as obligation/capability levels in [13, 14], dependency graphs [3, 6], timestamps [16] are statically associated with types, regardless of their recursive structure. In our case, unfolding a recursive type has the effect to "freshen" the events occurring therein. This significantly increases the range of well-typed processes. In particular, none of the aforementioned works is able to prove progress for non-trivial recursive processes interleaving (blocking) actions on different channels. For example, the (appropriate encoding of the) (4) is ill typed according to all previous type systems. More recently, the first author has studied a type system for deadlock and lock freedom which is capable of addressing non-trivial recursive process configurations, albeit in the context of the linear π-calculus [17]. The type system in [17] can prove that a configuration such as (4) is (dead)lock free, but only encoding the multiparty session s in terms of several binary sessions which, in turn, can be encoded using linear channels. In the present work instead we consider a calculus with a primitive notion of multiparty session, addressing scenarios that cannot be compiled down to binary sessions.

Naturally a type-based approach is only relevant if it can be taken into practice, so decidability is a fundamental property. We may argue that we can extract a decidable type-checking procedure from our type system, if we annotate restricted names with their types (as usual) and process recursion variables with the increment factor (together with confining unfoldings to a "just-in-time" setting). Inference is also an important issue as it allows to save the programmer's effort to specify the types and increase the probability that such advanced type system can actually be used in practice. Although we believe these are very important questions to address, we decided to leave them to future clarification and focus on the principles of our approach for now, so as to make further efforts worthwhile. Furthermore, observing that types are becoming very rich characterizations of process behavior (in our case how and when channels are used), one may ask if it is possible to deduce processes from types (e.g., [5]) and spare the "programmer" the effort of writing programs and just ask him to write the types.

Acknowledgments. This work was supported by MIUR PRIN CINA 2010LHT4KM, FCT through project Liveness, PTDC/ EIA–CCO/117513/2010, and LaSIGE Strategic Project, PEst–OE/EEI/UI0408/2014. We are grateful to the COORDINATION'14 reviewers whose comments helped us clarifying and improving the paper.

References

1. Amadio, R.M., Boudol, G., Lhoussaine, C.: On message deliverability and non-uniform receptivity. Fundam. Inform. 53, 105–129 (2002)
2. Baltazar, P., Caires, L., Vasconcelos, V.T., Vieira, H.T.: A type system for flexible role assignment in multiparty communicating systems. In: Palamidessi, C., Ryan, M.D. (eds.) TGC 2012. LNCS, vol. 8191, pp. 82–96. Springer, Heidelberg (2013)
3. Bettini, L., Coppo, M., D'Antoni, L., De Luca, M., Dezani-Ciancaglini, M., Yoshida, N.: Global progress in dynamically interleaved multiparty sessions. In: van Breugel, F., Chechik, M. (eds.) CONCUR 2008. LNCS, vol. 5201, pp. 418–433. Springer, Heidelberg (2008)
4. Caires, L., Vieira, H.T.: Conversation types. Theor. Comput. Sci. 411, 4399–4440 (2010)
5. Carbone, M., Honda, K., Yoshida, N.: Structured communication-centered programming for web services. ACM Trans. Program. Lang. Syst. 34, 8 (2012)
6. Coppo, M., Dezani-Ciancaglini, M., Padovani, L., Yoshida, N.: Inference of Global Progress Properties for Dynamically Interleaved Multiparty Sessions. In: De Nicola, R., Julien, C. (eds.) COORDINATION 2013. LNCS, vol. 7890, pp. 45–59. Springer, Heidelberg (2013)
7. Coppo, M., Dezani-Ciancaglini, M., Yoshida, N., Padovani, L.: Global progress for dynamically interleaved multiparty sessions. MSCS (to appear)
8. Dezani-Ciancaglini, M., de'Liguoro, U., Yoshida, N.: On progress for structured communications. In: Barthe, G., Fournet, C. (eds.) TGC 2007. LNCS, vol. 4912, pp. 257–275. Springer, Heidelberg (2008)
9. Gay, S.J., Hole, M.: Subtyping for session types in the pi calculus. Acta Inf. 42, 191–225 (2005)
10. Honda, K.: Types for dyadic interaction. In: Best, E. (ed.) CONCUR 1993. LNCS, vol. 715, pp. 509–523. Springer, Heidelberg (1993)
11. Honda, K., Vasconcelos, V.T., Kubo, M.: Language primitives and type discipline for structured communication-based programming. In: Hankin, C. (ed.) ESOP 1998. LNCS, vol. 1381, pp. 122–138. Springer, Heidelberg (1998)
12. Honda, K., Yoshida, N., Carbone, M.: Multiparty asynchronous session types. In: POPL 2008, pp. 273–284. ACM (2008)
13. Kobayashi, N.: A type system for lock-free processes. Inf. Comput. 177, 122–159 (2002)
14. Kobayashi, N.: A new type system for deadlock-free processes. In: Baier, C., Hermanns, H. (eds.) CONCUR 2006. LNCS, vol. 4137, pp. 233–247. Springer, Heidelberg (2006)
15. Milner, R., Parrow, J., Walker, D.: A calculus of mobile processes, part I and II. Inf. Comput. 100, 1–77 (1992)
16. Padovani, L.: From Lock Freedom to Progress Using Session Types. In: Proceedings of the 6th Workshop on Programming Language Approaches to Concurrency and Communication-cEntric Software (PLACES 2013). EPTCS, vol. 137, pp. 3–19 (2013)
17. Padovani, L.: Deadlock and lock freedom in the linear π-calculus. Technical report, HAL (2014)
18. Padovani, L., Vasconcelos, V.T., Vieira, H.T.: Typing liveness in multiparty communicating systems. Technical report (2014), http://hal.inria.fr/hal-00960879
19. Sangiorgi, D.: The name discipline of uniform receptiveness. Theor. Comput. Sci 221, 457–493 (1999)
20. Vasconcelos, V.T.: Typed concurrent objects. In: Pareschi, R. (ed.) ECOOP 1994. LNCS, vol. 821, pp. 100–117. Springer, Heidelberg (1994)
21. Vasconcelos, V.T.: Fundamentals of session types. Inf. Comput. 217, 52–70 (2012)
22. Torres Vieira, H., Thudichum Vasconcelos, V.: Typing progress in communication-centred systems. In: De Nicola, R., Julien, C. (eds.) COORDINATION 2013. LNCS, vol. 7890, pp. 236–250. Springer, Heidelberg (2013)

A Calculus of Self-stabilising Computational Fields[*]

Mirko Viroli[1] and Ferruccio Damiani[2]

[1] University of Bologna, Italy
mirko.viroli@unibo.it
[2] University of Torino, Italy
ferruccio.damiani@unito.it

Abstract. Computational fields are spatially distributed data structures created by diffusion/aggregation processes, designed to adapt their shape to the topology of the underlying (mobile) network and to the events occurring in it: they have been proposed in a thread of recent works addressing self-organisation mechanisms for system coordination in scenarios including pervasive computing, sensor networks, and mobile robots. A key challenge for these systems is to assure behavioural correctness, namely, correspondence of micro-level specification (computational field specification) with macro-level behaviour (resulting global spatial pattern). Accordingly, in this paper we investigate the propagation process of computational fields, especially when composed one another to achieve complex spatial structures. We present a tiny, expressive, and type-sound calculus of computational fields, enjoying self-stabilisation, i.e., the ability of computational fields to react to changes in the environment finding a new stable state in finite time.

1 Introduction

Computational fields [11,17] (sometimes simply *fields* in the following) are an abstraction traditionally used to enact self-organisation mechanisms in contexts including swarm robotics [1], sensor networks [3], pervasive computing [12], task assignment [22], and traffic control [6]. They are distributed data structures originated from pointwise events raised in some specific device (i.e., a sensor), and propagating in a whole network region until forming a spatio-temporal data structure upon which distributed and coordinated computation can take place. Example middleware/platforms supporting this notion include TOTA [12], Proto [13], and SAPERE [24,15]. The most paradigmatic example of computational field is the so-called *gradient* [4,12,15], mapping each node of the network to the minimum distance from the source node where the gradient has been injected. Gradients are key to get awareness of physical/logical distances, to project a single-device event into a whole network region, and to find the direction towards certain locations of a network, e.g., for routing purposes. A number of works

---

[*] This work has been partially supported by the EU FP7 project "SAPERE - Self-aware Pervasive Service Ecosystems" under contract No. 256873 (Viroli), by ICT COST Action IC1201 "BETTY: Behavioural Types for Reliable Large-Scale Software Systems" (Damiani), by the Italian PRIN 2010/2011 project "CINA: Compositionality, Interaction, Negotiation, Autonomicity" (Damiani & Viroli) and Ateneo/CSP project SALT (Damiani).

E. Kühn and R. Pugliese (Eds.): COORDINATION 2014, LNCS 8459, pp. 163–178, 2014.
© IFIP International Federation for Information Processing 2014

have been developed that investigate coordination models supporting fields [12,21], introduce advanced gradient-based spatial patterns [14], and develop catalogues of self-organisation mechanisms where gradients play a crucial role [8].

As with most self-organisation approaches, a key issue is to try to fill the gap between the system micro-level (the single-node computation and interaction behaviour) and the system macro-level (the shape of the globally established spatio-temporal structure), namely, ensuring that the programmed code results in the expected global-level behaviour. However, the issue of formally tackling the problem is basically yet unexplored in the context of spatial computing, coordination, and process calculi—some exceptions are [4,9], which however apply in rather ad-hoc cases. We note instead that deepening the problem will likely shed light on which language constructs are best suited for developing well-engineered self-organisation mechanisms based on computational fields, and to consolidate existing patterns or develop new ones.

In this paper we follow this direction and address the problem of finding an expressive calculus to specify the propagation process of those computational fields for which we can identify a precise mapping between system micro- and macro-level. We identified a core calculus with sound type systems formed by three constructs only: sensor fields (considered as an environmental input), pointwise functional composition of fields, and a form of *spreading* that tightly couples information diffusion and re-aggregation. The latter is constrained so as to enforce a special "terminating progressiveness" property that we identified, by which we derive self-stabilisation [7], that is, the ability of the system running computational fields to reach a stable distributed state in spite of perturbations (changes of network topology and of local data) from which it recovers in finite time. A consequence of our results is that the ultimate (and stable) state of an even complex computational field can be fully-predicted once the environment state is known (network topology and sensors state).

The remainder of this paper is organised as follows: Section 2 presents the proposed linguistic constructs by means of examples, Section 3 provides the formal calculus, Section 4 states soundness and self-stabilisation properties, and finally Section 5 discusses related works and concludes.

2   Computational Fields

From an abstract viewpoint, a computational field is simply a map from nodes of a network to some kind of value. They are used as a valuable abstraction to engineer self-organisation into networks of situated devices. Namely, out of local interactions (devices communicating with a small neighbourhood), global and coherent patterns (the computational fields themselves) establish that are robust to changes of environmental conditions. Such an adaptive behaviour is key in developing system coordination in dynamic and unpredictable environments [16].

Self-organisation and computational fields are known to build on top of three basic mechanisms [8]: diffusion (devices broadcast information to their neighbours), aggregation (multiple information can be aggregated back into a single sum-up value), and evaporation/decay (a cleanup mechanism is used to reactively adapt to changes). For instance, these mechanisms are precisely those used to create adaptive and stable

$$
\begin{array}{lr}
\texttt{e} ::= \texttt{x} \mid \texttt{v} \mid s \mid \texttt{g}(\texttt{e}_1, \ldots, \texttt{e}_n) \mid \{\texttt{e} : \texttt{g}(@, \texttt{e}_1, \ldots, \texttt{e}_n)\} & \text{expression} \\
\texttt{g} ::= \texttt{f} \mid \texttt{o} & \text{function} \\
\texttt{F} ::= \texttt{def T f}(\texttt{T}_1\ \texttt{x}_1, \ldots, \texttt{T}_n\ \texttt{x}_n)\ \texttt{is e} & \text{function definition}
\end{array}
$$

Fig. 1. Syntax of expressions and function definitions

gradients, which are building blocks of more advanced patterns [8,14]. A gradient is used to reify in any node some information about the path towards the nearest gradient source. It can be computed by the following process: value 0 is held in the gradient source; each node executes asynchronous computation rounds in which *(i)* messages from neighbours are gathered and *aggregated* in a minimum value, *(ii)* this is increased by one and is *diffused* to all neighbours, and *(iii)* the same value is stored locally, to replace the old one which *decays*. This continuous "spreading process" stabilises to a so called *hop-count gradient*, storing distance to the nearest source in any node, and automatically repairing in finite time to changes in the environment (changes of topology, position and number of sources).

2.1 Basic Ingredients

Based on these ideas, and framing them so as to isolate those cases where the spreading process actually stabilises, we propose a tiny calculus to express computational fields. Its syntax is reported in Figure 1. Following the general approach used in other languages for spatial computing [20,13], which the one we propose here can be considered as a core, our language is functional.

An atomic expression can be a variable x, a value v, or a sensor s. Variables are the formal parameters of a function. Values can be of different sorts: integers (0, 1, ... and INF meaning the maximum integer), floats (e.g., 1.0, -5.7), booleans (TRUE and FALSE), tuples (<1,TRUE>,<2,-3.5>,<1,FALSE,3>), and so on. Sensors are sources of input produced by the environment, available in each device (in examples, we shall use for them literals starting with symbol "#"). For instance, in a urban scenario we may want to use a crowd sensor #crowd yielding non-negative real numbers, to represent the perception of crowd level available in each deployed sensor over time [15].

Expressions can be composed functionally, by either a (built-in) operator o or a user-defined function f. Operators include usual mathematical/logical ones, used either in prefix or infix notation: e.g. to form expressions 2*#crowd and or(TRUE,FALSE). Operators 1st, 2nd, and so on, are used to extract the i-th component of a tuple. Functions are typed and can be declared by users; cyclic definitions are prohibited, and 0-ary function main is the program entry point. Types include int, float, bool, and tuple-types like <int,int>, <int,bool> and so on; each type T has a total ordered relation $\leq_{\text{T}}$— we use natural ordering, though in principle ad-hoc ordering relations could be used in a deployed specification language. As an example, we will use the following function restrict: def int restrict(int i, bool b) is b ? i : INF. It takes two arguments i and b, and yields the former if b is true, or INF otherwise—as we shall see, because of our semantics INF plays a role similar to an undefined value.

As in [20,13], expressions in our language have a twofold interpretation. When focussing on the *local* device behaviour, they represent values computed in a node at a given time. When reasoning about the *global* outcome of a specification instead, they represent whole computational fields: 1 is the immutable field holding 1 in each device, #crowd is the (evolving) crowd field, and so on.

The key construct of the proposed language is *spreading*, denoted by syntax $\{e : g(@, e_1, \ldots, e_n)\}$, where e is called *source* expression, and $g(@, e_1, \ldots, e_n)$ is called *progression* expression. The latter is an expression formed by an operator/function g: if it is a function, its body should not include a spreading construct or a sensor (nor the function it calls should). Additionally, the progression expression has one hole @ playing the role of a formal argument; hence the progression expression can be seen as the body of an anonymous, unary function, which we simply call *progression*. Viewed locally to a node, expression $e = \{e_0 : g(@, e_1, \ldots, e_n)\}$ is evaluated at a given time to value v as follows:

1. expressions $e_0, e_1, \ldots, e_n$ are evaluated to values $v_0, v_1, \ldots, v_n$;
2. the current values $w_1, \ldots, w_m$ of e in neighbours are gathered;
3. for each w_j in them, the progression function is applied as $g(w_j, v_1, \ldots, v_n)$, giving value w'_j;
4. the final result v is the minimum value among $\{v_0, w'_1, \ldots, w'_m\}$: this value is made available to other nodes.

Note that $v \leq_T v_0$, and if the device is isolated then $v = v_0$. Viewed globally, $\{e_0 : g(@, e_1, \ldots, e_n)\}$ represents a field initially equal to e_0; as time passes some field values can decrease due to smaller values being received from neighbours (after applying the progressive function).

The hop-count gradient created out of a #src sensor is hence simply defined as { #src : @ + 1 }, assuming #src holds what we call a zero-field, namely, it is 0 on source nodes and INF everywhere else. In this case #src is the source expression, and g is unary successor function.

2.2 Composition Examples

As a reference scenario to ground the discussion, we can consider crowd steering in pervasive environments [15]: computational fields run on top of a myriad of small devices spread in the environment (including smartphones), and are used to guide people in complex environments (buildings, cities) towards point of interested (POIs) across appropriate paths. There, a smartphone can perceive neighbour values of a gradient spread from a POI, and give directions towards smallest values so as to steer its owner and make him/her quickly descend the gradient [12]. Starting from the hop-count gradient, various kinds of behaviour useful in crowd steering can be programmed, based on the definitions reported in Figure 2. Note that as a mere syntactic sugar, we allowed there the use of functional compositions of built-in operators and user-defined functions as progression expressions. For instance, in function gradobs, the composition of restrict and + is used. A pre-processor could easily lift out such compositions into automatically-generated functions: e.g., for gradobs it could be

```
def int grad(int i) is { i : @ + #dist }
def int restrict(int i, bool b) is b ? i : INF
def int gradobs(int i, bool b) is { i : restrict(@ + #dist, b) }
def <int,bool> sum_or(<int,bool> x, <int,bool> y) is
                <1st(x) + 1st(y), 2nd(x) or 2nd(y)>
def bool sector(int i, bool b) is 2nd({ <i, b> : sum_or(@,<#dist, b>) }
def <int,int> add_to_1st(<int,int> x, int y) is <1st(x)+ y, 2nd(x)>
def <int,int> gradcast(int i, int j) is { <i, j> : add_to_1st(@, #dist) }
def int dist(int i, int j) is gradcast(restrict(j,j==0),grad(i))
def bool path(int i, int j, int w) is grad(i)+grad(j)-w < dist(i, j)
def int channel(int i, int j, int w) is gradobs(grad(j),not path(i, j, w))
```

Fig. 2. Definitions of examples

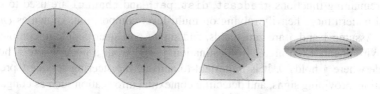

Fig. 3. A pictorial representation of various fields: hop-count gradient (a), gradient circumventing "crowd" obstacles (b), sector (c), and channel (d)

"def int gradobs$lifted(int x,int y,bool b) is restrict(x + y,b)",
so the body of gradobs could become "{ i : gradobs$lifted(@,#dist,b) }"
as the syntax of our calculus actually requires.

The first function in Figure 2 defines a more powerful gradient construct, called grad, which can be used to generalise over the hop-by-hop notion of distance: sensor #dist is assumed to exist that reifies an application-specific notion of distance as a positive number. It can be 1 everywhere to model hop-count gradient, or can vary from device to device to take into consideration contextual information. For instance, it can be the output of a crowd sensor, leading to greater distances when/where crowded areas are perceived, so as to dynamically compute routes penalising crowded areas as in [15]. In this case, note that function g maps (v_1, v_2) to $v_1 + v_2$. Figure 3 (a) shows a pictorial representation, assuming devices are uniformly spread in a 2D environment: considering that an agent or data items moves in the direction descending the values of a field, a gradient looks like a sort of uniform attractor towards the source, i.e., to the nearest source node. It should be noted that when deployed in articulated environments, the gradient would stretch and dilate to accommodate the static/dynamic shape of environment, computing optimal routes.

By suitably changing the progression function, it is also possible to block the diffusion process of gradients, as shown in function gradobs: there, by restriction we turn the gradient value to INF in nodes where the "obstacle" boolean field b holds TRUE. This can be used to completely circumvent obstacle areas, as shown in Figure 3 (b). Note that we here refer to a "blocking" behaviour, since sending a INF value has no effect on the target, and could hence be avoided for the sake of performance, e.g., not to flood the entire network. This pattern is useful whenever steering people in environments with prohibited areas—e.g. road construction in a urban scenario.

In our language it is also possible to keep track of specific situations during the propagation process, as function `sector` showcases. It takes a zero-field source i and a boolean field b denoting an area of interest: it creates a gradient of pairs, orderly holding distance from source and a boolean value representing whether the route towards the source crossed area b. As one such gradient is produced, it is wholly applied to operator 2nd, extracting a sector-like boolean field as shown in Figure 3 (c). To do so, we use a special progression function `sum_or` working on int,bool pairs, which sums the first components, and apply disjunction to the second. This pattern is useful to make people be aware of certain areas that the proposed path would cross, so as to support proper choices among alternatives [14].

The remaining functions `gradcast`, `dist`, `path` and `channel` are used to obtain a spatial pattern more heavily relying on multi-level composition, known as *channel* [20,13]. Assume i and j are zero-fields, and suppose to steer people in complex and large environments from area i to destination j, i.e., from a node where i holds 0 to a node where j holds 0. It is important to activate the steering service (spreading information, providing signs, and detecting contextual information such as congestion) only along the shortest path, possibly properly extended (of a distance width w to deal with some randomness of people movement)—see Figure 3 (d). Function `gradcast` generates a gradient, holding in each node a pair of the minimum distance to source i and the value of j in that source; this is typically used to broadcast along with a gradient a value held in its source. Function `dist` uses `gradcast` to broadcasts the distance d between i and j—i.e., the minimum distance between a node where i holds 0 and a node where j holds 0. This is done by sending a gradcast from the source of j holding the value of `grad(i)` there, which is exactly the distance d. Function `path` simply marks as positive those nodes whose distance from the shortest path between i and j is smaller than w. Finally, function `channel` generates from j a gradient confined inside `path(i,j,w)`, which can be used to steer people towards the POI at j without escaping the path area.

3   The Calculus of Self-stabilising Computational Fields

After informally introducing the proposed calculus in previous section, we now provide a formal account of it, in order to precisely state the self-stabilisation property in next section. We first discuss typing issues in Section 3.1, then formalise the operational semantics by first focussing on single-device computations in Section 3.2, and finally on whole network evolution (Section 3.3).

3.1   Typing and Self-stabilisation

The syntax of the calculus is reported in Figure 1. As a standard syntactic notation in calculi for object-oriented and functional languages [10], we use the overbar notation to denote metavariables over lists, e.g., we let $\bar{e}$ range over lists of expressions, written

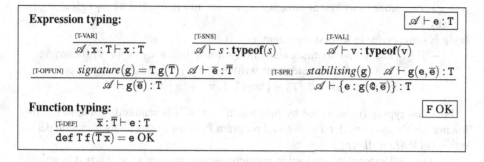

Fig. 4. Typing rules for expressions and function definitions

$e_1 \ e_2 \ \cdots \ e_n$, and similarly for $\bar{x}$, $\bar{T}$ and so on. We write $[\![T]\!]$ to denote the set of the values of type T, and *signature*(g) to denote the signature $T \ g(\bar{T})$ of g (which specifies the type T of the result and the types $\bar{T} = T_1, \ldots, T_n$ of the $n \geq 0$ arguments of g).

A program **P** in our language is a mapping from function names to function definitions, enjoying the following *sanity conditions*: *(i)* $\mathbf{P}(\mathtt{f}) = \mathtt{def} \ \mathtt{f} \ \cdots (\cdots) \ \mathtt{is} \ \cdots$ for every $\mathtt{f} \in dom(\mathbf{P})$; *(ii)* for every function name $\mathtt{f}$ appearing anywhere in **P**, we have $\mathtt{f} \in dom(\mathbf{P})$; *(iii)* there are no cycles in the function call graph (i.e., there are no recursive functions in the program); and *(iv)* $\mathtt{main} \in dom(\mathbf{P})$ and it has zero arguments.

The type system we provide aims to guarantee self-stabilisation: its typing rules are given in Figure 4. *Type environments*, ranged over by $\mathscr{A}$ and written $\bar{x} : \bar{T}$, contain type assumptions for program variables. The typing judgement for expressions is of the form $\mathscr{A} \vdash e : T$, to be read: e has type T under the type assumptions $\mathscr{A}$ for the program variables occurring in e. As a standard syntax in type systems [10], given $\bar{x} = x_1, \ldots, x_n$, $\bar{T} = T_1, \ldots, T_n$ and $\bar{e} = e_1, \ldots, e_n$ $(n \geq 0)$, we write $\bar{x} : \bar{T}$ as short for $x_1 : T_1, \ldots, x_n : T_n$, and $\mathscr{A} \vdash \bar{e} : \bar{T}$ as short for $\mathscr{A} \vdash e_1 : T_1 \ \cdots \ \mathscr{A} \vdash e_n : T_n$. Typing of variables, sensors, values, built-in operators and user-defined functions application are almost standard (in particular, values and sensors are given a type by construction). The only ad-hoc typing is provided for spreading expressions $\{e : g(@, \bar{e})\}$: they are trivially given the same type of $g(e, \bar{e})$, though additional conditions has to be checked to guarantee self-stabilisation, which are at the core of the technical result provided in this paper. In particular, any function g used in a spreading expression must be a *stabilising progression function*, according to the following definition.

Definition 1 (Stabilising progression). A function g with signature $T \ g(T_1, \ldots, T_m)$ is a *stabilising progression* (notation *stabilising*(g)) if the following conditions hold:

(i) $m > 0$ and $T = T_1$;

(ii) g is a so-called *pure operator*, namely, it is either a built-in operator o, or a user-defined function f whose call graph (including f itself) does not contain functions with spreading expressions or sensors in their body: in this case, we write $[\![g]\!]$ to denote the trivial mapping that provides the semantics of g symbol to a function;

(iii) T is so-called *locally noetherian*, to mean that $[\![T]\!]$ is equipped with a total order relation $\leq_T$, and for every element $v \in [\![T]\!]$, there are no infinite ascending chains of elements $v_0 <_T v_1 <_T v_2 \cdots$ such that (for every $n \geq 0$) $v_n <_T v$;

(iv) g is *monotone* in its first argument, i.e., $v \leq_T v'$ implies $[\![g]\!](v, \overline{v}) \leq_T [\![g]\!](v', \overline{v}))$ for any $\overline{v}$;

(v) g is *progressive* in its first argument, i.e.,
- if $[\![T]\!]$ has not a maximum element,[1] it holds that: $v <_T [\![g]\!](v, \overline{v})$ for any $\overline{v}$;
- if $[\![T]\!]$ has a maximum element[2] written $\text{top}(T)$, it holds that $[\![g]\!](\text{top}(T), \overline{v}) = \text{top}(T)$ and, for all $v \in [\![T]\!] - \{\text{top}(T)\}$, $v <_T [\![g]\!](v, \overline{v})$.

Function typing (represented by judgement "F OK") is standard. Then, in the following we always consider a *well-typed* program **P**, to mean that all the function declarations in **P** are well typed.

Note that all examples provided in previous section amount to well typed functions, with few inessential caveats. First, as already discussed, in spreading expressions we use compositions of functions: this is legitimate since it is easy to see that composition of stabilising progressions is stabilising. Second, more refined types are needed to correctly identify certain spreading expressions as stabilising. For instance, in function grad, the sensor #dist must have a positive integer type (e.g., posint), and operator + should be replaced by a sum operator that accepts a positive number only on right (e.g., +<int,posint>), and similarly for other cases. Third, to correctly type-check the functions that use tuples (which have not been explicitly modelled in the calculus) one would need to consider a polymorphic type system a la ML in the usual way. Handling all these advanced typing aspects, as well as presenting the formalisation of the *stabilising*$(\cdot)$ predicate (that is, an algorithm to check whether the conditions for a function to be stabilising hold), has not been considered here for the sake of space and since they are orthogonal aspects.

3.2 Device Computation

In the following, we let meta-variables ι and κ range over the denumerable set **I** of *device identifiers*, meta-variable I over finite sets of such devices, meta-variables u, v and w over values. Given a finite nonempty set $V \subseteq [\![T]\!]$ we denote by $\bigwedge V$ its minimum element, and write $v \wedge v'$ as short for $\bigwedge\{v, v'\}$.

To simplify the notation, we shall assume a fixed program **P** and write e_{main} to denote the body of the main function. We say that "device ι *fires*", to mean that expression e_{main} is evaluated on device ι. The result of evaluation is a *value-tree*, which is an ordered tree of values, tracking the result of any evaluated subexpression. Intuitively, such evaluation is performed against the value-trees of neighbours and the current value of sensors, and produces as result a new value-tree that is conversely made available to other neighbours for their firing.[3] The syntax of value-trees is given in Figure 5, together with the definition of the auxiliary functions $\rho(\cdot)$ and $\pi_i(\cdot)$ for extracting the root value and the i-th subtree of a value-tree, respectively—also the extension of these

---

[1] Like, e.g., the BigInteger type in JAVA.

[2] Like, e.g., the the double type in JAVA, which has top element Double.POSITIVE_INFINITY.

[3] Accordingly, since a function g used in a spreading expression $\{e_0 : g(@, e_1, \ldots, e_n)\}$ must be a pure operator (cf. Section 3.1), only the root of the produced sub-tree must be stored (c.f. rule [E-SPR]). Also, note that any implementation might massively compress the value-tree, storing only enough information for spreading expressions to be aligned.

functions to sequences of value-environments $\overline{\theta}$ is defined. We sometimes abuse the notation writing a value-tree with just the root as v instead of v(). The state of sensors σ is a map from sensor names to values, modelling the inputs received from the external world. This is written $\overline{s} \triangleright \overline{v}$ as an abuse of notation to mean $s_1 \triangleright v_1, \ldots s_n \triangleright v_n$. We shall assume that it is complete (it has a mapping for any sensor used in the program), and correct (each sensor s has a type written **typeof**(s), and is mapped to a value of that type). For this map, and for the others to come, we shall use the following notations: $\sigma(s)$ is used to extract the value that s is mapped to, $\sigma[\sigma']$ is the map obtained by updating σ with all the associations $s \triangleright v$ of σ' which do not escape the domain of σ (namely, only those such that σ is defined for s).

The computation that takes place on a single device is formalised by the big-step operational semantics rules given in Figure 5. The derived judgements are of the form $\sigma; \overline{\theta} \vdash e \Downarrow \theta$, to be read "expression e evaluates to value-tree θ on sensor state σ and w.r.t. the value-trees $\overline{\theta}$", where:

- σ is the current sensor-value map, modelling the inputs received from the external world;
- $\overline{\theta}$ is the list of the value-trees produced by the most recent evaluation of e on the current device's neighbours;
- e is the closed expression to be evaluated;
- the value-tree θ represents the values computed for all the expressions encountered during the evaluation of e— in particular $\rho(\theta)$ is the local value of field expression e.

The rules of the operational semantics are *syntax directed*, namely, the rule used for deriving a judgement $\sigma; \overline{\theta} \vdash e \Downarrow \theta$ is univocally determined by e (cf. Figure 5). Therefore, the shape of the value-tree θ is univocally determined by e, and the whole value-tree is univocally determined by σ, $\overline{\theta}$, and e.

The rules of the operational semantics are almost standard, with the exception that rules [E-OP], [E-FUN] and [E-SPR] use the auxiliary function $\pi_i(\cdot)$ to ensure that, in the judgements in the premise of the rule, the value-tree environment is aligned with the expression to be evaluated.

The most important rule is [E-SPR] which handles spreading expressions formalising the description provided in Section 2.1. It first recursively evaluates expressions e_i to value-trees η_i (after proper alignment of value-tree environment by operator $\pi_i(.)$) and top-level values v_i. Then it gets from neighbours their values w_j for the spreading expression, and for each of them g is evaluated giving top-level result w_j. The resulting value is then obtained by the minimum among v_0 and the values w_j (which equates to v_0 if there are currently no neighbours).

3.3 Network Evolution

We now provide an operational semantics for the evolution of whole networks, namely, for modelling the distributed evolution of computational fields over time. Figure 6 (top) defines key syntactic elements to this end. F models the overall computational field (state), as a map from device identifiers to value-trees. τ models *network topology*,

Value-trees and sensor-value maps:

$$\theta, \eta ::= \mathbf{v}(\overline{\theta}) \qquad\qquad\qquad\qquad \text{value-tree}$$
$$\sigma ::= \overline{s} \rhd \overline{\mathbf{v}} \qquad\qquad\qquad\qquad \text{sensor-value map}$$

Auxiliay functions:

$$\rho(\mathbf{v}(\overline{\theta})) = \mathbf{v} \qquad\qquad\qquad\qquad \pi_i(\mathbf{v}(\theta_1, \ldots, \theta_n)) = \theta_i$$
$$\rho(\theta_1, \ldots, \theta_n) = \rho(\theta_1), \ldots, \rho(\theta_n) \qquad\qquad \pi_i(\theta_1, \ldots, \theta_n) = \pi_i(\theta_1), \ldots, \pi_i(\theta_n)$$

Rules for expression evaluation: $\qquad\qquad\qquad \boxed{\sigma; \overline{\theta} \vdash \mathbf{e} \Downarrow \theta}$

$$[\text{E-SNS}] \quad \frac{}{\sigma; \overline{\theta} \vdash s \Downarrow \sigma(s)} \qquad\qquad [\text{E-VAL}] \quad \frac{}{\sigma; \overline{\theta} \vdash \mathbf{v} \Downarrow \mathbf{v}}$$

$$[\text{E-OP}] \quad \frac{\iota; \pi_1(\overline{\theta}) \vdash \mathbf{e}_1 \Downarrow \eta_1 \quad \cdots \quad \sigma; \pi_n(\overline{\theta}) \vdash \mathbf{e}_n \Downarrow \eta_n \qquad \mathbf{v} = [\![\mathbf{o}]\!](\rho(\eta_1), \ldots, \rho(\eta_n))}{\sigma; \overline{\theta} \vdash \mathbf{o}(\mathbf{e}_1, \ldots, \mathbf{e}_n) \Downarrow \mathbf{v}(\eta_1, \ldots, \eta_n)}$$

$$[\text{E-FUN}]$$
$$\frac{\mathtt{def}\ \mathsf{T}\ \mathtt{f}(\mathsf{T}_1\ \mathtt{x}_1, \ldots, \mathsf{T}_n\ \mathtt{x}_n) = \mathbf{e} \qquad \sigma; \pi_1(\overline{\theta}) \vdash \mathbf{e}_1 \Downarrow \eta_1 \quad \cdots \quad \sigma; \pi_n(\overline{\theta}) \vdash \mathbf{e}_n \Downarrow \eta_n \qquad \sigma; \pi_{n+1}(\overline{\theta}) \vdash \mathbf{e}[\mathtt{x}_1 := \rho(\theta_1') \quad \cdots \quad \mathtt{x}_n := \rho(\theta_n')] \Downarrow \mathbf{v}(\overline{\eta})}{\sigma; \overline{\theta} \vdash \mathtt{f}(\mathbf{e}_1, \ldots, \mathbf{e}_n) \Downarrow \mathbf{v}(\theta_1', \ldots, \theta_n', \mathbf{v}(\overline{\eta}))}$$

$$[\text{E-SPR}]$$
$$\frac{\begin{array}{c} \sigma; \pi_0(\overline{\theta}) \vdash \mathbf{e}_0 \Downarrow \eta_0 \quad \cdots \quad \sigma; \pi_n(\overline{\theta}) \vdash \mathbf{e}_n \Downarrow \eta_n \\ \rho(\eta_0, \ldots, \eta_n) = \mathbf{v}_0 \ldots \mathbf{v}_n \qquad \rho(\overline{\theta}) = \mathbf{w}_1 \ldots \mathbf{w}_m \\ \sigma; \emptyset \vdash \mathtt{g}(\mathbf{w}_1, \mathbf{v}_1, \ldots, \mathbf{v}_n) \Downarrow \mathbf{u}_1(\cdots) \quad \cdots \quad \sigma; \emptyset \vdash \mathtt{g}(\mathbf{w}_m, \mathbf{v}_1, \ldots, \mathbf{v}_n) \Downarrow \mathbf{u}_m(\cdots) \end{array}}{\sigma; \overline{\theta} \vdash \{\mathbf{e}_0 : \mathtt{g}(@, \mathbf{e}_1, \ldots, \mathbf{e}_n)\} \Downarrow \bigwedge\{\mathbf{v}_0, \mathbf{u}_1, \ldots, \mathbf{u}_m\}(\eta_0, \eta_1, \ldots, \eta_n)}$$

Fig. 5. Big-step operational semantics for expression evaluation

namely, a directed neighbouring graph, as a map from device identifiers to set of identifiers. Σ models *sensor (distributed) state*, as a map from device identifiers to (local) sensors (i.e., sensor name/value maps). Then, E (a couple of topology and sensor state) models the system's environment. So, a whole network configuration N is a couple of a field and environment.

We define network operational semantics in terms of small-steps transitions of the kind $N \xrightarrow{\ell} N'$, where ℓ is either a device identifier in case it represents its firing, or label ε to model any environment change. This is formalised in Figure 6 (bottom). Rule [N-FIR] models a computation round (firing) at device ι: it reconstructs the proper local environment, taking local sensors ($\Sigma(\iota)$) and accessing the value-trees of ι's neighbours; then by the single device semantics we obtain the device's value-tree θ, which is used to update system configuration. Rule [N-ENV] takes into account the change of the environment to a new well-formed environment E'. Let $\iota_1, \ldots, \iota_n$ be the domain of E'. We first construct a field F_0 associating to all the devices of E' the default value-trees $\theta_1, \ldots, \theta_n$ obtained by making devices perform an evaluation with no neighbours and sensors as of E'. Then, we adapt the existing field F to the new set of devices: $F_0[F]$ automatically handles removal of devices, map of new devices to their default value-tree, and retention of existing value-trees in the other devices.

Upon this semantics. we introduce the following definitions and notations:

Initiality. The empty network configuration $\langle \emptyset \rhd \emptyset, \emptyset \rhd \emptyset; \emptyset \rhd \emptyset \rangle$ is said *initial*.

System configurations and action labels:

$$F ::= \bar{\iota} \triangleright \bar{\theta} \qquad\qquad\qquad\qquad\qquad \text{computational field}$$
$$\tau ::= \bar{\iota} \triangleright \bar{I} \qquad\qquad\qquad\qquad\qquad\qquad \text{topology}$$
$$\Sigma ::= \bar{\iota} \triangleright \bar{\sigma} \qquad\qquad\qquad\qquad\qquad \text{sensors-map}$$
$$E ::= \tau, \Sigma \qquad\qquad\qquad\qquad\qquad\qquad \text{environment}$$
$$N ::= \langle E; F \rangle \qquad\qquad\qquad\qquad \text{network configuration}$$
$$\ell ::= \iota \mid \varepsilon \qquad\qquad\qquad\qquad\qquad\qquad \text{action label}$$

Environment well-formedness:

$WFE(\tau, \Sigma)$ holds if τ, Σ have same domain, and τ's values do not escape it.

Transition rules for network evolution: $\boxed{N \xrightarrow{\ell} N}$

$$\text{[N-FIR]} \; \frac{E = \tau, \Sigma \qquad \tau(\iota) = \bar{\iota} \qquad \Sigma(\iota); F(\bar{\iota}) \vdash \mathsf{e_{main}} \Downarrow \theta}{\langle E; F \rangle \xrightarrow{\iota} \langle E; F[\iota \triangleright \theta] \rangle}$$

$$\text{[N-ENV]}$$
$$\frac{WFE(E') \qquad E' = \tau, \iota_1 \triangleright \sigma_1, \dots, \iota_n \triangleright \sigma_n \qquad}{\sigma_1; \emptyset \vdash \mathsf{e_{main}} \Downarrow \theta_1 \quad \cdots \quad \sigma_n; \emptyset \vdash \mathsf{e_{main}} \Downarrow \theta_n \qquad F_0 = \iota_1 \triangleright \theta_1, \dots, \iota_n \triangleright \theta_n}{\langle E; F \rangle \xrightarrow{\varepsilon} \langle E'; F_0[F] \rangle}$$

Fig. 6. Small-step operational semantics for network evolution

Reachability. Write $N \xRightarrow{\bar{\iota}} N'$ as short for $N \xrightarrow{\ell_1} N_1 \xrightarrow{\ell_2} \cdots \xrightarrow{\ell_n} N'$: a configuration N is said *reachable* if $N_0 \xRightarrow{\bar{\iota}} N$ where N_0 is initial. Reachable configurations are the well-formed ones, and in the following we shall implicitly consider only reachable configurations.

Firing. A firing evolution from N to N', written $N \Longrightarrow N'$, is one such that $N \xRightarrow{\bar{\iota}} N'$ for some $\bar{\iota}$, namely, where only firings occur.

Stability. A system state N is said *stable* if $N \xrightarrow{\iota} N'$ implies $N = N'$, namely, the computation of fields reached a fixpoint in the current environment. Note that if N is stable, then it also holds that $N \Longrightarrow N'$ implies $N = N'$.

Fairness. We say that a sequence of device fires is *k-fair* ($k \geq 0$) to mean that, for every h ($1 \leq h \leq k$), the h-th fire of any device is followed by at least $k - h$ fires of all the other devices. Accordingly, a firing evolution $N \xRightarrow{\bar{\iota}} N'$ is said *k-fair*, written $N \xRightarrow{\bar{\iota}}_k N'$, to mean that $\bar{\iota}$ is k-fair. We also write $N \Longrightarrow_k N'$ if $N \xRightarrow{\bar{\iota}}_k N'$ for some $\bar{\iota}$. This notion of fairness will be used to characterise finite firing evolutions in which all devices are given equal chance to fire when all others had.

Self-stabilisation. A system state $\langle E; F \rangle$ is said to *self-stabilise* to $\langle E; F' \rangle$ if there is a $k > 0$ and a field F' such that $\langle E; F \rangle \Longrightarrow_k \langle E; F' \rangle$ implies $\langle E; F' \rangle$ is stable, and F' is univocally determined by E. Self-stability basically amounts to the inevitable reachability of a stable state depending only on environment conditions, through a sufficiently long fair evolution. Hence, the terminology is abused equivalently saying that a field expression $\mathsf{e_{main}}$ is self-stabilising if for any environment state E there exists a unique stable field F' such that *any* $\langle E; F \rangle$ self-stabilises to $\langle E; F' \rangle$.

3.4 An Example Application of the Semantics

Consider the function definition def int main() is { #src : @ + #dist },
where #src is a sensor of type int (with default value 0), #dist is a sensor of type
posint (positive integers, with default value 1) and + is a built-in sum operator which
can be given signature int +(int,posint). Note that operator + (which is the progression function used in this spreading expression) is a self-stabilising progression,
according to the definition in 3.1.

Starting from an initial empty configuration, we move by rule [N-ENV] to a new
environment with the following features:

- the domain is formed by $2n$ $(n \geq 1)$ devices $\iota_1, \ldots, \iota_n, \iota_{n+1}, \ldots, \iota_{2n}$;
- the topology is such that any device ι_i is connected to ι_{i+1} and ι_{i-1} (if they exist);
- sensor #dist gives 1 everywhere;
- sensor #src gives 0 on the devices ι_i ($1 \leq i \leq n$, briefly referred to as *left devices*)
  and a value u ($u > n+1$) on the devices ι_j ($n+1 \leq j \leq 2n$, briefly referred to as
  right devices).

Accordingly, the left devices are all assigned to value-tree $0(0,1)$, while the right ones
to $u(u,1)$: hence, the resulting field maps left devices to 0 and right devices to 1—
remember such evaluations are done assuming nodes are isolated, hence the result is
exactly the value of the source expression. With this environment, the firing of a device
can only replace the root of a value-tree, making it the minimum of the source expression's value and the minimum of the successor of neighbour's values. Hence, any firing
of a device that is not ι_{n+1} does not change its value-tree. When ι_{n+1} fires instead by
rule [N-FIR], its value-tree becomes $1(u,1)$, and it remains so if more firings occur next.

Now, only a firing at ι_{n+2} causes a change: its value-tree becomes $2(u,1)$. Going on
this way, it easy to see that after any n-fair firing sequence the network self-stabilises
to the field state where left devices still have value-tree $0(u,1)$, while right devices
$\iota_{n+1}, \iota_{n+2}, \iota_{n+3}, \ldots$ have value-trees $1(u,1), 2(u,1), 3(u,1), \ldots$, respectively. That is, the
root of such trees form a hop-count gradient, measuring minimum distance to the source
nodes, namely, the left devices.

It can also be shown that any environment change, followed by a sufficiently long
firing sequence, makes the system self-stabilise again, possibly to a different field state.
For instance, if the two connections of ι_{2n-1} to/from ι_{2n-2} break (assuming $n > 2$), the
part of the network excluding ι_{2n-1} and ι_{2n} keeps stable in the same state. The values
at ι_{2n-1} and ι_{2n} start raising instead, increasing of 2 alternatively until both reach the
initial value-trees $u(u,1)$—and this happens in finite time by a fair evolution thanks to
the local noetherianity property of stabilising progressions. Note that the final state is
still the hop-count gradient, though adapted to the new environment topology.

An example of field that is *not* self-stabilising is { #src : @ }: there, progression
function is the identity, which is not a stabilising progression (cf. Definition 1). Assuming a connected network, and #src holding value v_s in one node and top(int)
in all others, then *any* configuration where all nodes hold the same value v less than
or equal to v_s is trivially stable. This would model a source gossiping a fixed value v_s
everywhere: if the source suddenly gossips a value v'_s smaller than v, then the network
would self-organise and all nodes would eventually hold v'_s. However, if the source then

gossips a value v_s'' greater than v_s', the network would *not* self-organise and all nodes would remain stuck to value v_s'.

4 Properties

In this section we state the main property of the proposed calculus, namely, self-stabilisation. Few preliminaries and results are given first. Given an expression e such that $\overline{x} : \overline{T} \vdash e : T$, the set $WFVT(\overline{x} : \overline{T}, e, T)$ of the *well-formed* value-trees for e, is inductively defined as follows: $\theta \in WFVT(\overline{x} : \overline{T}, e, T)$ if there exist

- a sensor mapping σ,
- well-formed tree environments $\overline{\theta} \in WFVT(\overline{x} : \overline{T}, e, T)$; and
- values $\overline{v}$ such that $length(\overline{v}) = length(\overline{x})$ and $\emptyset \vdash \overline{v} : \overline{T}$;

such that $\sigma; \overline{\theta} \vdash e[\overline{x} := \overline{v}] \Downarrow \theta$ holds. As this notion is defined we can state the following two theorems, guaranteeing that from a properly typed environment, evaluation of a well-typed expression yields a properly typed result and always terminates, respectively.

Theorem 1 (Device computation type preservation). If $\overline{x} : \overline{T} \vdash e : T$, σ is a sensor mapping, $\overline{\theta} \in WFVT(\overline{x} : \overline{T}, e, T)$, $length(\overline{v}) = length(\overline{x})$, $\emptyset \vdash \overline{v} : \overline{T}$ and $\sigma; \overline{\theta} \vdash e[\overline{x} := \overline{v}] \Downarrow \theta$, then $\emptyset \vdash \rho(\theta) : T$.

Proof (sketch). By induction on the application of the rules in Fig. 5 (by observing that, in rules [E-OP], [E-FUN] and [E-GRD], the use of the auxiliary function $\pi_i(\cdot)$ preserves the well formedness of the value-trees $\overline{\theta}$).

Theorem 2 (Device computation termination). If $\overline{x} : \overline{T} \vdash e : T$, σ is a sensor mapping, $\overline{\theta} \in WFVT(\overline{x} : \overline{T}, e, T)$, $length(\overline{v}) = length(\overline{x})$ and $\emptyset \vdash \overline{v} : \overline{T}$, then $\sigma; \overline{\theta} \vdash e[\overline{x} := \overline{v}] \Downarrow \theta$ for some value-tree θ.

Proof (sketch). By induction on the syntax of expressions and on the number of function calls that may be encountered during the evaluation of the closed expression $e[\overline{x} := \overline{v}]$ (cf. sanity condition *(iii)* in Section 3.1).

The two theorems above basically state soundness and termination of local computations, that is, from a well-typed input computation completes without errors. On top of them we state the main technical result of the paper, namely, self-stabilisation of any well-constructed field expression in any environment.

Theorem 3 (Network self-stabilisation). Given a well-typed program, any reachable network configuration $\langle F; E \rangle$ self-stabilises.

Proof (sketch). By induction on the syntax of closed expressions e and on the number of function calls that may be encountered during the evaluation of e. Let F_e denote the computation field associated to the closed expression e, so $F = F_{e_{\text{main}}}$. The idea is to prove the following auxiliary statements:

1. For every network configuration N, there exists $k \geq 0$ such that: $N \Longrightarrow_k N'$ implies N' is stable.

2. For every network configuration $\langle F_e; E \rangle$, there exist a stable field F_e' and an evolution $\langle F_e; E \rangle \Longrightarrow_h \langle F_e'; E \rangle$ ($h \geq 0$) such that: (i) F_e' is univocally determined by E; and (ii) for every stable network configuration $\langle F_e''; E \rangle$ it holds that $F_e'' = F_e'$.

For both the statements, the key case of the proof is that of a spreading expression, $e = \{e_0 : g(@, e_1, \ldots, e_n)\}$, which exploits the following auxiliary results: (i) If e_0 stabilises to F_{e_0}, and $\langle F_e; E \rangle \Longrightarrow_1 \langle F_e'''; E \rangle$ then the field F_e''' is *pre-stable*, i.e., for every device ι it holds that $F_e'''(\iota) \leq F_{e_0}'''(\iota) = F_{e_0}(\iota)$; (ii) Pre-stability is preserved by firing evolution (i.e., if N_1 is pre-stable and $N_1 \Longrightarrow N_2$, then N_2 is pre-stable); and (iii) Every stable network configuration is pre-stable. Moreover, statement 2 above is proved by: (i) Building an evolution $\langle F_e; E \rangle \Longrightarrow_1 \langle F_e'''; E \rangle \Longrightarrow_{h-1} \langle F_e'; E \rangle$ together with a set of stable devices **S** such that: (i.a) at the beginning of the evolution the set **S** is empty; (i.b) at the end of the evolution the set **S** contains all the devices of the network; (i.c) during the construction of the evolution, if a device ι is added to **S**, then ι is stable, its value is the minimum about the values of the devices $\notin$ **S** both in the current network configuration and in the final network configuration $\langle F_e'; E \rangle$, and that value is univocally determined by E; and (ii) Showing that, for any stable network configuration $\langle F_e''; E \rangle$, if the devices fire in the same order they fire in the evolution $\langle F_e'''; E \rangle \Longrightarrow_{h-1} \langle F_e'; E \rangle$ than each device must assume the same value it has in F_e'. So, since $\langle F_e''; E \rangle$ is stable, it must hold that $F_e'' = F_e'$. The construction of the evolution $\langle F_e'''; E \rangle \Longrightarrow_{h-1} \langle F_e'; E \rangle$ exploits the fact that g is a stabilising progression and that $\langle F_e'''; E \rangle$ is pre-stable.

The fact that any well-typed program self-stabilises in any well-formed environment independently of any intermediate computation state is a result of key importance. It means that any well-typed expression can be associated to a final and stable field, reached in finite time by fair evolutions and adapting to the shape of the environment. This acts as the sought bridge between the micro-level (field expression in program code), and the macro-level (expected global outcome).

5   Conclusion, Related and Future Work

This paper aims at contributing to the general problem of identifying sound techniques for engineering self-organising applications. In particular: we introduce a tiny yet expressive calculus of computational fields, we show how it can model several spatial patterns of general interest (though focussing on examples of crowd steering scenarios in ad-hoc networks) and then prove self-stabilisation. Some of the material presented here was informally sketched in [18]: the present paper fully develops the idea, providing a type-sound calculus, a precise definitions of self-stabilisation, and proved sufficient conditions for self-stabilisation.

The problem of identifying self-stabilising algorithms in distributed systems is a long investigated one [7]. Creating a hop-count gradient is considered as a preliminary step in the creation of the spanning tree of a graph in [7]: an algorithm known to self-stabilise. Our main novelty in this context is that self-stabilisation is not proved for a specific algorithm/system: it is proved for all fields inductively obtained by functional composition of fixed fields (sensors, values) and by a gradient-inspired spreading process. As argued in [8], there is a whole catalogue of self-organisation patterns can be derived this way.

To the best of our knowledge, the only work aiming at a mathematical proof of stabilisation for the specific case of computational fields is [4]. There, a self-healing gradient algorithm called CRF (constraints and restoring forces) is introduced to estimate physical distance in a spatial computer, where the neighbouring relation is fixed to unit-disc radio, and node firing is strictly connected to physical time. Compared to our approach, the work in [4] tackles a more specific problem, and is highly dependent on the underlying spatial computer assumptions.

Our work is aimed to find applications to a number of models, languages, and architectures rooted on spatial computations and computational fields, a thorough review of which may be found in [5]. Examples of such models include the Hood sensor network abstraction [23], the $\sigma\tau$-Linda model [21], the SAPERE computing model [15], and TOTA middleware [12], which all implement computational fields using similar notions of spreading. More generally, Proto [13,3] and its formalisation [19,20], provides a functional model which served as a starting point for our approach. Proto is based on a wider set of constructs than the one we proposed, though, which makes it very hard to formally address general self-stabilisation properties. In particular, it was key to our end to neglect recursive function calls (in order to ensure termination of device fires), stateful operations (in our model, the state of a device is always cleaned up before computing the new one), and to restrict aggregation to minimum function and progression to what we called "self-stabilising" functions. In its current form, we believe our result already implies self-stabilisation of certain Proto fields, like those intertwining constructs rep (state), nbr (access to neighbours), and min-hood+ (min-aggregation) as follows: (rep x (inf) (min F (g (min-hood+ (nbr x)) F_1 .. F_n))). One such connection, however, needs to formally addressed in future works, along with the possibility of widening the applicability of our result by releasing some assumption. Additionally, we plan to develop an algorithm to check whether the progression function at hand is actually self-stabilising. Another interesting future thread concerns finding a characterisation of expressiveness of computational field mechanisms and spatial computing languages [2], with clear implications in the design of new mechanisms.

Acknowledgements. We thank the anonymous COORDINATION referees for comments and suggestions for improving the presentation.

References

1. Bachrach, J., Beal, J., McLurkin, J.: Composable continuous space programs for robotic swarms. Neural Computing and Applications 19(6), 825–847 (2010)
2. Beal, J.: A basis set of operators for space-time computations. In: Spatial Computing Workshop (2010), http://www.spatial-computing.org/scw10/
3. Beal, J., Bachrach, J.: Infrastructure for engineered emergence in sensor/actuator networks. IEEE Intelligent Systems 21, 10–19 (2006)
4. Beal, J., Bachrach, J., Vickery, D., Tobenkin, M.: Fast self-healing gradients. In: Proceedings of ACM SAC 2008, pp. 1969–1975. ACM (2008)
5. Beal, J., Dulman, S., Usbeck, K., Viroli, M., Correll, N.: Organizing the aggregate: Languages for spatial computing. In: Mernik, M. (ed.) Formal and Practical Aspects of Domain-Specific Languages: Recent Developments, ch. 16, pp. 436–501. IGI Global (2013), A longer version available at, http://arxiv.org/abs/1202.5509

6. Claes, R., Holvoet, T., Weyns, D.: A decentralized approach for anticipatory vehicle routing using delegate multiagent systems. IEEE Transactions on Intelligent Transportation Systems 12(2), 364–373 (2011)
7. Dolev, S.: Self-Stabilization. MIT Press (2000)
8. Fernandez-Marquez, J.L., Serugendo, G.D.M., Montagna, S., Viroli, M., Arcos, J.L.: Description and composition of bio-inspired design patterns: a complete overview. Natural Computing 12(1), 43–67 (2013)
9. Giavitto, J.-L., Michel, O., Spicher, A.: Spatial organization of the chemical paradigm and the specification of autonomic systems. In: Wirsing, M., Banâtre, J.-P., Hölzl, M., Rauschmayer, A. (eds.) Software Intensive Systems. LNCS, vol. 5380, pp. 235–254. Springer, Heidelberg (2008)
10. Igarashi, A., Pierce, B.C., Wadler, P.: Featherweight Java: A minimal core calculus for Java and GJ. ACM Transactions on Programming Languages and Systems 23(3) (2001)
11. MacLennan, B.: Field computation: A theoretical framework for massively parallel analog computation, parts i-iv. Technical Report Department of Computer Science Technical Report CS-90-100, University of Tennessee, Knoxville (February 1990)
12. Mamei, M., Zambonelli, F.: Programming pervasive and mobile computing applications: The tota approach. ACM Trans. on Software Engineering Methodologies 18(4), 1–56 (2009)
13. MIT Proto. software available at, http://proto.bbn.com/ (retrieved January 1, 2012)
14. Montagna, S., Pianini, D., Viroli, M.: Gradient-based self-organisation patterns of anticipative adaptation. In: Proceedings of SASO 2012, pp. 169–174. IEEE (September 2012)
15. Montagna, S., Viroli, M., Fernandez-Marquez, J.L., Di Marzo Serugendo, G., Zambonelli, F.: Injecting self-organisation into pervasive service ecosystems. In: Mobile Networks and Applications, pp. 1–15 (September 2012) (online first)
16. Omicini, A., Viroli, M.: Coordination models and languages: From parallel computing to self-organisation. The Knowledge Engineering Review 26(1), 53–59 (2011)
17. Tokoro, M.: Computational field model: toward a new computing model/methodology for open distributed environment. In: Proceedings of the Second IEEE Workshop on Future Trends of Distributed Computing Systems, 1990, pp. 501–506 (1990)
18. Viroli, M.: Engineering confluent computational fields: from functions to rewrite rules. In: Spatial Computing Workshop (SCW 2013), AAMAS 2013 (May 2013)
19. Viroli, M., Beal, J., Usbeck, K.: Operational semantics of Proto. Science of Computer Programming 78(6), 633–656 (2013)
20. Viroli, M., Damiani, F., Beal, J.: A calculus of computational fields. In: Canal, C., Villari, M. (eds.) ESOCC 2013. CCIS, vol. 393, pp. 114–128. Springer, Heidelberg (2013)
21. Viroli, M., Pianini, D., Beal, J.: Linda in space-time: an adaptive coordination model for mobile ad-hoc environments. In: Sirjani, M. (ed.) COORDINATION 2012. LNCS, vol. 7274, pp. 212–229. Springer, Heidelberg (2012)
22. Weyns, D., Boucké, N., Holvoet, T.: A field-based versus a protocol-based approach for adaptive task assignment. Autonomous Agents and Multi-Agent Systems 17(2), 288–319 (2008)
23. Whitehouse, K., Sharp, C., Brewer, E., Culler, D.: Hood: a neighborhood abstraction for sensor networks. In: Proceedings of the 2nd International Conference on Mobile Systems, Applications, and Services. ACM Press (2004)
24. Zambonelli, F., Castelli, G., Ferrari, L., Mamei, M., Rosi, A., Serugendo, G.D.M., Risoldi, M., Tchao, A.-E., Dobson, S., Stevenson, G., Ye, J., Nardini, E., Omicini, A., Montagna, S., Viroli, M., Ferscha, A., Maschek, S., Wally, B.: Self-aware pervasive service ecosystems. Procedia CS 7, 197–199 (2011)

The Stochastic Quality Calculus

Kebin Zeng, Flemming Nielson, and Hanne Riis Nielson

DTU Compute, Technical University of Denmark, 2800 Kgs. Lyngby

Abstract. We introduce the Stochastic Quality Calculus in order to model and reason about distributed processes that rely on each other in order to achieve their overall behaviour. The calculus supports broadcast communication in a truly concurrent setting. Generally distributed delays are associated with the outputs and at the same time the inputs impose constraints on the waiting times. Consequently, the expected inputs may not be available when needed and therefore the calculus allows to express the absence of data.

The communication delays are expressed by general distributions and the resulting semantics is given in terms of *Generalised Semi-Markov Decision Processes*. By restricting the distributions to be continuous and by allowing truly concurrent communication we eliminate the non-determinism and arrive at *Generalised Semi-Markov Processes (GSMPs)*; further restriction to exponential distributions gives rise to *numerically analysable GSMPs*, in particular using techniques from stochastic model checking.

1 Introduction

Networked communication is the key for modern *distributed systems* as found in Systems of Systems [1] – encompassing service-oriented systems as well as cyber-physical systems – and including systems that are essential for the infrastructure in the 21st century. *Safety* as well as *security* are key concerns for many of these systems and in particular denial of service attacks have received attention. Massive amounts of requests may be sent to a process thereby making it unavailable for genuine communication and in the case of wireless communication the actual communication may also be disrupted by interference with the frequency band and physically shielding the antennas of senders and receivers.

The Quality Calculus. The classical *"super-optimistic"* programming style of traditional software development no longer suffices – we need to take into account that the expected communications might not occur and that the systems still have to coordinate to the extent possible: we have to turn to a *"realistic-pessimistic"* programming style. The Quality Calculus introduced in [2] is a first step towards a calculus supporting this change of paradigm; the communication paradigm is point-to-point (as in the π-calculus [3]) and is accompanied by a

E. Kühn and R. Pugliese (Eds.): COORDINATION 2014, LNCS 8459, pp. 179–193, 2014.

SAT-based analysis for checking whether the processes are vulnerable to unreliable communication. Probabilistic reasoning is added to the calculus in [4] in a setting where each input binder is annotated with a probability distribution indicating the trustworthiness of the inputs received with respect to a security lattice; a probabilistic trust analysis is then developed in order to identify the extent to which a robust programming style has been adhered to. Furthermore, a broadcast version of the calculus is developed in [5]; here it is additionally extended with cryptographic primitives and the focus is on the development of a rewriting semantics allowing us to reason – in a discrete setting – about unsolicited messages as well as the absence of expected communications.

Our contribution. The Stochastic Quality Calculus (SQC) presented in this paper is an extension of the previous works, and it differs in several aspects. First, it supports *truly concurrent broadcast communication* meaning that several processes may send messages at the same time (also over the same channel) and all processes that are ready to receive these messages must do so. Another main difference it that the *timing aspect* plays a central role. The time for completing a communication depends on the hardware architecture and the communication protocols but also the cyber environment. Hence *real time* considerations are relevant for those communications taking exact duration, and *stochastic time* considerations are relevant for those taking random time influenced by the cyber environment.

In our calculus, we use *generally distributed* random variables to characterise communication delays, so that both continuous stochastic time and real (exact duration) time can be expressed. An output process has the form $t_1!^G t_2.P$ specifying that the value t_2 should be communicated over the channel t_1 within some time determined by the general distribution G. A unique feature of the Stochastic Quality Calculus is an input binder of the form:

$$\&_q^{[a,a']}(c_1?x_1,\cdots,c_n?x_n).$$

It specifies that the process is waiting for n inputs over the channels $c_1,\cdots,c_n$; it is waiting for at least a time units and at most a' time units, where $a < a'$. The quality predicate q determines when sufficient inputs have been achieved and will then allow the process to continue before a' time units have passed (provided that a time units already have passed). The quality predicate q may be $\exists$ meaning that at least one of the n inputs must have been received, it may be $\forall$ meaning that all the n inputs must have been received, but other combinations are also possible. The continuation process will then have to inspect which inputs have been received and take appropriate actions in each case – thereby enforcing the "realistic-pessimistic" programming style alluded to above.

Related work. The challenge of combining concurrency and stochasticity has been addressed in previous stochastic process calculi as PEPA [6] and IMC [7]; the challenge of combining concurrency, stochasticity and mobility have been addressed in the stochastic π-calculus [8] and StoKLAIM [9]; the challenge of combining concurrency and real time have been addressed in timed CCS [10] and PerTiMo [11]. Most stochastic calculi make use of exponential distributions (denoted Exp) to express random delay, and can then use classic techniques and tools for Markov chain analysis. However, it is well-known that Exp distributions often are inadequate to faithfully model many phenomena, where the systems contain real time delays or highly variable distributed durations. The work of e.g. [12, 13] go one step further and incorporate general distributions thereby expressing a rich class of randomness. However, the real time (exact duration) delays are much less frequently incorporated in stochastic process calculi.

A CCS-like process algebraic framework introduced in [14] considers both discrete real time and generally distributed stochastic time. It uses a "spent-lifetime" semantics to track the time passed since activation to perform a race among parallel processes without a clock. Differently, SQC utilizes a clock to keep tracking residual lifetimes for the race, which avoids the complexity of time additivity mentioned in [14]. Besides, the transformational semantics of SQC gives a clear picture of the separation of the stochastic aspect and the real time aspect:

- for local processes, process transitions replace all stochastic time variables by sampled clock values with no consideration of time features;
- for global systems, real timed system transitions generate events and update the clocks with no consideration of stochastic features.

Overview. In Section 2 we introduce the syntax of the Stochastic Quality Calculus. The operational semantics of processes is presented in Section 3; it makes use of general distributions and in Section 4 we show that it amounts to *Generalised Semi-Markov Decision Processes (GSMDPs)* [15] by modelling truly concurrent broadcast communication as discrete events. Some of the discrete events in GSMDPs are controllable, which introduces a decision dimension to execute controllable events nondeterministically; a *policy* (as in Markov decision processes [16]) is introduced to deal with the nondeterminism. The classical problem is then to find an optimal strategy to maximise some reward function on GSMDPs and we refer to [15, 17] for the analysis.

In order to avoid the decision dimension and perform purely stochastic reasoning on the systems, in Section 5 we introduce two *analysable fragments of SQC* that both admit truly concurrent behaviour. The first fragment does not contain the non-determinism thereby obtaining *Generalised Semi-Markov Processes (GSMPs)* [18, 19] that can be analysed using statistical model checking [20, 21]. The second fragment maps further to *numerically analysable GSMPs* [22] that can be analysed using stochastic model checking techniques for Continuous Time Markov Chains [23] and Continuous Stochastic Logic [24]. We conclude and present future work in Section 6.

2 Syntax of SQC

The syntax of the Stochastic Quality Calculus (SQC) consists of *processes* P, input *binders* b and *terms* t, as given in Table 1. A *system* S consists of a number of process definitions and a main process:

$$\text{define } A_1 \triangleq P_1$$
$$\vdots$$
$$A_n \triangleq P_n$$
$$\text{in} \quad P_*$$
$$\text{using } c_1, \cdots, c_m$$

Here A_i is the name of a process, P_i is its body, P_* is the initial main process and $c_1, \cdots, c_m$ is a list of all the global channel names.

A *process* can have the form $(\nu c)\, P$ introducing a new channel c with scope P, and it can be an *empty process* denoted 0; we shall feel free to dispense with trailing occurrences of the process 0. An *output process* has the form $t_1!^G t_2.P$ specifying that value t_2 is transmitted over channel t_1 with a communication delay specified by the general distribution G. In SQC, we use *broadcast* transmission, so that all the receivers waiting on channel t_1 receive the value t_2. An *input process* has the general form $b.P$, where b is a *binder* specifying the desired inputs with real time constraints to be satisfied before continuing with P.

A binder may have the form $t?x$ stating that some value should be received over channel t, and stored in the variable x. More generally, a binder has the form $\&_q^I(t_1?x_1, \cdots, t_n?x_n)$ indicating that n inputs are simultaneously active: a *quality predicate* q determines whether sufficient inputs have been received to continue; a non-empty semi-closed *time interval* I determines when control is transferred to the continuation processes. The quality predicate q expresses when enough inputs have been received to continue; it can be $\exists$ meaning that one input is required, or it can be $\forall$ meaning that all inputs are required; formally $\exists(x_1, \cdots, x_n) \Leftrightarrow x_1 \vee \cdots \vee x_n$ and $\forall(x_1, \cdots, x_n) \Leftrightarrow x_1 \wedge \cdots \wedge x_n$. For more expressiveness, we shall allow quality predicates as for example $[1 \vee (2 \wedge 3)](x_1, x_2, x_3) \Leftrightarrow x_1 \vee (x_2 \wedge x_3)$. A non-empty semi-closed time interval I takes the form $[a, a')$ meaning that the binder has the minimum waiting time a and maximum waiting time a' (for $0 \leq a < a' \leq \infty$). As special cases a may be 0 or a' may be ∞ and the subsequent development can be simplified in these cases; we shall feel free to leave the interval field empty when $I = [0, \infty)$.

As an example, the system $\&_{\exists}^{[a,a')}(c_1?x_1, c_2?x_2).P \parallel c_1!^{G_1}t_1 \parallel c_2!^{G_2}t_2$ expresses that two output processes are simultaneously active at time 0, and wait for their output to be accomplished; the quality predicate $\exists$ of the input process will be evaluated at time a for the first time and the input process will continue with P if at least one of the two inputs has arrived. If not, the input process shall wait until one input arrives in the period $[a, a')$; if no input has arrived at time a', the process shall stop waiting (i.e. time-out) and continue with P even though no input has been received.

Table 1. Syntax of the Stochastic Quality Calculus

$$P ::= (\nu c) P \mid 0 \mid t_1!^G t_2.P \mid b.P \mid \text{case } x \text{ of some}(y) \colon P_1 \text{ else } P_2$$
$$\mid P_1 \parallel P_2 \mid A$$
$$b ::= t?x \mid \&_q^I(t_1?x_1, \cdots, t_n?x_n)$$
$$t ::= y \mid c$$

In SQC, communication delays are associated with outputs. Thus, a process takes a generally distributed time to send some data out on the channel, but it takes instantaneous time for receiving and storing the data. This is reflected in the syntax where we write $t_1!^G t_2$ for output and $t?x$ for input. Associating delays with outputs rather than inputs is a deliberate design decision that is helpful for identifying analysable fragments of SQC later.

As a consequence of using a general binder, some variables might not obtain proper values as the corresponding inputs are missing. To model this we shall use optional data types as known for example from Standard ML [25]. Let y denote *data variables* and let x denote *optional data variables*. Also, let some$(\cdots)$ express the presence of some data and none the absence of data. The *case construct* case x of some$(y)\colon P_1$ else P_2 has the following meaning: if x evaluates to a value some(c) then we bind c to y and continue with P_1; otherwise x evaluates to none and we continue with P_2.

Continuing with the processes we also have parallel composition $P_1 \parallel P_2$. A process can also be a *recursive call* A to one of the defined processes.

We forbid recursion through parallel composition, thereby ensuring that the resulting semantics has a finite state space. We shall say that $A \triangleq P$ has no recursion through parallel composition if the syntax tree for P does not contain any process name B in a descendant of a $\parallel$ construct, such that B might (perhaps indirectly) call A.

We also forbid the creation of new channels in recursion, so that we have a finite number of channels that can be used. Let $\mathsf{fc}(P)$ be the set of free channel names in the process P; for $A_i \triangleq P_i$ we define $\mathsf{fc}(A_i)$ as the least solution to the simultaneous equation system $\mathsf{fc}(A_i) = \mathsf{fc}(P_i)$ (for $i = 1 \cdots n$). We say that $A \triangleq P$ has no creation of new channels in recursion if the syntax tree for P does not contain any process name in a descendant of a (νc) construct.

Finally, for a system of the form displayed above we shall require that the initial main process P_* as well as the bodies P_i have no free variables over neither data nor optional data, and that their free constants are among $c_1, \cdots, c_m$.

3   Semantics of SQC

The semantics consists of a structural congruence and a transition relation for processes and on top of this we define a transition relation for systems. To facilitate this we need to define the semantics of binders and this includes a

Table 2. The structural congruence

$P \equiv P$	$(\nu c)\, P \equiv P$ if $c \notin \mathsf{fc}(P)$
$A \equiv P$ if $A \triangleq P$	$P_1 \equiv P_2 \Rightarrow C[P_1] \equiv C[P_2]$
$P \parallel 0 \equiv P$	$P_1 \parallel P_2 \equiv P_2 \parallel P_1$
$P_1 \equiv P_2 \Rightarrow P_2 \equiv P_1$	$P_1 \equiv P_2 \wedge P_2 \equiv P_3 \Rightarrow P_1 \equiv P_3$
$(\nu c)\,(P_1 \parallel P_2) \equiv ((\nu c)\, P_1) \parallel P_2$	if $c \notin \mathsf{fc}(P_2)$
$(\nu c_1)\,(\nu c_2)\, P \equiv (\nu c_2)\,(\nu c_1)\, P$	if $c_1 \neq c_2$

Table 3. Transition relation for processes

[INPUT] $\dfrac{b::_{\mathsf{tt}} \theta}{b.P \to P\theta}$ [OUTPUT] $\dfrac{\omega \sim G}{c!^G d.P \to c!^\omega d.P}$

[CONGRU] $\dfrac{P \equiv Q \quad Q \to R}{P \to R}$ [PARA] $\dfrac{P_1 \to P_1'}{P_1 \parallel P_2 \to P_1' \parallel P_2}$

[CASE1]   case some(c) of some(y): P_1 else $P_2 \to P_1[y \mapsto c]$

[CASE2]   case none of some(y): P_1 else $P_2 \to P_2$

transformation, a test on when the binder is satisfied and a transition relation for binders. Throughout this section we need to take care of the generally distributed output delays and the timing requirements.

The structural congruence defined in Table 2 is standard. The contexts C are defined by:

$$C ::= [\,] \mid (\nu c)\, C \mid C \parallel P \mid P \parallel C$$

As usual we apply α-conversion whenever needed to avoid accidental capture of names during substitution.

The transition relation for processes has the form $P \to P'$ and describes how a process P evolves into another process P'. The relation is defined in Table 3 and we notice that the rules [CONGRU] and [PARA] are standard. The two axioms [CASE1] and [CASE2] are straightforward and this leaves us with the rules for input and output; before explaining those we need some preliminaries.

Transforming the binders. We take a transformational approach to give the semantics to binders such that all the real time constraints from the binders are encoded as *Dirac distributed* delays. For clarity we shall write TSQC for the transformed version of SQC and observe that TSQC will be a fragment of SQC.

In the following let $\Re_{\geq 0}$ be the set of nonnegative real numbers, let δ_a denote a Dirac distribution with parameter $a \in \Re_{\geq 0}$, and let ω be a clock value generated according to the δ_a distribution (written $\omega \sim \delta_a$); then we have $\mathbb{P}(\omega \leq a) - \mathbb{P}(\omega < a) = 1$. Thus real time delays can be expressed because a Dirac distribution δ_a is a special case of a general distribution G.

The idea is now to transform an SQC process of the form $\&_q^I(t_1?x_1, \cdots, t_n?x_n).P$ into a process using specific channels for keeping track of the time and to let a modified version of the binder react when the time signals arrive. Depending on the interval I used in $\&_q^I(t_1?x_1, \cdots, t_n?x_n)$, different transformations are considered; here we shall only consider the case where I is $[a, a')$ (and $0 < a < a' < \infty$) and note that simpler transformations are mandatory in the special cases where a is 0 and/or a' is ∞. Then we shall replace the SQC process $\&_q^{[a,a')}(t_1?x_1, \cdots, t_n?x_n).P$ with the TSQC process

$$(\nu c_a)(\nu c_{a'})\left(\&_{\dot{q}}(t_1?x_1, \cdots, t_n?x_n, c_a?x_a, c_{a'}?x_{a'}).P \parallel c_a!^{\delta_a}\bullet \parallel c_{a'}!^{\delta_{a'}}\bullet\right),$$

Here two fresh outputs with Dirac distributed delays make use of fresh channels c_a and $c_{a'}$ to send the signals corresponding to the beginning and the end of the time interval. The binder itself is modified to listen for these signals and x_a and $x_{a'}$ are fresh variables used only to store the real time signal $\bullet$. Finally, the quality predicate is modified to record this by taking $\dot{q}(x_1, \cdots, x_n, x_a, x_{a'}) = (q(x_1, \cdots, x_n) \wedge x_a) \vee x_{a'}$.

We shall apply the above transformation rules for all the binders in the system, and we call $\&_{\dot{q}}(t_1?x_1, \cdots, t_n?x_n, c_a?x_a, c_{a'}?x_{a'})$ a *transformed binder* of TSQC. To shorten the notation (by keeping $c_a?x_a$, $c_{a'}?x_{a'}$ implicit), we write $\&_{\dot{q}}(t_1?x_1, \cdots, t_n?x_n)$ for the transformed binder.

Evaluation of binders. Now we introduce the relation

$$b ::_v \theta$$

to record whether all required inputs in b have been performed, by means of $v \in \{\text{tt}, \text{ff}\}$, as well as the composite substitution that has been constructed, by means of θ; it is defined in Table 4 and assumes that we have extended syntax

$$d ::= c \mid \bullet$$
$$b ::= t?x \mid \&_{\dot{q}}(sb_1, \cdots, sb_n)$$
$$sb ::= t?x \mid [x \mapsto \mathsf{some}(d)]$$

where $[x \mapsto \mathsf{some}(d)]$ is the substitution θ that maps the variable x to $\mathsf{some}(d)$. We shall use id for the identity substitution and $\theta_2\theta_1$ for the composition of two substitutions, so $(\theta_2\theta_1)(x) = \theta_2(\theta_1(x))$ for all x.

Returning to the definition of the transition relation $P \to P'$ in Table 3 we now see that the rule [INPUT] simply checks whether the binder is satisfied and if so it will apply the corresponding substitution to the continuation process.

Table 4. Evaluation of binders

$$t?x ::_{\text{ff}} [x \mapsto \text{none}] \quad [x \mapsto \text{some}(c)] ::_{\text{tt}} [x \mapsto \text{some}(c)] \quad [x \mapsto \text{some}(\bullet)] ::_{\text{tt}} [x \mapsto \text{some}(\bullet)]$$

$$\frac{sb_1 ::_{v_1} \theta_1 \quad \cdots \quad sb_n ::_{v_n} \theta_n}{\&_{\dot{q}}(sb_1, \cdots, sb_n) ::_v \theta_n \cdots \theta_1}, \text{ where } v = \dot{q}(v_1, \cdots, v_n).$$

Table 5. Transition relation for binders

[AX1] $(c_i!^\omega d_i)_{i=1}^m \vdash c?x \overset{\omega,(c_i)_{i=1}^m}{\longrightarrow} [x \mapsto \text{some}(d_i)]$, if $c = c_i$

[AX2] $(c_i!^\omega d_i)_{i=1}^m \vdash c?x \overset{\omega,(c_i)_{i=1}^m}{\longrightarrow} c?x$, if $c \notin \{c_1, \ldots, c_m\}$

[AX3] $(c_i!^\omega d_i)_{i=1}^m \vdash [x \mapsto \text{some}(d)] \overset{\omega,(c_i)_{i=1}^m}{\longrightarrow} [x \mapsto \text{some}(d)]$

[AX4] $\dfrac{\bigwedge_{j \in \{1,\ldots,n\}} (c_i!^\omega d_i)_{i=1}^m \vdash sb_j \overset{\omega,(c_i)_{i=1}^m}{\longrightarrow} sb_j'}{(c_i!^\omega d_i)_{i=1}^m \vdash \&_{\dot{q}}(sb_1, \cdots, sb_n) \overset{\omega,(c_i)_{i=1}^m}{\longrightarrow} \&_{\dot{q}}(sb_1', \cdots, sb_n')}$.

Active and inactive outputs. To define the transition relation for binders we shall distinguish between *active* and *inactive* outputs. An output is *active* when it starts to send data over some channel, otherwise it is *inactive*. As soon as an output becomes active, we replace its delay distribution G with a clock $\omega \in \Re_{\geq 0}$ to track the residual time for the output to complete. The clock ω is initialised by a sampled nonnegative value according to the distribution of the channel (written $\omega \sim G$). Note that the case where $\omega = 0$ indicates that the output completes instantaneously. To formalise that an inactive output becomes active, we extend the syntax by replacing the delay distribution with an explicit clock value like $c!^\omega d$. This is depicted by the rule [OUTPUT] in Table 3.

Furthermore, we assume that all the distributed processes share a global clock, and that the time of an output will be updated after each system transition (to be introduced below). In this manner, all active outputs implicitly remember the entire history of the time that has passed; we shall discuss this point later when we define the rule for system transitions.

Transition relation for binders. The transition relation for binders takes the form

$$(c_i!^\omega d_i)_{i=1}^m \vdash b \overset{\omega,(c_i)_{i=1}^m}{\longrightarrow} b'$$

where $(c_i!^\omega d_i)_{i=1}^m$ records the m concurrently active outputs that will modify the binder b so that it becomes b' and where the annotation $\omega, (c_i)_{i=1}^m$ records the communication over the channels at the specified time. The relation is defined by the axioms [AX1] to [AX4] in Table 5 and is explained below.

The first axiom [AX1] records the change of a simple input $c?x$ by receiving some value d_i from the channel c_i in $(c_i)_{i=1}^m$ at time ω. In the special case where

Table 6. Transition relation for systems

$$[\text{MATCH}] \quad \frac{(c_i!^{\omega}d_i)_{i\in I} \vdash b_k \xrightarrow{\omega,(c_i)_{i\in I}} b'_k \text{ for all } k \in K}{\text{define}\cdots\text{in } P \text{ using } f \xrightarrow{\omega,(c_i)_{i\in I}} \text{define}\cdots\text{in } P' \text{ using } f, e}, \text{ if } \begin{cases} \{f\} \cap \{e\} = \emptyset, \\ I \neq \emptyset, \end{cases}$$

where $P \to^* \equiv (\nu e)\left((\|_{i\in I} c_i!^{\omega}d_i.P_i) \| (\|_{j\in J} c_j!^{\omega+\omega_j}d_j.P_j) \| (\|_{k\in K} b_k.P_k) \right)$ for $\omega_j \in \Re_{>0}$,
and $\quad P' = (\|_{i\in I} P_i) \| (\|_{j\in J} c_j!^{\omega_j}d_j.P_j) \| (\|_{k\in K} b'_k.P_k)$.

the $(c_i!^{\omega}d_i)_{i=1}^m$ contains both $c!^{\omega}d_1$ and $c!^{\omega}d_2$ (i.e. two broadcasts take place over the same channel at the same moment), it is nondeterministic whether d_1 or d_2 shall be received for the input, so the axiom specialises to

$$c!^{\omega}d_1, c!^{\omega}d_2 \vdash c?x \xrightarrow{\omega,(c,c)} [x \mapsto \text{some}(d_i)], \text{ where } i \in \{1,2\}.$$

This is a deliberate design decision and alternatives, as for example that none of the two values are received due to the collision, can be modelled if wanted.

The axiom [AX2] records that no data is received for a simple input at time ω because of the mismatch between inputs and outputs whereas [AX3] records that an already received input retains its value. From the individual records, we express the change of a transformed binder as the collection of individual input changes as recorded in the rule [AX4].

The transition relation for systems. Let us now turn to the semantics of systems; it is defined in Table 6 by a transition relation of the form

$$\text{define}\cdots\text{in } P \text{ using } f \xrightarrow{\omega,(c_i)_{i\in I}} \text{define}\cdots\text{in } P' \text{ using } f'$$

The annotation on the arrow describes the truly concurrent communications $(c_i)_{i\in I}$ happening at time ω. The rule [MATCH] expresses that the main process P of the system first executes all the local steps from each distributed component; for this we use the reflexive transitive closure of the transition relation for processes $\to^*$ composed with the structural congruence $\equiv$. Note that the execution of the subprocesses may introduce new channels into the system; they are denoted e.

The distributed components of the processes resulting from this can be classified into three cases:

(1) $\|_{i\in I} c_i!^{\omega}d_i.P_i$ are processes that will perform outputs at time ω;
(2) $\|_{j\in J} c_j!^{\omega+\omega_j}d_j.P_j$ are the processes that will perform outputs at time $\omega + \omega_j$ for $\omega_j \in \Re_{>0}$ and hence later than at time ω; and
(3) $\|_{k\in K} b_k.P_k$ are the processes that are ready to perform inputs.

Given a set of broadcasts over $(c_i)_{i\in I}$ at time ω, the resulting system will be composed of the processes obtained from (1), (2) and (3). The processes of (1) will have completed their outputs so they will become $\parallel_{i \in I} P_i$. The processes of (2) are still waiting to perform their outputs and their clock values will now be reduced so they become $\parallel_{j \in J} c_j!^{\omega_j} d_j . P_j$. Finally, the processes of (3) will simply be updated to record which inputs they have performed as in $\parallel_{k \in K} b'_k . P_k$.

This completes the semantics of SQC as transformed into TSQC.

4   SQC is GSMDP

The transition systems obtained from the operational semantics turn out to constitute Generalised Semi-Markov Decision Processes (GSMDPs).

Definition 1. *A Generalised Semi-Markov Decision Process (motivated by [15]) is a tuple* $(S, E, A, \{E_s\}_{s \in S}, \{G_e\}_{e \in E}, \{\Omega_e\}_{e \in E}, \Longrightarrow)$, *where*

- S *is a finite and non-empty set of states,*
- E *is a finite and non-empty set of events,*
- $A \subseteq E$ *is a set of so-called controllable events,*
- $E_s \subseteq E$ *specifies for a state* $s \in S$ *a set of events enabled at* s,
- G_e *specifies for an event* $e \in E$ *a general probability distribution,*
- Ω_e *specifies for an event* $e \in E$ *a real-valued clock; when the event* e *becomes enabled,* $\omega_e \in \Re_{\geq 0}$ *is initialised by sampling from the distribution* G_e *to express the residual time until event* e *occurs,*
- $\Longrightarrow: S \times \{\Omega_e\}_{e \in E} \times E \times S$ *is a transition relation: given* $s, s' \in S$, $\omega \in \{\Omega_e\}_{e \in E}$, $e \in E_s$, *the transition* $s \xrightarrow{\omega, e} s'$ *expresses that a transition from* s *to* s' *is triggered by an event* e *with* ω *being the sojourn time in state* s; *the sojourn time* ω *in state* s *is determined by the smallest clock value over* $\{\Omega_e\}_{e \in E_s}$.

The dynamics of GSMDPs are described by *execution paths*. An execution path ρ for a GSMDP is a sequence $\rho = s_0 \xrightarrow{\omega_0, e_0} s_1 \xrightarrow{\omega_1, e_1} s_2 \xrightarrow{\omega_2, e_2} \cdots$ with $s_i \in S$, $e_i \in E_{s_i}$ and $\omega_i \geq 0$ being the sojourn time in state s_i. The *length* of an execution path equals the number of transitions along the path, which can be either finite or infinite. The decision dimension of GSMDPs arises in the situation where $s \xrightarrow{\omega, e} s_1$, $s \xrightarrow{\omega, e} s_2$ and $s_1 \neq s_2$. A *policy* (as in Markov Decision Processes [16]) picks an event in the set of enabled controllable events of a state to generate a partial execution path. Thereafter, the optimal strategy over different policy executions over a GSMDP can be obtained using the techniques of [15,17].

For a system expressed in TSQC, we model a sequence (more precisely a multiset) of truly concurrent broadcast communications as an event of a GSMDP. Therefore, when more than one output take place at the same time on the same channel, there exists a nondeterministic choice of the potential successive system configurations.

Theorem 1. *The semantics of systems in SQC amounts to GSMDPs.*

Proof. To see this we shall now define a GSMDP for a system of the Stochastic Quality Calculus as transformed into TSQC. First let $S/\equiv$ denote the quotient set obtained by using the structural congruence $\equiv$ over a set S of systems. We then define the GSMDP $(S, E, A, \{E_s\}_{s \in S}, \{G_e\}_{e \in E}, \{\Omega_e\}_{e \in E}, \Longrightarrow)$ as follows:

- The set of states S is the quotient

    {define $\cdots$ in P using $\cdots$ | define $\cdots$ in P using $\cdots$ is generated by the rules in Table 6 from define $\cdots$ in P_* using $\cdots$ }/$\equiv$.

    The obtained state space is finite, because recursion through parallel composition is forbidden.

- An event e in the state $s =$ define $\cdots$ in P using $\cdots$ is defined as a sequence $(c_i)_{i \in I}$ such that each c_i is used as an active output $c_i!^\omega d_i$ in the body P of s and all c_i share the same clock value ω. The set E_s is the set of events e enabled in the state s.

- The set of events is the union of all the enabled events: $E = \bigcup_{s \in S} E_s$.

- The set of controllable events is the union: $A = \bigcup_{s \in S} A_s$, where $A_s = \{e \mid s \overset{\omega, e}{\Longrightarrow} s_1, s \overset{\omega, e}{\Longrightarrow} s_2$ and $s_1 \neq s_2$ for some s, s_1, s_2, ω, and $e \in E_s\}$.

- The distribution of an event is defined as follows:
    - if the event is c where $c!^G d$ occurs in define $\cdots$ in P_* using $\cdots$, the distribution is G;
    - if the event is $(c_i)_{i \in I}$ where $(c_i!^\omega d_i)_{i \in I}$ occurs in define $\cdots$ in P_* using $\cdots$, the distribution of the event $(c_i)_{i \in I}$ is δ_ω;
    - for all c_a where c_a is introduced by the transformation of a binder b in define $\cdots$ in P_* using $\cdots$, the distribution is δ_a.

- The real valued clock Ω_e associated with the event e is ω whenever e is a sequence $(c_i)_{i \in I}$ where $(c_i!^\omega d_i)_{i \in I}$ occurs in define $\cdots$ in P_* using $\cdots$, or is introduced by the transformation of a binder in the same system.

- $\Longrightarrow = \{\overset{\omega, (c_i)_{i \in I}}{\Longrightarrow} | \overset{\omega, (c_i)_{i \in I}}{\Longrightarrow}$ generated by the rules in Table 6}. $\quad\square$

The GSMDP semantics of SQC captures the most general behaviour of the systems expressed by the Stochastic Quality Calculus:

1. Output makes use of general probability distributions (expressing both stochastic and real time delay), and runs concurrently using clocks.
2. Input makes use of stochastic quality binders (expressing both real time and quality constraints), and enforces the "realistic-pessimistic" programming style.
3. A sequence of broadcast communications may occur at the same time, such that the data is determined nondeterministically when more than one communication makes use the same channel at the same time.

The classical analysis of GSMDPs is to find an optimal strategy to maximise some reward function, which may use techniques such as policy iteration [16,17].

5   Analysable Fragments of SQC

In order to perform more standard stochastic reasoning on the systems, we introduce two analysable fragments of SQC sitting at different levels of generality, so that more established analysing methods become available.

5.1   SQC with Continuous Distributions

To exclude the nondeterminism, we introduce a fragment of SQC disallowing non-continuous distributions for outputs.

Definition 2. *The* Stochastic Quality Calculus with continuous distributions *(SQC$_{con}$) is the untransformed Stochastic Quality Calculus in Table 1 with the condition that all the probability distributions for the outputs have continuous Cumulative Density Functions (CDFs).*

Note that the continuous CDF restriction of SQC$_{con}$ does not exclude the real time (Dirac) output delays that are created during the binder transformation and that are explicit in the TSQC form of SQC$_{con}$. However, these real time (Dirac) output delays take place over freshly created channels. Therefore, when more than one binder in SQC$_{con}$ uses the same real time constraint, more than one communication may occur at the same time, but only over freshly created channels. Hence, by allowing truly concurrent transitions where all such communications take place at the same time we avoid any non-deterministic behaviour.

Proposition 1. *The system expressed by SQC$_{con}$ does not have nondeterministic communications.*

Proof. By the continuity of continuous probability distributions (be aware that Dirac distributions do not have continuous CDFs), the probability of two continuous random delays to be exactly the same is strictly zero, and hence we feel free to ignore the possibility that more than one output complete at the same time using the same channel. Hence nondeterministic communications are excluded (with probability 1). ☐

Without the nondeterminism, the semantics of SQC$_{con}$ turns out to become a Generalised Semi-Markov Process, which is a subclass of GSMDPs.

Definition 3. *A Generalised Semi-Markov Process (GSMP) (motivated by [19]) is a Generalised Semi-Markov Decision Process (cf. Definition 1) with the controllable event set $A = \emptyset$ and the transition relation $\Longrightarrow$ becoming a functional relation (meaning that $s \overset{w,e}{\Longrightarrow} s_1$ and $s \overset{w,e}{\Longrightarrow} s_2$ imply $s_1 = s_2$).*

A GSMP can be analysed using discrete event simulation or statistical model checking. We refer to [17, 20] for the technical details.

Theorem 2. *The semantics of systems in the Stochastic Quality Calculus with continuous distributions amounts to GSMPs.*

Proof. The semantics of SQC is a GSMDP, and SQC$_{con}$ is a fragment of SQC without the nondeterminism. Removing the nondeterminism from a GSMDP, one obtains a GSMP system corresponding to SQC$_{con}$. The construction of the GSMP from SQC$_{con}$ follows Theorem 1, and we shall omit the details due to space limitation. ☐

5.2 SQC with Exponential Distributions

Despite the fact that statistical methods can be used to analyse the GSMPs obtained from SQC$_{con}$, the general continuous probability distributions make numerical methods infeasible. Statistical methods scale better with the size of the state space, however a precise result often requires a large number of samples. Therefore, for state space $|S| < 10^5$ (based on a set of case studies over CTMCs in [21]), numerical methods seem to be preferable. To enable numerical methods, we introduce another fragment of SQC by restricting output delays further to be only exponentially distributed (denoted Exp). We first introduce a subclass of GSMPs with only Exp and real time events, such that the numerical analysis approach in [22] is applicable, which indicates that numerical verification techniques like stochastic model checking are also applicable.

Definition 4. *A numerically analysable GSMP is a generalised semi-Markov process, such that the general probability distributions are restricted to* Exp *distributions and Dirac distributions.*

Numerical analysable GSMPs retain both stochastic (Exp distributions) and real time (Dirac distributions) behaviour. Next, we introduce a fragment of SQC that amounts to numerically analysable GSMP.

Definition 5. *The* Stochastic Quality Calculus with Exp distributions (SQC$_{exp}$) *is the untransformed Stochastic Quality Calculus in Table 1 with the condition that all the probability distributions for the outputs are exponentially distributed (denoted* Exp*).*

Theorem 3. *The semantics of systems in the Stochastic Quality Calculus with* Exp *distributions amounts to numerically analysable GSMPs.*

Proof. Theorem 2 shows that the semantics of SQC$_{con}$ amounts to GSMPs, where the probability distributions have continuous CDFs. By Definition 5, the systems in SQC$_{exp}$ are special cases of SQC$_{con}$, where the continuous probability distributions are restricted to be Exp distributions, which amounts to numerically analysable GSMPs by definition.   □

Both analysable fragments of SQC retain real time constraints on inputs to enforce the "realistic-pessimistic" programming style. Therefore, it is not possible to reduce the semantics further into continuous–time Markov chains. However, the stochastic behaviour (Exp distributed) and the real time behaviour (Dirac distributed) can often be split into a pure stochastic behaviour (Exp distributed) in the form of a Continuous Time Markov Chain [23] and a pure real time behaviour (Dirac distributed) embodied in a query in Continuous Stochastic Logic [24]. These ideas are developed in [26].

6 Conclusion

The motivation behind the Quality Calculus [2] is that many of the security errors in modern distributed systems are due to an overly "optimistic" programming style. Programmers tend to think of benign communication environments, and hence focus on getting the software to perform as many functions as possible. To a much lesser extent, they consider malign environments and the need to focus on avoiding errors that can be provoked by outside attackers. We believe future programming languages need to support a more robust ("pessimistic") programming style: What conceivably might go wrong, probably will go wrong. A major cause of disruption is due to the *networked communication* between distributed software components.

This paper developed the Stochastic Quality Calculus (SQC) to model and reason about truly concurrent broadcast communications. A distinguishing feature of SQC is to consider both stochastic and real time communications that express the influences from cyber physical environment. Furthermore, the stochastic quality binder enforces the "realistic-pessimistic" programming style: to program the ideal as well as default behaviour depending on the availability or absence of desired data.

The semantics of SQC amounts to generalised semi-Markov decision processes. To avoid the decision dimension and enable purely stochastic analysis, we introduce two analysable fragments of SQC to express the systems in different levels of generality. The first fragment of SQC amounts to Generalised Semi-Markov Processes (GSMP) that can be analysed using statistical model checking, while the second amounts to a numerically analysable GSMP that can be further analysed using stochastic model checking.

These analyses lay a foundation for supporting a new discipline of robust programming. We believe that with the quantitative information obtained from the analysis, it will be possible to better determine whether or not the software continues to deal appropriately with risks and threats in the new application environment.

Acknowledgment. The research has been supported by IDEA4CPS, granted by the Danish Research Foundations for Basic Research (DNRF86-10). The research question addressed was largely motivated by the European Artemis project SESAMO (www.SESAMO-PROJECT.eu).

References

[1] CONNECT, U.A.D.: Report from the European Union workshop on Directions in Systems of Systems Engineering as part of Horizon 2012 (July 2012)

[2] Nielson, H.R., Nielson, F., Vigo, R.: A calculus for quality. In: Păsăreanu, C.S., Salaün, G. (eds.) FACS 2012. LNCS, vol. 7684, pp. 188–204. Springer, Heidelberg (2013)

[3] Milner, R.: Communicating and Mobile Systems: the Pi-Calculus. Cambridge University Press (1999)

[4] Nielson, H.R., Nielson, F.: Probabilistic analysis of the quality calculus. In: Beyer, D., Boreale, M. (eds.) FORTE 2013 and FMOODS 2013. LNCS, vol. 7892, pp. 258–272. Springer, Heidelberg (2013)

[5] Vigo, R., Nielson, F., Nielson, H.R.: Broadcast, denial-of-service, and secure communication. In: Johnsen, E.B., Petre, L. (eds.) IFM 2013. LNCS, vol. 7940, pp. 412–427. Springer, Heidelberg (2013)

[6] Hillston, J.: A compositional approach to performance modelling. Cambridge University Press, New York (1996)

[7] Brinksma, E., Hermanns, H.: Process Algebra and Markov Chains. In: Brinksma, E., Hermanns, H., Katoen, J.-P. (eds.) FMPA 2000. LNCS, vol. 2090, pp. 183–231. Springer, Heidelberg (2001)

[8] Priami, C.: Stochastic π-calculus. The Computer Journal 38(7), 578–589 (1995)

[9] De Nicola, R., Katoen, J.P., Latella, D., Massink, M.: Stoklaim: A stochastic extension of klaim. CNR-ISTI Technical Report number ISTI-2006-TR-01 (2006)

[10] Yi, W.: CCS + time= an interleaving model for real time systems. In: Leach Albert, J., Monien, B., Rodríguez-Artalejo, M. (eds.) ICALP 1991. LNCS, vol. 510, pp. 217–228. Springer, Heidelberg (1991)

[11] Ciobanu, G., Koutny, M.: PerTiMo: A Model of Spatial Migration with Safe Access Permissions. Newcastle University, Computing Science (2011)

[12] Bravetti, M., Bernardo, M., Gorrieri, R.: Towards performance evaluation with general distributions in process algebras. In: Sangiorgi, D., de Simone, R. (eds.) CONCUR 1998. LNCS, vol. 1466, pp. 405–422. Springer, Heidelberg (1998)

[13] Nielsen, B.F., Nielson, F., Riis Nielson, H.: Model checking multivariate state rewards. In: QEST 2010, Seventh International Conference on the Quantitative Evaluation of Systems, pp. 7–16. IEEE Computer Society (2010)

[14] Markovski, J.: Real and stochastic time in process algebras for performance evaluation. PhD thesis, Ph. D. Thesis, Eindhoven University of Technology (2008)

[15] Doshi, B.T.: Generalized semi-markov decision processes. Journal of Applied Probability, 618–630 (1979)

[16] Puterman, M.L.: Markov Decision Processes: Discrete Stochastic Dynamic Programming, 1st edn. John Wiley & Sons, Inc., New York (1994)

[17] Younes, H.L., Simmons, R.G.: Solving generalized semi-markov decision processes using continuous phase-type distributions. In: Proceedings of the National Conference on Artificial Intelligence, pp. 742–748 (2004)

[18] Matthes, K.: Zur theorie der bedienungsprozesse. In: Trans. of the 3rd Prague Conf. on Information Theory, Stat. Dec. Fns. and Random Processes, pp. 513–528 (1962)

[19] Glynn, P.W.: A GSMP formalism for discrete event systems. Proceedings of the IEEE 77(1), 14–23 (1989)

[20] Younes, H.L.: Ymer: A statistical model checker. In: Etessami, K., Rajamani, S.K. (eds.) CAV 2005. LNCS, vol. 3576, pp. 429–433. Springer, Heidelberg (2005)

[21] Younes, H., Kwiatkowska, M., Norman, G., Parker, D.: Numerical vs. statistical probabilistic model checking. International Journal on Software Tools for Technology Transfer (STTT) 8(3), 216–228 (2006)

[22] Lindemann, C., Thümmler, A.: Numerical Analysis of Generalized Semi-Markov Processes. Dekanat Informatik, Univ. (1999)

[23] Kwiatkowska, M., Norman, G., Parker, D.: Stochastic model checking. In: Bernardo, M., Hillston, J. (eds.) SFM 2007. LNCS, vol. 4486, pp. 220–270. Springer, Heidelberg (2007)

[24] Aziz, A., Sanwal, K., Singhal, V., Brayton, R.K.: Verifying continuous time Markov chains. In: Alur, R., Henzinger, T.A. (eds.) CAV 1996. LNCS, vol. 1102, pp. 269–276. Springer, Heidelberg (1996)

[25] Milner, R.: A proposal for standard ML. In: Proceedings of the 1984 ACM Symposium on LISP and functional Programming, pp. 184–197. ACM (1984)

[26] Nielson, F., Nielson, H.R., Zeng, K.: Stochastic Model Checking for the Stochastic Quality Calculus (2014) (submitted for Publication)

Author Index

Printed in the United States
By Bookmasters